BACKYARD GUIDE
TO THE BIRDS
BIRDS
OF NORTH AMERICA

SECOND EDITION

BACKYARD GUIDE
TO THE BIRDS
OF NORTH AMERICA

SECOND EDITION

JONATHAN ALDERFER
AND NOAH STRYCKER

NATIONAL GEOGRAPHIC
WASHINGTON, D.C.

CONTENTS

The energetic Black-capped Chickadee is a common year-round visitor to rural and suburban backyards.
Previous pages: Sleek, silky Cedar Waxwings feed on berries and other fruit.

HOW TO USE THIS BOOK

Of all the creatures in nature, birds are the most visible and accessible—they are right in your backyard! With minimal effort, your life can intersect with theirs, and both you and the birds around you will benefit. This book is a concise guide to enjoying and identifying the common birds in your area, wherever you live in North America, north of Mexico.

Backyard Basics

The first section of this book presents basic information on bird feeding, birdhouses, landscaping for birds, and birding skills. Installing a bird feeder in your backyard is a sure way to get great looks at some of your backyard birds, and a pair of binoculars will multiply your enjoyment. Enticing a pair of birds to raise a family in a birdhouse you have provided and maintained is a special joy, and bird-friendly landscaping will coax even more species to take up residence in your yard. All the information you need to get started is located here.

Guide to 150 Species

Millions of people have discovered that the pleasures of bird-watching increase when they know what they're looking at. We have designed the identification section to help you along that path. The features found in every species account are detailed on the sample pages opposite. The following additional features will help you locate any of the 150 species using different search criteria.

Visual Index: Inside covers (front and back). Images of all 150 species shown in taxonomic order, followed by a page number.

Quick-Find Index: Front cover flap. Alphabetical listing of common bird names.

Map Key: Front cover flap. Key to the colors used on the range maps.

Parts of a Bird: Back cover flap. Illustration labeling the various feather groups.

Glossary: Page 240. Definitions of specialized birding terms.

The sequence of birds in the identification section may seem arbitrary to beginners, but it is based on taxonomy—the science of evolutionary relationships—and proceeds from the oldest (most primitive) species to the most recent in origin. Almost all birding field guides follow this convention, so it's helpful to become familiar with it. You can always turn to the Visual Index on the inside covers for a quick reminder of the sequence. The sequence is subdivided into bird families—scientific groupings of related bird species—and each family is introduced with a short description.

Online Resources

The National Geographic website features news, pictures, and facts about birds. See page 244 for additional resources and information about birds and bird-watching.

SPECIES

The common name for each bird is given, followed by its official genus and species designations in Latin. Sizes (lengths) are also indicated.

ILLUSTRATION

Paintings of each species, often shown with common variations within species, are drawn to highlight noteworthy characteristics.

♂ male

♀ female

SIDEBAR

Interesting or helpful information about birds and birding is highlighted in side essays throughout the field guide section.

SIGHTINGS

A row of boxes at the bottom of each species description allows you to keep track of your own sightings by month throughout the year.

RANGE MAPS

The extent of each species' range and migratory routes aid identification in your part of the country. See the key on the front flap.

FAMILY

Common groupings of bird species are described in greater detail at the start of their section.

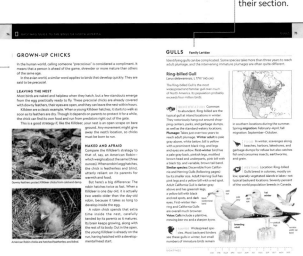

BACKYARD
BASICS

With a friendly attitude and perhaps a few enticements, anyone can get to know their neighborhood birds. The backyard is a perfect place to make introductions. Like other guests, birds will reward attention with their distinct personalities, stories, and dramas—and it helps to learn each one by name.

NOAH STRYCKER

THE BACKYARD

Take a look outside. What do you see? You might be surrounded by trees, concrete, saguaro cacti, strip malls, tomato fields, or glaciers. Perhaps you reside on a quiet cul-de-sac, along a sandy beach, or on the 82nd floor. Look closely. From the heart of the Bronx to the peak of Denali, birds are everywhere around us. No matter where you live, your home is their home, too.

MEET AND GREET

Just as no two backyards are the same, neither are the neighbors. The birds next door might be noisy and loud, but more likely they're a bit shy. Many people don't even realize how many birds are out there—these neighbors don't exactly introduce themselves.

With a little effort, your backyard inhabitants can literally become feathered friends. They are never far away and they are always up to something. Put out a bird feeder, build a birdhouse or birdbath, and tenants will probably move right in, repaying the favor with intimate, unabashed vignettes of their daily lives.

It's hard to say how many people enjoy birds, but millions of North American backyards are decked out with feeders. If you don't know what a bird is called, chances are you know someone who does. You certainly don't have to call yourself a birder to watch them; bring up the topic at a cocktail party, though, and you may be deluged with enthusiastic stories, along with curious questions.

This book aims to answer some of those questions by way of a general introduction. As colorful characters with beautiful songs and fascinating behaviors, backyard birds bring nature up close. Admiring them in your yard is gratifyingly different from watching TV; it's a raw, unpredictable, completely analog encounter, experienced with your eardrums and eyeballs and an inner sense of wonder. This show never goes off air, and it's always free.

Rufous
Hummingbird

The Great Horned Owl is the classic wizard's owl—wise-looking and with a call that sounds like *"Who-who!"*

THE PLAYING FIELD

A backyard may be fenced and secluded, or it could be more intangible—a city block or that little park down the street. Whatever it looks like, your backyard is the bubble of personal space around your residence.

Familiarity is the premier advantage of watching birds at home. You could travel to a foreign place and see exotic birds, but you wouldn't get to know them in the same way. And many of the friendliest birds are pinups; who couldn't spot their first Steller's Jay or Northern Cardinal without a little frisson of admiration and attraction?

Like any circle of friends, birds reward regular contact and some basic hospitality. Getting to know them requires, at first, only the willingness to pay attention. Once you begin to notice birds, you might find it impossible to keep them off your radar. For some, bird-watching is the gateway to a broader interest in nature and the outdoors.

HOW MANY BIRDS?

Your backyard may host a dozen or more common birds in a season. Keen observers like to keep a "yard list" of all the birds they've spotted at home. Sometimes these lists get a little competitive between neighbors; yards in productive places, such as waterways and flyways, have been known to record more than 100 species—and experts have documented more than 200 species in one yard.

For reference, about 700 bird species nest in North America, and at last count 10,585 species were recognized worldwide.

GETTING STARTED

Birds transcend all kinds of borders: They symbolize freedom and peace, love and resurrection. Anyone, anywhere can get interested in birds, because birds are among the most universal creatures on Earth.

Fortunately, it's never been easier to nurture this interest. No definition of "bird-watcher" can possibly encompass all the ways we appreciate birds, from aesthetic to scientific, from environmental to pure sport, but there are common threads.

You don't need much equipment to look at birds. Technically, bird-watching requires no gear at all, though a good pair of binoculars helps bring subjects into better focus. A reasonable mid-range model with 7x to 10x magnification might run $200 to $300. A camera with a nice zoom could be fun, especially as feeders bring birds close for photo ops. And you'll need a field guide. The one in your hands is a great resource, as it covers most of the birds you're likely to find at home.

Flip through this guide to get a feel for what's possible. It's helpful to learn up front how to identify a few common birds, so that when you see a new one you have some reference points. Range maps quickly let you know if a particular species lives in your area.

For beginners, a pair of binoculars is a good investment.

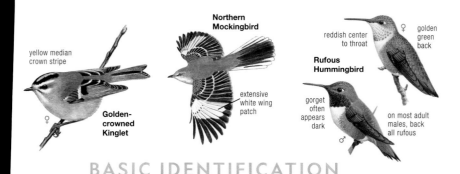

yellow median
crown stripe

Golden-
crowned
Kinglet

♀

Northern
Mockingbird

extensive
white wing
patch

reddish center
to throat

Rufous
Hummingbird

gorget
often
appears
dark

♂

♀

golden
green
back

on most adult
males, back
all rufous

BASIC IDENTIFICATION

Whenever you spot an interesting bird, watch it intently. Consciously describe it to yourself as you note each feature, working from general to specific. First, where is it—on the ground, in a tree, diving down your chimney? Then, what is it doing? Behaviors like flight style, flocking, vocalizations, feeding, interactions, and wariness are as helpful as appearance for identifying species. Like picking out a friend in a distant crowd (and after you've gotten to know a species), nailing a bird identification is often based on snap impressions.

Keep your eyes on the bird for as long as you can see it, and note its characteristics. How large is it, and how is it shaped? Compare the size to other birds you know; you might say, for instance, that a Mourning Dove is about the size of a Blue Jay with a longer, lankier profile. Only when you have absorbed the bird's location, behavior, and overall impression should you begin to examine its looks in detail.

Analyzing field marks is the strange alchemy of birdwatching. If you observe the field marks closely enough, you can identify almost any bird—although some confusing ones still stump the pros. Note any features that stand out, like a crest or bold pattern. Then, as deliberately as possible, look at each part of the bird and describe its colors.

When your subject flies away, write down your impressions so they are not later blurred by suggestion. Then look through this guide and try to match your observations with a species. Sometimes it works, and sometimes the jury stays out! With experience, you'll learn more and the process will get easier.

Even if you can't identify every bird, following the basic ID steps will help you watch birds more carefully. Remember, not every backyard bird with an admirer needs a name.

A YEAR OF BIRDS

As seasons change, birds follow predictable patterns. Many of their habits are tied to the calendar in an intricate balance of energy, productivity, and survival. Throughout the year, look for these seasonal behaviors in your backyard birds.

MONTH BY MONTH

January
Winter birds include many resident species, like Northern Cardinals and Carolina Wrens. Watch their social behavior: Do you see them moving around in pairs? Residents are much more likely to be monogamous, mating for multiple years or for life (though if one dies, its partner will seek a new mate). These species usually maintain permanent territories, so you'll see the same individuals in your yard year-round.

February
On cold nights, small birds have trouble conserving energy because their metabolism is so high. Long hours of winter darkness exacerbate this problem, as there are fewer daylight hours to forage—birds can't see in the dark and must rest at night. Some species, like chickadees, can lower their heart rate and slow their breathing, reducing internal temperature by several degrees. They may also roost snuggled together in cavities or dense trees to save body heat.

March
While northern states remain locked in winter, early spring migrants begin to push up from the south. The first Purple Martins show up along the Gulf Coast during January, and scouts reach the Midwest by mid-March. Tree Swallows, another early migrant, cross the Canadian border in March. On the West Coast, Rufous Hummingbirds arrive at bird feeders in Washington and begin to filter inland, having buzzed up from Mexico.

April

Courtship season kicks into gear for many local birds: Males sing to defend territories and attract mates, and perform all kinds of antics to impress females. Even paired-up, monogamous birds get frisky, feeling the allure of nesting season. Watch a city pigeon bob his head, coo several times, bow deeply, fan his tail, and fast-walk after a decidedly unimpressed female—it is a simultaneously comical and ultraserious performance.

May

The floodgates of migration release millions of birds in northward streams from coast to coast, many of them coming from wintering grounds in Central America, the Caribbean, and even South America. So-called "Neotropical migrants" like Baltimore Orioles, Scarlet Tanagers, and dozens of warbler species may use your yard as a rest stop during their long journeys, appearing like colorful confetti to forage for insects in any tree or shrub. Some will fly on as far as the boreal forests of northern Canada or Alaska before staking out a summer territory.

During migration, Baltimore Orioles frequently stop in backyards to rest and forage for food.

Spotted Towhee

juvenile

June

For resident and migrant songbirds alike, nesting peaks in early summer to midsummer. Things suddenly become quiet when birds stealthily disappear to incubate eggs. Then parents begin bringing food to their rapidly developing broods, making hundreds or even thousands of trips in just a couple of weeks to stuff their chicks full of protein-rich insects. If you follow a bird with food in its beak at a respectful distance, it may eventually lead you to its nest.

July

Juvenile birds may appear in odd plumages. Towhees, juncos, finches, cowbirds, starlings, and many others keep their brown feathers for a few weeks after leaving the nest, causing all sorts of backyard ID confusion. Their parents continue feeding them for a while, often bringing the fledglings to feeders before they become fully independent. Young, dispersing birds can show up in strange habitats as they search for new territories throughout late summer and fall.

August

All birds must replace their feathers at certain intervals, and many North American species do so in late summer. This process is energetically demanding, so birds wait until the nesting season is finished before they molt. You may find feathers on the ground and be tempted to collect them, but remember that the Migratory Bird Treaty Act forbids possession of feathers or any part of a native species. Male ducks have a special "eclipse plumage" in late summer, when they briefly resemble females before acquiring colorful feathers again.

September

Fall migration tends to be more drawn out than the spring rush, extending from July through November as birds straggle south. Many fall migrants are dull-looking juveniles making their first journey to wintering grounds. Shorebirds depart first in July and August, followed by Neotropical songbirds in September, raptors into October, and waterfowl through November. Watch for unusual birds in your yard; sometimes young migrants get lost and end up in unexpected places.

October

Fruit-eating birds like waxwings and robins gorge on berries in the fall. Sometimes the fruit has fermented enough to make birds tipsy; they perch glassy-eyed or fly erratically under the influence. At the same time, nut-eating birds like jays and Acorn Woodpeckers frantically store food for later consumption. They will rely on their caches during the coming winter.

November

Visitors from the far north begin to appear, including occasional Snowy Owls in northern states. Small flocks of Common Redpolls and American Tree Sparrows may visit your feeders to hunker down for the winter. In southern parts of the United States, seasonal arrivals include Fox and White-throated Sparrows, Ruby-crowned and Golden-crowned Kinglets, and Yellow-rumped Warblers. These hardy songbirds spend their winters in North America instead of the tropics.

December

Many birders take down their hummingbird feeders after summer is over, but leaving one up could attract an exciting guest. The birds migrate according to daylight, so your feeder won't make one linger unnecessarily. On the West Coast, Anna's Hummingbirds naturally reside from Mexico to Canada, and will drink at your feeders year-round. They are very hardy.

Yellow-rumped Warblers spend their winters in North America instead of migrating farther south.

In cold weather, a backyard feeder might attract flocks of Common Redpolls.

BIRD FEEDING

A bird feeder can be an easy and inexpensive way to attract birds year-round. There are a variety of feeders and foods, but most fall into a few traditional categories. Some are better than others, and each will entice certain species. It is important to keep feeders clean and to place them in safe locations—but if you take proper care, feeding will benefit the birds, helping them survive and reproduce.

TYPES OF FEEDERS

Ground
Some birds, like juncos and towhees, prefer to stay at ground level and tend to avoid hanging setups. These visitors will often eat spilled seed underneath feeders. If you scatter extra seed on the ground, only use a little at a time so that it does not spoil.

Platform
A flat tray with mesh or drainage holes, mounted atop a post or hanging, can be stocked with almost any food and serves a broad spectrum of birds. Platform feeders—especially with a roof—are tidier, safer, and better protected than ground feeding. Try mixed seed, cracked corn, peanuts, and fruit—and see what shows up.

Hopper
Many styles of hopper feeders are available, but all share the same general design: Seed is kept in an enclosed bin and portioned out as it is eaten. These setups often have a peaked wooden roof, clear sides, and rails for birds to perch on while they eat. It's best to fill a hopper with black-oil sunflower seed, and hang it in a spot where predators can't sneak up close.

Window
Particularly nice for classrooms, visitor centers, and urban apartments, window feeders stick to glass with suction cups. They

Tubes hold large seeds.

Finch feeders have tiny holes.

Hoppers may tempt mammals.

Tables attract mockingbirds.

Globes keep seeds dry.

Window mounts bring birds close.

Platform feeders serve many birds.

Suet cakes nourish woodpeckers.

Fruit beckons orioles.

American
Goldfinch

are usually made of clear plastic to allow close viewing, and often have a small hopper-type design. You can stand inches away without disturbing the action! Mounting a feeder directly on a window also helps break up reflections, so that birds are less likely to fly into the glass. (If you have an issue with window strikes, place a screen, branches, or other shapes in front of the problem area.)

Tube

The most common type of backyard feeder is a simple tube with holes and perches for small birds, like finches. It's best to keep tube feeders stocked with black-oil sunflower seed, which will attract a variety of species including chickadees, titmice, goldfinches, cardinals, and grosbeaks. Larger birds, like jays and pigeons, may attempt all kinds of acrobatics, but are generally too big to perch on tube feeders.

Finch

Specialized tubes with tiny holes, finch feeders are designed to be filled with delicate nyjer seed. Goldfinches, siskins, and redpolls go especially crazy for nyjer, which is similar to thistle. You can also offer these seeds in a hanging "sock" of fine mesh, but tube feeders are better at keeping things dry. Some finch tubes have holes below the perches so that birds must hang upside down to eat, which permits goldfinches but not other species.

Suet

Cakes of beef fat, sometimes combined with seeds, peanut butter, or other delicacies, will considerably broaden the variety of birds attracted to your feeding station—especially in winter. Blocks of suet are usually offered in a specialized metal cage, but suet mixtures can also be spread on logs, pine cones, or other natural features. Woodpeckers, starlings, jays, chickadees, warblers, and many other birds enjoy suet. Because suet can go rancid in warm temperatures, suet feeders should be placed in trees or hung from feeder stations in a shaded, cool area with just enough food for birds to eat in a day or two—and they should be kept at least five feet from the ground to be out of the reach of dogs.

TYPES OF FOOD

The gold standard in North American bird feeding is black-oil sunflower seed, which attracts many species of birds and can be stocked in almost any feeder. These seeds are high in fat and protein, with thin shells and meaty hearts.

Other types of food are worth mentioning. Safflower is an alternative for chickadees, titmice, finches, and cardinals (all of which will happily eat black-oil). Jays and woodpeckers sometimes enjoy striped sunflower seeds, larger and thicker than black-oil. Small, round, white proso millet will attract doves and ground-feeding birds, and is best provided on platforms or in hopper feeders. Nyjer (also known as thistle) is a finch specialty.

Be careful of commercial birdseed mixes packed with cheap fillers, like red millet, milo, and oats, which most backyard species ignore. Birds will often pick out the sunflower seeds while the rest of the mix is wasted.

Black-oil sunflower seeds

If you want to give your jays a treat, try scattering a few whole peanuts on a platform feeder or on the ground. And cracked corn, strewn on a platform feeder or on the ground, is a cheap way to entertain flocks of blackbirds, sparrows, and other gregarious visitors. Suet, either raw or in processed cakes, is a wintertime staple.

Orioles, robins, tanagers, and warblers will sometimes eat fruit (especially oranges, halved and skewered in place) and fruit-flavored jelly. Instead of throwing away your bacon grease, drizzle it in a small, open container or on a piece of wood—the birds will eat it up! Not all human food is nutritional for birds (try cracked corn, barley, oats, other grains, or duck feed pellets instead of white bread, especially for ducks), but animal fat is high energy and easily metabolized.

Nyjer for finches

For insect-eaters, mealworms—either alive or dried—are a delectable snack. You can buy mealworms at local pet stores and bait shops, or online. Bluebirds particularly love mealworms, and will not eat other backyard bird foods. Leave the worms in a dish or tray where birds can see them.

Fruits of all kinds

FEEDING HUMMINGBIRDS

The fighter-jet antics and dazzling personalities of humming-birds liven up any yard. Especially in spring and summer, these turbocharged gems provide constant entertainment for just a little investment.

You'll need a nectar feeder. These feeders come in many designs from "rocket ship" to "flying saucer" shapes. All that matters is that hummingbird beaks can reach the sugar water through each feeding port.

It's easy and inexpensive to make nectar yourself. Dissolve one part refined white sugar (don't use brown sugar, honey, sweeteners, or red food coloring) in four parts water. Pour some in the feeder, and hang it in a visible spot! Extra nectar can be kept in the fridge for several weeks for refills.

Change the nectar every few days or if it starts to look cloudy. In hot weather, give the feeders a gentle clean at least twice a week.

In most of North America, you should put up nectar feeders by mid-March and leave them out through October. Hummingbirds migrate according to daylight levels, so a feeder won't affect their timing. In some places, it's possible to attract hummers at any time of year.

Don't worry about indulging the birds' sweet tooth; they also eat a lot of insects to balance their diet. The metabolism of hummingbirds is so high that they need all the calories they can get.

FEEDER ETIQUETTE

All bird feeders should be placed in safe locations, out of reach of cats and close enough to shelter (a tree or shrub) that birds can dart for cover if a predator appears. If a Sharp-shinned Hawk or Cooper's Hawk stakes out a feeder, you can take it down for a few days until the hungry hawk moves on.

Keep a sharp eye out for mold, which can make birds sick. Wet birdseed and rotten fruit should be discarded immediately, and all feeders should be cleaned regularly to avoid the spread of disease. You can use a mild solution of vinegar or bleach as disinfectant.

Hummers, such as this Anna's Hummingbird, crave nectar.

It's a good idea to protect your bird feeder with a squirrel baffle.

If a male stakes out your feeder and defends it against all comers, you can add additional feeders in other corners of the yard. Hummingbirds are known for their territorial and acrobatic behavior—all part of the entertainment.

SQUIRRELS AND OTHER GUESTS

Love 'em or hate 'em, squirrels are likely to crash the party. Even the most ingenious barriers are vulnerable to marauding squirrels, which can jump, squeeze, tiptoe, and chew their way through practically any obstacle.

You can buy a "squirrel-proof" feeder with a wire cage, allowing small birds entry but not larger species. Or you can install a squirrel baffle, a slippery dish-shaped piece of plastic that guards the feeder's pole or wire. Try hanging your feeders on monofilament line, at least four feet high and 10 feet from any horizontal launching points. If all else fails, either distract your squirrels with a feeder of their own (they love dried corncobs), or be prepared to feed all comers.

Birdseed may also attract opossums, raccoons, deer, bears, and other wildlife. Platform and hopper feeders are most vulnerable, but even wire-covered tube feeders can be ransacked by large animals. The best defense is placement; hanging feeders out of reach is the only sure way to deter unwanted guests.

BIRDHOUSES

As winter transitions to spring, birds begin to think about nesting. A birdhouse, also called a nest box, offers shelter for birds to raise their chicks. In many ways, it is like a human house; its main purpose is to protect residents from weather and predators. Birds can be remarkably choosy when deciding where to start a family, but most species look for similar features in a good home.

IDENTIFYING THE MARKET

Many backyard birds do not use birdhouses. Robins, doves, cardinals, jays, orioles, hummingbirds, towhees, catbirds, and tanagers build their nests in trees or shrubs.

Woodpeckers are the developers of avian real estate, excavating cavities in snags. Most woodpeckers dig a new hole each year, leaving a large secondary supply of old cavities for other birds to nest in. But in many suburban areas, snags are removed, so natural cavities are in short supply. This shortage of cavities creates a market for birdhouses that you can supply.

Western Screech-Owl

Chickadees, titmice, wrens, swallows, martins, and bluebirds nest exclusively in cavities and will happily move into a birdhouse of the right dimensions. Great Crested Flycatchers, Prothonotary Warblers, Western and Eastern Screech-Owls, American Kestrels, and Wood Ducks can also be tempted by nest boxes.

The habitat in your backyard determines which species might move in. Fields and pastures attract swallows and bluebirds; suburban yards attract chickadees and wrens. Open areas are generally better than deep, dark shade.

SPECIFICATIONS

A birdhouse must have a few standard features, no matter which tenants it targets. Untreated wood is best, at least three-quarter-inch thick for proper insulation. Cedar works especially

Well-designed birdhouses offer shelter and safety for birds like this Tree Swallow.

well, but other types of wood are also fine. Resist the urge to paint or decorate; it might seem cute, but birds prefer a natural look. The birdhouse should be well constructed, preferably with galvanized screws, as nails can loosen over time.

To keep out rain, the roof should slope down and overhang by a couple of inches on all sides. Ventilation holes should be on each side near the roof, and at least four drainage holes should be placed in the floor.

A perch on the outside is not necessary—cavity-nesting birds have strong feet for clinging to vertical surfaces, and a perch simply adds a toehold for predators. But on the inside, it is a good idea to roughen the wood by scraping it with a chisel or knife just below the entrance hole so that young birds have an easier time climbing out when they are ready to fly.

The house should be easy to reach for regular monitoring and cleaning. Ideally, the front or side panel should swing open on a hinge for this purpose—but make sure it latches securely shut.

SIZE MATTERS

The diameter of the entrance hole determines which birds can fit into the house. House Wrens and chickadees can squeeze through a one-inch hole, which will also exclude non-native House Sparrows.

Swallows, titmice, bluebirds, and most smaller backyard birds need a 1.5-inch hole, which will exclude aggressive, non-native, and generally unwanted European Starlings. As long as a bird can fit inside, it will consider moving in.

PLACEMENT

Safety and comfort are key considerations for any home. Make sure to install your birdhouse where it is protected from predators and the elements.

Nesting season begins in early spring, so put up the house by March. Sometimes a little weathering can help the house feel more natural to birds.

Mounting a nest box on a freestanding pole provides the greatest safety. For added security, attach a baffle to the

Erecting birdhouses is a fun family activity.

Birdhouses can attract another family to the backyard.

DO IT YOURSELF

Build it and they will come! Constructing a birdhouse is a satisfying project requiring minimal materials and tools—great for kids and families. A standard nest box requires only a five-foot board and a few screws. You'll also need a saw, drill (for the entrance, ventilation, and drainage holes), and screwdriver.

Species-specific plans and blueprints can be downloaded for free courtesy of the Cornell Lab of Ornithology's NestWatch program *(nestwatch .org/learn/all-about-birdhouses)*.

pole below the nest box; the best guards are shaped like stovepipes or cones to deter climbing snakes, cats, and other predators.

You can also attach birdhouses to fence posts or trees, like a natural cavity. Be aware of surroundings, though: Areas with heavy pesticides, near reflective windows, and with dense cat populations are hazardous for birds.

Placing a birdhouse 5 to 20 feet high is about right for most small birds. Put it in a spot with a good view and nearby cover. Bonus points if you can see it from your kitchen window!

MONITORING

All native North American birds are protected by the Migratory Bird Treaty Act, which prohibits tampering with nests. It is illegal to remove an active nest or handle birds and nestlings without a permit, except for non-native European Starlings and House Sparrows.

You can, however, discreetly monitor your birdhouse. If it has a hinged side, peek in every few days to see if any birds are nesting. Once tenants move in, you can still check on their progress; it is a myth that birds will not return to a nest once a human has touched it. But be respectful, especially if there are eggs or chicks. When chicks are close to fledging, stop checking the birdhouse to avoid accidentally scaring them out of the nest early. You can keep watch from a distance, so you don't miss the big moment when fledglings leave the nest.

Once the birds have definitely left, clean out their old nest. Adults are more likely to return for a second brood if the house is unoccupied and empty. You can leave the birdhouse up throughout winter, which will give birds a place to roost on cold nights, but do a thorough spring cleaning for cobwebs, wasps, the old nest, and other debris in February or March.

You might like to contribute to Cornell's NestWatch program *(nestwatch.org),* which gathers data on nesting birds all over North America.

BLUEBIRD BOXES

One of our most popular backyard birds, the Eastern Bluebird, suffered a population decline in the early to mid-1900s. Reasons for this decline and subsequent recovery varied, but one thing certainly helped: Beginning in the 1970s, bird lovers made a concerted effort to install birdhouses specifically for bluebirds.

Today, significant numbers of Eastern Bluebirds depend on nest boxes throughout their range. You can do your part by putting up a birdhouse in the proper habitat. Bluebirds like open pastures, fields, hedgerows, and fence lines with short grass and places to perch. You might space multiple houses along a route where they can be monitored during nesting season.

To attract bluebirds to your yard year-round, offer mealworms and a birdbath with a dripper. These friendly neighbors will more than reward you for the effort.

MARTIN CONDOS

Special rules apply to the Purple Martin, a large, colonial swallow that nests in birdhouses across North America.

Historically, Purple Martins occupied natural woodpecker cavities in snags. But at some point, Native Americans discovered that hollowed-out gourds, hung up with a hole cut in one side, would attract martins. Early European settlers copied

Purple Martins are the condo lovers of the bird world.

the practice, and today all Purple Martins east of the Rockies nest in man-made birdhouses. (Some martins in the Pacific Northwest still use natural snags, and a few in the desert Southwest use saguaro cacti.)

Modern martin houses are custom built. Multiple gourds hung in groups are still popular, usually artificial ones that can be opened and cleaned. Some people also install martin-size condominiums in their backyard with many separate nesting compartments. Large operations can host dozens, hundreds, or even a thousand nesting pairs in a single, dense colony.

If you want to host Purple Martins, you'll need a large open space, preferably near human habitation (which helps the birds feel safe) and water. Attracting the first birds to establish your colony is the tricky part, but once they are nesting, the martins will return year after year.

Purple Martin

Becoming a Purple Martin landlord is its own subject with many intricacies. You can learn more at the Purple Martin Conservation Association *(purplemartin.org)*.

JUST ADD WATER

All birds need water. Some birds get moisture from the foods they eat, but most have to drink water every day. Many kinds of birds like birdbaths—especially during the summer and in dry areas. Most people picture a birdbath as a round, concrete basin on an isolated pedestal. Such ornaments may be sold in lawn shops, but they aren't the best option for wild birds, which have specific preferences for drinking and bathing.

LOW AND SHALLOW

Common Redpoll

Because wild birds are used to finding water in puddles, they will be less attracted to a raised birdbath. A tall pedestal may be necessary if cats are around; otherwise, keep it within a foot of the ground.

Many commercial birdbaths have steep, slippery sides and a deep basin, which complicates bathing for small birds. They want a gradual slope for wading into shallow water. You can put rocks in the bath for a better grip, with a variety of depths up to about two inches. Give birds some dry places to perch around the water's edge where they can lean down to drink.

PLACEMENT

A shady spot keeps the water cool and slows evaporation. Position the bath close to protective cover, such as a hedge or dense shrub, so that birds will feel safe—they are vulnerable to predators when their feathers are wet. After splashing around, birds typically go to a nearby perch and preen themselves dry.

Make sure to place the bath where you can see it! Stick it outside your kitchen window, or somewhere you will notice any action.

Birds like these American Robins appreciate clean water for drinking and bathing.

DRIPPERS AND MISTERS

Adding a dripper is the best way to turbocharge your birdbath. You can make one yourself by hanging up a gallon-size jug with a pinhole or by rigging a garden hose to drip steadily. Commercial drippers can be installed for a more permanent setup.

Keep the water moving so that it doesn't breed mosquitoes and algae. You might try a recirculating pump, a mister (particularly alluring for hummingbird baths), or even mini cascading waterfalls.

MAINTENANCE

Scrub out your bath at the first sign of algae or mold; birds really like clean and fresh water. You may use a dilute solution of bleach to disinfect droppings while rinsing.

In freezing weather, birds bathe less but still need to drink—and open water may be difficult for them to find. You can keep your birdbath open with an inexpensive, immersion-style water heater, or put a lightbulb inside a flowerpot underneath the bath to keep water from icing over. Ceramic and concrete baths are liable to crack when they freeze, so durable plastic tends to work better in cold places.

GARDENING FOR BIRDS

Lawn grass canvases about 60,000 square miles of North America—enough to carpet the entire state of Illinois. Manicured turf looks nice, but grass alone won't attract many birds, especially if it's soaked in weed killer. To boost the diversity of your backyard and make it more bird-friendly, consider replacing grass with flowers, vines, shrubs, and trees that can furnish food and shelter.

GETTING STARTED

Rose-breasted Grosbeak

You don't need a green thumb to fix up your yard, just a little motivation and vision. Birds have predictable tastes. With a few strokes, you can turn your yard into an attractive oasis for both avian and human visitors.

What are the natural features of your backyard? Look at it from a bird's-eye view. On paper, draw a map of your house and yard, filling in the foliage and topography. This exercise will help you evaluate what's already there and visualize gaps where new plants might be added.

Birds use vegetation for perching, eating, nesting, hiding, roosting, and many things in between. Different birds prefer different plants, and what thrives in your garden will depend on its location. Wherever you live, try to offer a variety of plantings for food and shelter throughout the year.

Food

Some plants produce nectar, seeds, berries, and fruit that are irresistible to birds, like a naturally replenishing bird feeder. You might plant a row of sunflowers—when they bloom, finches and chickadees will love harvesting the seeds. Hummingbirds are attracted to many different flowers, especially tube-shaped red and orange varieties. Vines like Virginia creeper hold delectable fruit into the winter months, while elderberry and serviceberry shrubs attract a wide array of waxwings, thrushes, catbirds, grosbeaks, jays, woodpeckers, and other species. If you have space for a fruiting tree, such as a cherry or crab apple, you can entice birds to your yard year after year when the fruits ripen. Growing different plants will allow birds to glean foliage, and dramatically increase the number of birds attracted to your yard. Applying pesticides will only keep birds away.

Native plants are better than exotic ones, as native species are familiar to birds and harbor more insects than non-native varieties. Exotic plants may also invade, as their seeds in bird droppings spread far beyond your yard. Native plants are ideally adapted to the local climate, so they stand the best chance of growing strong and healthy.

The indirect foods produced by your garden are even more significant. Some birds won't touch fruit, but virtually all North American songbirds raise their chicks on a protein-rich insect diet. A hungry nestling can consume astonishing quantities of bugs: Researchers have estimated that it takes nearly 10,000 caterpillars to raise one brood of chickadees!

Many birds love to eat berries, including this Cedar Waxwing in a serviceberry tree.

Milkweed flowers draw insects—nutritious meals for some birds.

Common elderberries attract birds from grosbeaks to woodpeckers.

Shelter

Think about the structure of your yard: Is it balanced? Even in a small area, you should aim for a nice mix of shade and sun, short and tall plants, dense thickets and open spaces. Designing a garden is like composing a painting, with all the elements benefiting birds beyond their aesthetic merit. Edge zones, where one natural environment meets another, promote higher diversity because they attract birds from multiple habitats.

Trees and shrubs give shelter for nesting, roosting, and foraging, and a variety of trees offer different things in different seasons. A deciduous tree may be wonderfully lush in spring and summer, but bare during the cold winter months. Dense evergreens provide excellent year-round cover.

If you have space, perhaps designate one corner where plants can grow wild, with a layer of leaf litter and even a few "weeds." What may seem untidy to humans can be particularly appealing to birds that like to scratch around in the dirt. Resist the urge to trim away dead branches, which make good perches and harbor insects in their crevices. Standing snags attract woodpeckers, bluebirds, flycatchers, and raptors; if a lifeless tree looks like an eyesore, use it as a rose trellis instead of cutting it down.

You can recycle branches and cuttings into a brush pile where birds take shelter. Put down larger limbs first, then build up smaller twigs to create open spaces inside the pile. Sparrows, quail, thrashers, and many other species will appreciate the cover when resting or hiding from predators. If the brush pile is within a short flight of your backyard feeders, birds will use it as a launching point. A well-built brush pile can attract birds for years.

BIRD-FRIENDLY PLANTS

If you plant, the birds will come. The possibilities may be overwhelming, but your local nursery can help with ideas. Just remember that native plants are usually more attractive to birds. To get started, here are 20 tried-and-true plants for backyard bird-watchers:

COMMON NAME	SPECIES	TYPE	RANGE	PROVIDES
Milkweed	*Asclepias* spp.	Flower	Widespread	Insects
Sunflower	*Helianthus* spp.	Flower	Widespread	Seeds
Purple coneflower	*Echinacea purpurea*	Flower	East	Seeds
Goldenrod	*Solidago* spp.	Flower	Widespread	Seeds
Trumpet honeysuckle	*Lonicera sempervirens*	Vine	East	Nectar flowers
Virginia creeper	*Parthenocissus quinquefolia*	Vine	East	Fruit, cover
Wild grape	*Vitis* spp.	Vine	Widespread	Fruit
Elderberry	*Sambucus* spp.	Shrub	West, Northeast	Fruit
Bayberry	*Myrica pensylvanica*	Shrub	East	Fruit
Prickly pear	*Opuntia* spp.	Shrub	Southwest	Cover
Great Basin sagebrush	*Artemisia tridentata*	Shrub	Interior West	Cover, insects
Saw palmetto	*Serenoa repens*	Shrub	Southeast	Cover
Serviceberry	*Amelanchier* spp.	Shrub/Tree	Widespread	Fruit
American holly	*Ilex opaca*	Shrub/Tree	East	Fruit, cover
Pacific dogwood	*Cornus nuttallii*	Tree	West	Cover
Crab apple	*Malus* spp.	Tree	Widespread	Fruit, cover
Sumac	*Rhus* spp.	Tree	Widespread	Cover, fruit
Pacific madrone	*Arbutus menziesii*	Tree	Pacific Northwest	Cover, fruit
California juniper	*Juniperus californica*	Tree	West	Cover, fruit
Oak	*Quercus* spp.	Tree	Widespread	Cavities, insects, acorns

CONSERVATION

You don't have to leave your neighborhood to connect with nature, even if the closest park is miles away. The tiniest habitats can attract birds. As cities grow, our yards occupy an increasingly significant part of the landscape and become ever more important as natural refuges. Not all backyards are created equal, but in the big picture your yard could help make a real difference for wildlife.

A BIRD-FRIENDLY YARD

Think of your backyard like a miniature bird community. Does it have places to sleep, eat, and nest? The more needs you can fulfill, the more birds will linger.

If you already put up bird feeders, think about installing a birdhouse or two. If you have a lawn, plant native plants instead—and maybe create a brush pile in one corner. Try adding a dripper to your birdbath if it doesn't already have one. Every yard is different, and every yard can be spruced up to help birds thrive.

Suburbs host a remarkably high diversity of birdlife, from transitory migrants like Rufous Hummingbirds and Baltimore Orioles to year-round residents such as Steller's Jays and Northern Cardinals. According to some research, more species of birds use suburban habitats than temperate forest, partly because suburbs create an "edge" between multiple habitat types. From a conservation standpoint, our neighborhoods offer a useful reserve for bird populations.

By improving your yard, you can improve the long-term survival of birds. They will repay the favor by bringing nature right to your back door.

Ecological Traps

Be wary of false advertising. Do not attract birds if they will be unsafe in your yard. Nobody wants to lure birds to their demise, but some threats are nearly invisible.

A scenario that draws wildlife to risky habitat is called an "ecological trap." Imagine a field that is mowed midsummer: The birds think it's good breeding territory, only to have their nests flattened. What might seem attractive at first leads to hidden, and tragic, consequences.

Suburbs are full of ecological traps. If birds cannot sustain their numbers, your neighborhood could even become a population sink, sucking individuals from other areas instead of producing new generations. So, while enticing birds with habitat enhancements, think about the possible dangers in your backyard.

CATS

Cats can make good pets, but feral and domestic cats also prey on hundreds of millions, if not billions, of birds in North America each year—taking the deadliest toll on bird populations of any factor besides habitat loss and climate change. Cats not only kill common backyard birds, but they have likely contributed to the extinction of more than 30 bird species,

A North Carolina garden offers houses, trees, flowers, and bushes for birds.

House cats make good bird-watchers—but only from the indoors.

and they continue to threaten birds at risk of extinction, such as the Piping Plover and the Hawaiian Goose.

This isn't the cats' fault; their instincts are hardwired. Domestic cats are not native, yet they now inhabit the continent in staggering numbers. The cumulative loss of so many wild birds to an introduced predator spells trouble for already stressed populations.

In your backyard, the solution is simple: Be diligent about keeping cats away from feeders and birdhouses, and exclude them from your yard if possible. If you have a cat, it is better off indoors. (Collars with bells are not very effective.) Many birders are also proud cat owners—you don't have to choose one or the other—but owners of all kinds of pets bear the responsibility for their animals' behavior.

WINDOWS

Thud! That is the sound of a bird hitting glass. Perhaps you've discovered stunned, injured, or dead birds beneath your windows. Many millions of common and rare birds meet their fate this way each year, most frequently White-throated Sparrows, Dark-eyed Juncos, Ruby-throated Hummingbirds, and Wood Thrushes. But the problem can be effectively solved with the right approach.

Installing a mosquito screen on the outside of your windows can eliminate bird strikes entirely, as the screen cuts reflections. Likewise, products involving tape, dots, curtains, or ribbons—or other obscuring devices—have been shown to dramatically reduce collisions. Just putting an isolated decal on a window does not work, though, as birds try to fly around it.

You can buy glass with embedded patterns designed to be visible to birds. Glass coated with ultraviolet material can be seen by birds but not humans, making the window appear transparent to us but not to birds.

Increasingly, cities are mandating the use of bird-safe glass in new construction. The most dangerous buildings for birds are low-rises surrounded by trees and shrubs where birds often hang out—like suburban houses. Treating your windows will benefit the birds.

CITIZEN SCIENCE

Several long-term projects aim to study bird movements using the observations of backyard birders. By becoming a citizen scientist and contributing your sightings, you assist researchers in tracking migration patterns and population trends. Get the whole family involved!

Project FeederWatch

Each winter, tens of thousands of people count the birds in their backyards as part of an effort co-sponsored by the Cornell Lab of Ornithology and Bird Studies Canada. Keep track of your sightings from November to April, as often as once a week, and your observations will join a decades-long data set spanning North America.

Scientists have used FeederWatch *(feederwatch.org)* data to study migration, irruptions, disease, food preferences, and many other topics over the years. This is a great activity for classrooms and bird clubs (to find a bird club near you, check Facebook or search online for the American Birding Association, the Bird Watcher's Digest Bird Club Finder, Audubon, and other birding organizations). You can find a research kit, including complete instructions, online.

Great Backyard Bird Count

Wood Thrush

For four days each February, birders contribute backyard bird counts to a global catalog. Results are displayed on the internet in near real time so you can see how your area stacks up! Spend as little as 15 minutes or as many hours as you like recording birds during the count period, then submit your observations online. Led by the National Audubon Society and the Cornell Lab of Ornithology, the Great Backyard Bird Count creates a unique

A flock of swallows might offer interesting citizen science data.

snapshot of bird populations that can be compared from one year to the next, and it is a fun activity with kids. Learn more at *gbbc.birdcount.org*.

Journey North

Founded in 1994 and funded by the Annenberg Foundation, Journey North offers an easy way to get started in citizen science. This project crowdsources the spectacle of spring migration, inviting everyone to watch and report the first waves of Ruby-throated Hummingbirds, Barn Swallows, American Robins, and other species as they make their way north.

To join in, report the first date that you observe spring migrants in your yard. Each sighting is included on interactive maps and tables. You can also observe butterflies, frogs, earthworms, tulips, daylight, and other signs of spring, and track these seasonal changes throughout the year. Submit a sighting or browse past data at *journeynorth.org*.

Christmas Bird Count

At the turn of the 20th century, luminary ornithologist Frank Chapman proposed a bird count as a friendly alternative to the then-popular Christmas "side hunt," in which participants would compete to bag all kinds of quarry. Armed with field glasses instead of guns, 27 participants recorded 89 species of birds on December 25, 1900.

More than a century later, the side hunt has fallen away as a forgotten footnote. Meanwhile, the Christmas Bird Count, spanning North America and beyond, attracts tens of thousands of intrepid volunteers who brave midwinter conditions for birds and holiday camaraderie. One-day counts are held between December 14 and January 5 in designated areas, including virtually all major cities, each described by a circle 15 miles in diameter. Your backyard may lie inside a count circle; if not, one is probably nearby. For more details, see *audubon.org/conservation/science/christmas-bird-count*.

eBird

Launched in 2002, eBird has quickly grown into the world's largest biodiversity project with citizen scientists, and it has transformed modern bird-watching. Through a mobile phone app and website, hundreds of thousands of users have submitted hundreds of millions of sightings (and millions of photos) representing nearly every bird species on Earth. All the eBird citizen scientists have to do is go bird-watching, anytime and anywhere, and keep track of the birds—it's that easy!

Try keeping a daily list of the birds that visit your yard. The site summarizes all of your observations, and you can use eBird's many tools to explore its full database. Scientists have published an incredible variety of papers with eBird data, which is archived by the Cornell Lab of Ornithology. Check out the website, or create a free account to submit observations, at *ebird.org* (which offers a free smartphone app to make it easy to record bird sightings while you're away from home).

When you track your sightings with eBird, you not only benefit science—you can also access your bird records whenever you want to answer your own questions about the birds you saw and when and where you saw them.

URBAN BIRDING

Even the densest concrete jungles have a wild side, and all kinds of birds can be found in metro areas. In recent years, urban birding has suddenly become fashionable—as an accessible pursuit, a gritty back-to-nature movement, and even a millennial art form. City dwellers might cultivate a more figurative notion of their "backyard," but they can definitely take bird-watching to the streets.

THE OASIS EFFECT

In a parched desert, life congregates around any green water hole. The same is true in cities, where developed landscapes are studded with tiny patches of nature.

Migratory birds will drop into any available habitat to rest and refuel. This could be as small as a Boston rooftop garden or a palm tree along the Las Vegas Strip, as long as a bird can perch and forage. Try looking at your neighborhood through the eyes of a warbler: Where would you land?

Massive numbers of birds migrate through North American cities in spring and fall, mostly unseen as they fly overhead after dark. On busy nights, songbirds can be so numerous that they appear on weather radar! Yet if you're not looking for them, these migrants are practically invisible. Tracking them down is like a treasure hunt for urban birders.

Because of the oasis effect, isolated green spaces, like Central Park in New York City, can host unnaturally dense concentrations of birds during migration. In other words, more birds crowd into the park than would be found there if it were part of a larger forest, because it is the only hospitable fragment. Urban birders try to identify such hot spots— ponds, lakefronts, leafy neighborhoods, and parks—amid the sprawl of development, and visit often during spring and fall.

If you have space, you can create your own urban oasis. Even a small flower planter can attract hummingbirds, and a window feeder offers food for passersby. To make your backyard friendlier for your natural neighbors, choose native

Scarlet
Tanager

A Red-tailed Hawk and her chick occupy an Upper West Side fire escape in New York City.

plants to give birds a refuge and access to nutritious nuts, seeds, insects, nectar, and fruit. Visiting birds will appreciate the effort.

Regular Residents

A few birds have adopted city life with ease, thriving in the province of human civilization. We often belittle these species as lowly commoners, but they deserve our admiration for their success and adaptability. Perhaps we see parts of ourselves reflected in these birds' cosmopolitan lives, or just take them for granted. In any case, even the most familiar urban birds can be a joy to watch.

Consider the regular city pigeon, or Rock Pigeon, *Columba livia*. For millions of years, pigeons lived wild in rocky parts of Europe, Africa, and Asia. When humans intruded on the scene, pigeons were domesticated for meat, feathers, and message carrying. The reason pigeons are so omnipresent today is that they have been highly regarded by people for thousands of years.

If you think pigeons are dumb, think again: In different studies, they have been taught letters of the alphabet and abstract mathematical concepts, and have been suspected of recognizing individual human faces—mental feats usually attributed to just a few primates and smart animals. Pigeons are highly trainable and flexible. They are also socially monogamous, with courtship rituals evident year-round.

In general, cities are perfect places to study behavior because many birds are unfazed by the presence of people. They go about their business underfoot, giving occasional

TIPS FOR URBAN BIRDING

- **Take a local patch under your wing.** Find the closest interesting spot (perhaps your own backyard) and visit it regularly throughout the year. When you know a place intimately, its birds become familiar friends. Finding a new bird patch is just as exciting as the rarity across town.

- **Stay safe.** City parks can be hot spots for all kinds of activity, so tread carefully. Cemeteries, botanical gardens, and public monuments often have beautiful habitat with good security. When in doubt, ask around before visiting a new neighborhood.

- **Don't be embarrassed!** People do much weirder things in public than carry around binoculars, especially in urban zones. Be ready to point out birds to pedestrians who might wonder what you're watching. Many birders were hooked because someone was kind enough to show them a cool sighting. Still, don't overdo it. Slinking around backyards with high-powered optics may give the wrong impression, especially if you're alone. Be aware of what's behind your target when you focus on a bird.

- **Dress in your own style.** Full jungle attire isn't necessary in cities, where camouflage makes no difference. Birder street fashion tends toward scrappy and practical, but really anything goes.

- **Be social.** Urban birders are an accepting, laid-back crowd with many young people, minorities, and spunky characters. There are feminist bird clubs, brew-loving bird clubs, and teen bird clubs (ask Google or your nearest Audubon chapter about opportunities). Local groups often host walks in city hot spots, all comers welcome. Just bring a smile and an appreciation for feathered friends.

This city-dwelling Rock Pigeon enjoys the view from atop the Empire State Building.

Two Monk Parakeets, perhaps escaped pets, rest in a cabbage palm tree in Florida.

moments of utter captivation. Cell phone videos of urban birds (riding the subway, playing with toys, harassing cats) have become a staple of social media, showing all kinds of humorous, intelligent, and unexpected encounters.

EXPECT THE UNEXPECTED

Don't be surprised if you spot a parrot flying around downtown. Escaped or released pet parrots have started wild flocks in many North American cities, including Los Angeles, San Francisco, Houston, and Miami.

Depending on the neighborhood, you might see a variety of parrots and parakeets, of which at least 30 species have been documented free-flying in U.S. cities. Rose-ringed Parakeets are well established in Bakersfield, California, which has similar temperature and precipitation to India, where they're from. Red-crowned Parrots have adapted so well to urban areas in California, Texas, and Florida that their U.S. population now rivals that of their native Mexico. Monk Parakeets, native to South America, are the most widespread of U.S. exotic species—and have set up colonies all over the country, including in Chicago, New York City, Long Island, Florida, New Orleans, Texas, Southern California, and even Washington. Green Parakeets, native to Mexico, have crossed the border into Texas' Lower Rio Grande Valley. In San Francisco, a local flock of Red-masked Parakeets even inspired a documentary, *The Wild Parrots of Telegraph Hill.*

Escaped Red-masked Parakeets, native to Ecuador and Peru, are reproducing in the wild around San Francisco.

None of these bird species is native, but survive on exotic fruit trees in suburban neighborhoods. Because cities have a unique mishmash of landscaping and microhabitats, they present novel environments for birds, and many non-native species have adapted to urban life.

Do not release pets of any kind into the wild—it is illegal, unethical, and environmentally hazardous (if you need to surrender a pet, contact your local animal shelter). But *do* appreciate the sight of free-flying parrots without having to visit the tropics. These newcomers certainly spice up our regular avifauna.

AN INSPIRING URBAN SUCCESS

In recent years, cities have been embraced by a startling bird: the Peregrine Falcon.

Things were looking grim for the world's fastest animal 50 years ago, when the pesticide DDT had nearly wiped out all of North America's Peregrine Falcons (it caused eggshells to become so thin that they broke while being incubated). By the time DDT was officially banned in 1972, the Peregrine had gone completely extinct east of the Mississippi River, and was listed as an endangered species.

Peregrines are built like jet fighters with a 40-inch wingspan, aggressively hooked beak, and black bandit hood. They can exceed an interstate speed limit in level flight and have been clocked at 200 miles an hour while diving. Their steep population decline set off alarms that helped spur the

Peregrine Falcon

environmental movement of the 1960s and '70s. Once DDT was banned, a group called the Peregrine Fund set out to reintroduce falcons to their wild haunts. Through breeding programs, thousands of Peregrine chicks were "hacked" and released all over the United States and Canada.

Initially, falcons were returned to natural cliff nests, but the young, captive-raised birds were easy prey for Great Horned Owls. So researchers tried something new: They released Peregrine Falcons at artificial nest ledges on skyscrapers, bridges, smokestacks, and other man-made sites.

These metropolitan falcons flourished, devouring pigeons and other urban prey. Tall buildings mimicked natural cliffs, and soon Peregrines were nesting in downtown New York City, Chicago, Atlanta, Philadelphia, Detroit, Norfolk, Salt Lake City, Los Angeles, and many other cities.

Today, Peregrine Falcons are common urban residents throughout North America, and are no longer on the endangered species list. To find out whether Peregrines are nesting near you, try a quick internet search for your area or ask your local Audubon group.

Peregrine Falcons, like this one in Chicago, can adapt to cityscapes.

GUIDE
TO 150 SPECIES

Millions of people have discovered that
the pleasures of bird-watching increase when
they can identify what they are looking at.
This identification section is designed
to help you along that path.

JONATHAN ALDERFER

sts and forested backyards in North America are home to White-breasted Nuthatches

DUCKS, GEESE, & SWANS   Family Anatidae

A worldwide family of web-footed, gregarious birds, ranging from small ducks to large swans. Largely aquatic, but some species also graze on land.

honking calls lower pitched than Cackling Goose

long, black neck

white chin strap

Canada Goose
Branta canadensis, L 30–43" (76–109 cm)

Nonmigratory populations have exploded in the last 50 years and are regarded as pests in many locations.

 IDENTIFICATION Common and increasing. "Canadian Geese" or (as hunters often refer to them) "honkers" are well known and easy to identify. **Plumage:** Long black neck (like a black stocking); black head with white "chin strap"; brown body, paler below. Downy **goslings** are a patchy blend of yellow and brown.
Similar species: Cackling Goose (not illustrated) is a tiny look-alike that occasionally winters with "normal-size" Canada Geese.
Voice: Call is a deep, musical but nasal *honk-a-lonk* or two-syllable *ka-ronk*.

RANGE Widespread species; year-round resident throughout much of its range. Nonmigratory (feral) geese abound in many suburban locations, such as parks, golf courses, and reservoirs, as well as more natural locations. Flocks of wild migrating birds fly in V-formation. Spring **migration** of wild geese: February–April; fall migration: September–November.

 FOOD Grazes on grass, but diet is usually supplemented with a variety of pond plant life. Migrating birds seek out waste grain in agricultural fields.
Feeding: Canada Geese are very attracted to corn and other grains.

U-shaped rump b[...]

NESTING *Location:* On the ground near water. *Nest:* Bulky construction of plant material. *Eggs:* Usually 5–6; incubated by female for 25–30 days, while male stands guard. *Fledging:* Downy gosling leaves the nest soon after hatching and can feed itself; able to fly at about 9 weeks. Parents and young remain together as a family group until the following spring.

| JAN | FEB | MAR | APR | MAY | JUN | JUL | AUG | SEP | OCT | NOV | DEC |

blue speculum

Mallard
Anas platyrhynchos, L 23" (58 cm)

The Mallard is the most abundant duck in the world and the ancestor of almost all domestic ducks. The world population is estimated at over 30 million birds, with about 18 million in North America.

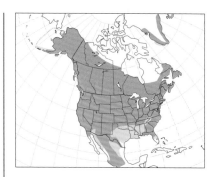

dark saddle on orange bill

♀

mostly white tail

IDENTIFICATION Common. The Mallard and related ducks, known as dabbling or puddle ducks, are strong, agile fliers able to spring directly into flight.

Plumage: Male has metallic green head, chestnut breast, and yellow bill; **female** is a nondescript, mottled brown, with orange bill with a black saddle mark.

Ducklings are flightless, fluffy balls of yellow and brown.

Similar species: City and suburban parks host a bewildering mix of Mallard-like domestic ducks with plumages from all white to ancestral looking, and everything in between.

Voice: Male's **call** is a soft, raspy *rab;* female gives the loud, familiar *Quack!,* often in a descending series: *Quack, Quack, quackquackquack.*

RANGE Widespread species. Mallards are found around almost any freshwater habitat, and many birds are year-round residents. Spring **migration** is very early, with breeding birds usually arriving during the spring thaw; fall migration: September–November.

FOOD During the breeding season, feeds almost entirely on animal pond life (insect larvae, snails). At other seasons, they are opportunistic feeders that seek out seeds from wild plants and farm crops. Most food is obtained by "tipping up"—using the familiar "butt-in-the-air-and-head-underwater" position that allows food to be gleaned from the pond bottom.

Feeding: In many city and suburban parks, the local birds will see you coming and demand a handout, even if it's only some bread crumbs. Cracked corn makes a healthier meal.

NESTING *Location:* On the ground, usually near water. *Nest:* Hollow of plant material, lined with feathers and down. *Eggs:* Usually 10–12; incubated by female for about 28 days. *Fledging:* Duckling can swim and feed itself soon after hatching. The female accompanies young until they can fly at 7–8 weeks.

green head

yellow bill

curled central tail feathers

♂

Parks with water features provide habitat for many ducks, geese, and other waterfowl.

CITY DUCKS

City parks—especially those with ponds or lakes—are bird magnets. Even the tiniest spaces with standing water can be oases for ducks.

These birds aren't bashful around people, either. In densely populated areas, waterfowl become accustomed to humans and are quite approachable. For close observation or photography, you can't beat a metropolitan duck pond.

WHAT TO EXPECT

In much of North America, Mallards and Canada Geese dominate urban landscapes to the point of being pests. (An adult Canada Goose can poop every 20 minutes, totaling two pounds a day—twice as much as a healthy human.) But flocks of these commoners help entice other, wilder visitors to your local park, especially during the winter months.

On city ponds, look out for shier species, such as Wood Ducks, American Wigeon, Ring-necked Ducks, and Lesser Scaup. These wild birds can become incredibly tame when they join throngs of habituated park ducks, giving a great opportunity for intimate scrutiny.

You might also see some strange varieties that don't appear in field guides. Domestic breeds of waterfowl, dumped or abandoned by their owners, often survive and even hybridize with wild birds to create odd pairings. Entirely black or white Mallards with potbellied profiles, Chinese and barnyard geese, and Black Swans inhabit many North American parks. Some exotics have even established self-sustaining, feral populations: Domestic Muscovy Ducks and Egyptian Geese are now widespread in suburban parts of Florida, Texas, and California, where they seldom stray far from golf course lakes, mall ponds, and other fabricated water features.

NEW WORLD QUAIL   Family Odontophoridae

All New World quail have chunky bodies, crests or head plumes, and a terrestrial lifestyle. In North America, most species live in the West.

slight crest — white supercilium
buffy superculium
♂ white throat
buffy throat
♀
juvenile

Similar species: None.
Voice: The male's rising, whistled **call**—*bob-WHITE!*—is heard mostly in spring and summer. Both sexes give soft *hoy* or louder *koi-lee* contact calls.

Northern Bobwhite
Colinus virginianus, L 9¾" (25 cm)

Named for the male's whistled call, these birds are the only native quail in the East. Except in parts of Texas, this species has dramatically declined during the past 30 years, probably a victim of suburban sprawl, feral cats, and other small predatory mammals.

IDENTIFICATION Uncommon. The bobwhite is a chunky, ground-dwelling bird with a short tail. If frightened, it runs for cover and freezes before flushing with a loud whir of wings. When not breeding, forms coveys of 5–30 birds.
Plumage: Overall reddish brown with irregular streaks and spots. **Male**'s head is boldly patterned in blackish brown and white; **female**'s head is brown and buff; **juvenile** is smaller and duller.

RANGE Eastern species; year-round resident. Found in rural and agricultural areas, rarely in suburbia.

FOOD Forages on the ground—often in dense cover—for seeds, berries, vegetation, and insects.
Feeding: Will come to seed or cracked corn scattered on the ground or at a platform feeder. Offering water is important, especially during droughts.

NESTING *Location:* On the ground in a sheltered location. *Nest:* Shallow hollow of plant material, often completely arched over, with an entrance at one side. *Eggs:* Usually 12–14; incubated mostly by female for about 23 days. *Fledging:* Downy young leaves the nest almost immediately and can feed itself, accompanied by parents; able to fly at 7–10 days.

California Quail
Callipepla californica, L 10" (25 cm)

This handsome and sociable quail inhabits westernmost North America. During the nonbreeding season, large coveys form. An old name for it is "Valley Quail." State bird of California.

brown crown

teardrop-shaped crest

♂

scaled belly

small topknot

♀

coastal females are browner

RANGE Western species; year-round resident. Lives in scrubby lowlands and on brushy slopes to about 5,000 feet. Comes to suburban backyards if there is suitable cover and a supply of water.

FOOD Vegetable matter, especially buds and fresh shoots in spring, and insects. In winter, subsists largely on seeds, small fruits, and berries. **Feeding:** Comes to grain scattered on the ground or on a platform feeder.

NESTING *Location:* On the ground. *Nest:* Shallow depression lined with grass. *Eggs:* Usually 10–17; incubated by female for 18–23 days. *Fledging:* Downy young leaves the nest almost immediately and can feed itself, accompanied by parents; able to fly at 10–14 days.

IDENTIFICATION Common. Ground-dwelling bird that looks beautifully ornate up close. You're most likely to see them at dawn or in the late afternoon; during the heat of the day, they stick to cover.
Plumage: Curved topknot feathers overhang bill; scaly belly. Fancy **male** has dark head with white stripes and chestnut patch on belly. **Female** is browner and more subtly marked, lacks strong face pattern, and has smaller topknot. **Juvenile** is browner and has tiny topknot.
Similar species: Desert-dwelling Gambel's Quail (opposite) overlaps slightly in range. The male Gambel's has a redder crown and a black belly patch.
Voice: The most characteristic **call** is a loud, emphatic *chi-CA-go*—often heard in the background of Hollywood Westerns.

SIGHTINGS

JAN   FEB   MAR   APR   MAY   JUN   JUL   AUG   SEP   OCT   NOV   DEC

Gambel's Quail

Callipepla gambelii, L 11" (28 cm)

This close relative of the California Quail is a familiar and beautiful desert bird. Tame and sociable, it has adapted to the increasing human development of its desert home.

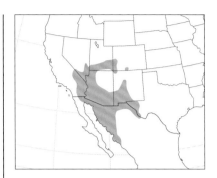

 IDENTIFICATION Common. This gregarious bird is often seen in small family groups or large winter coveys. When frightened they scurry for cover; if pressed further, they scatter in all directions on loudly whirring wings. At night, coveys roost in low trees.
Plumage: Curved topknot feathers overhang bill. **Male** has white stripes on head, reddish crown, and black belly patch surrounded by white. **Female** is more subtly marked and has an unmarked white belly and smaller topknot. **Juvenile** is gray and tan with a tiny topknot.
Similar species: California Quail (opposite), with a small overlap in range, is browner and has a scaly belly.
Voice: Most characteristic **call** is a loud, emphatic *chi-CA-go-go*—similar to the California Quail's, but higher pitched and usually with four notes, not three; also a plaintive *qua-el.*

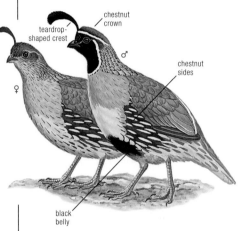

teardrop-shaped crest

chestnut crown

♂

chestnut sides

♀

black belly

RANGE Desert Southwest and Great Basin species; year-round resident. Inhabits low-lying desert washes, river valleys, and arroyos with scrubby vegetation. Frequents suburban backyards and urban parks with nearby desert vegetation.

 FOOD Vegetable matter, especially buds and fresh shoots in spring, and some insects. In winter, feeds mostly on seeds, small fruits (including cactus fruit), and berries.

Cannot survive without a permanent water source.
Feeding: Is attracted to grain scattered on the ground or on a platform feeder, but is vulnerable to free-roaming cats.

NESTING *Location:* On the ground, sheltered by a shrub, tree, or clump of prickly pear cactus. *Nest:* Shallow depression lined with grass. *Eggs:* Usually 12–17; incubated by female for 21–23 days, with male nearby on sentry duty. *Fledging:* Downy young leave the nest almost immediately and can feed themselves, accompanied by parents; able to fly at 10–14 days.

SIGHTINGS

| JAN | FEB | MAR | APR | MAY | JUN | JUL | AUG | SEP | OCT | NOV | DEC |

PIGEONS & DOVES   Family Columbidae

A large family with over 300 species worldwide. The larger species of these birds are usually called pigeons, the smaller ones doves. They feed their young a regurgitated liquid "pigeon's milk" for the first few days of life.

color variations

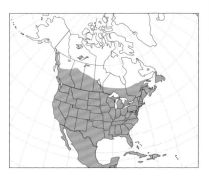

Rock Pigeon
Columba livia, L 12½" (32 cm)

Non-native species. Introduced from Europe to eastern North America in the early 17th century. The adaptable "city pigeon" spread across the continent and remains closely tied to human-dominated landscapes.

IDENTIFICATION Common to abundant. Highly variable plumage, but usually instantly recognizable by structure and behavior. Found in small to large flocks, these tame birds strut, bob, and peck their way around most city parks and squares.

Plumage: The ancestral—and most prevalent—type is gray (darker on head, with iridescent neck) with two blackish wing bars, white rump, and blackish tail band. Many color variants exist. Variants often retain the two dark wing bars and whitish rump of the ancestral type, but solidly colored birds do not. All birds have pinkish red legs and feet.

Similar species: The larger, shyer Band-tailed Pigeon (next page) of the West has similar plumage coloration. Note the Band-tailed's yellow-based bill, yellow feet, white crescent on the nape, and broad, pale gray (not black) tail band.

Voice: Soft **call** *coo-cuk-cuk-cuk-cooo*.

RANGE Widespread species; year-round resident. Found in cities, towns, and farms; able to survive in the most urbanized landscapes.

ancestral natural coloration

FOOD Seeds, waste grain, and fruits. Park birds greedily gather around anyone handing out bread crumbs. Visits bird feeders, but is usually an unwelcome guest.

white rump

NESTING *Location:* Usually on or in a man-made structure—a bridge, apartment windowsill, farm building, and so forth. *Nest:* Loose construction of twigs and debris. *Eggs:* Usually 2; incubated by both parents for 17–19 days. *Fledging:* Leaves nest at 25–32 days. *Broods:* Breeds year-round in most areas and may raise 5 or more broods per year.

Band-tailed Pigeon
Patagioenas fasciata, L 14½" (37 cm)

A big, sociable pigeon found in the West. It can be common in urban parks and suburban neighborhoods, including at backyard bird feeders.

white band

yellow-based bill

lacks white band on nape

duller bill

juvenile

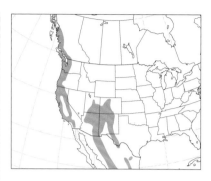

IDENTIFICATION Fairly common. Larger and shier than the Rock Pigeon, but both species are usually found in flocks.
Plumage: Grayish overall with purplish tint on head and breast. Nape is iridescent with a white crescent above; tail has a broad pale band at tip. Bill is yellow with a black tip; feet are also yellow. **Juvenile** is less colorful and lacks white nape crescent.
Similar species: Compare to Rock Pigeon (opposite page), which lacks white nape crescent and has a dark tail tip, reddish feet, and often a white rump (Band-tailed never has a white rump). Band-taileds perch in trees, a location usually avoided by Rock Pigeons. In Band-tailed flocks, birds look uniform;

rather long tail with broad pale tail band

in most Rock Pigeon flocks, there is lots of variation from bird to bird.
Voice: Often silent; **call** is an owl-like, low-pitched *whoo-whoo.*

RANGE Western species. Two separate populations: mountains of the interior West, and West Coast (see map). Year-round resident in some areas (including some northern cities, such as Vancouver, Seattle, and Portland). Nomadic winter flocks wander in search of food, and northernmost breeders move south for the winter. Spring **migration:** February–late May; fall migration: mid-August–November.

FOOD Seeds, berries, grain, acorns, pine nuts, and tree buds. Fruit and nut orchards are also visited. Feeds on the ground on spilled or waste grain, but more often feeds in trees.
Feeding: Comes to platform feeders and grain scattered on ground; also eats berries of holly and other fruiting residential trees and shrubs.

NESTING *Location:* In a tree or shrub, 8–20 feet up. *Nest:* Shallow twiggy platform. *Eggs:* 1; incubated by both parents for 18–20 days. *Fledging:* Leaves nest at 25–30 days.

Eurasian Collared-Dove
Streptopelia decaocto, L 12½″ (32 cm)

Non-native species. Accidentally introduced to the Bahamas and spread to Florida in 1978. Now found across much of the U.S. and into southern Canada, a colonization of North America astonishing for its speed and success.

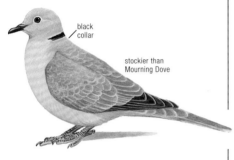

black collar

stockier than Mourning Dove

IDENTIFICATION Common. Large, pale dove; conspicuous and vocal. Feeds on the ground, but often perches on buildings and overhead wires. Flaps on broad, black-tipped wings, sometimes soars briefly, and floats down to a landing with tail spread.
Plumage: Light grayish tan overall with black hindneck collar; squared-off tail with large white tip and black base (most noticeable from below). **Juvenile** Similar; black collar obscured or missing.
Similar species: Often occurs with Mourning Dove (page 61), a darker and slimmer dove with a long pointed tail. White-winged Dove (page 60) is also darker overall; it has white wing patches, but a similar tail pattern and shape.
Voice: Three-syllable **call** *coo-COO-cup* is repeated monotonously.

RANGE Widespread species; year-round resident. Continues to colonize new areas, but is not migratory. Notably absent from New England.

Found in towns, suburbs, and farms; seems to avoid city centers and heavily forested areas.

FOOD Seeds, waste grain, and some berries and insects. Feeds on the ground; takes handouts from humans.
Feeding: Frequents platform feeders and grain scattered on ground. Rapidly becoming a well-known backyard bird in many areas.

NESTING *Location:* In tree, shrub, or sheltered building ledge, at mid-level. *Nest:* Flimsy platform of sticks and twigs. *Eggs:* Usually 2; incubated by both parents for 14–19 days. *Fledging:* Leaves nest at 16–20 days. *Broods:* 2 or more per year; probably breeds throughout the year in southern areas.

three-toned wing

grayish

large white tip

Inca Dove
Columbina inca, L 8¼" (21 cm)

These dainty little doves are closely associated with towns, suburbs, and cities and are slowly spreading to the north and east. The repetitive, melancholy call sounds like *no hope,* earning it the nickname "Doomsday Dove."

 IDENTIFICATION Common. Small and slender, with a long tail. Small groups of these tame doves some-times huddle tightly together on a single perch. The wing and tail patterns are best seen on stretching or flying birds. Flight is direct, and takeoffs from the ground are explosive, often from nearly under-foot. Forages on open ground and lawns; moves around with a shuffling gait.

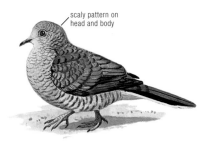
scaly pattern on head and body

Plumage: Grayish overall, paler below; black fringes on feathers create a scaly pattern. Bright chestnut on wings and white outer tail feathers (features mostly hidden on perched birds). **Juvenile** is browner and less scaly.
Similar species: Shape recalls a miniature Mourning Dove (page 61), but Mourning Dove lacks "scaly" plumage and chestnut in wings. Common Ground-Dove (not illustrated) has chestnut in wing and over-laps in range, but is slightly smaller; it has a scaly pattern only on head and breast (not on back), and a short tail.

Voice: Low-pitched, two-syllable **call** *kooo-poo* ("no hope"), given repeatedly throughout the day.

 RANGE Southwestern and Texas species; year-round resident. Closely associated with human develop-ment—cities, towns, suburbs, parks, farms, and feedlots; avoids extensive forest and dense brush.

 FOOD Weed and grass seeds, grains, and birdseed.
Feeding: Common feeder bird. Comes to seed scattered on the ground or to an elevated platform feeder. Needs a source of water.

NESTING *Location:* In a medium-height tree, shrub, or cactus; often exposed to direct sun. *Nest:* Small, com-pact platform of twigs and weed stalks. *Eggs:* 2; incubated by both parents for 13–15 days. *Fledging:* Leaves nest at 12–16 days. *Broods:* Up to 5 per year.

rufous primary patches

long tail with white edges

White-winged Dove
Zenaida asiatica, L 11½" (29 cm)

Flocks of these doves are a common sight in summer in areas near the Mexican border. The adaptable White-wing is increasing in numbers, and its range on the Great Plains is expanding northward.

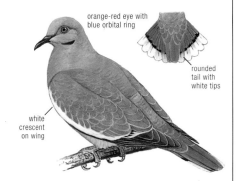

orange-red eye with blue orbital ring

rounded tail with white tips

white crescent on wing

IDENTIFICATION Common. Medium-large dove with a bulky body, square-tipped tail, and broad wings. The bill appears long (for a dove) and slightly downcurved. Its orange-red eyes are surrounded by blue skin.
Plumage: Brownish gray upperparts, grayer below. Large white wing patch, conspicuous in flight; appears as a white stripe when wing is folded. Blackish tail with white terminal band, prominent when spread, mostly hidden when perched.
Similar species: Similar in color and overall length to Mourning Dove (opposite). Mourning Dove lacks the white wing patches and has a slender body and long, pointed tail. Eurasian Collared-Dove (page 58) is much paler, has a black band across the hindneck, and also lacks white wing patches.
Voice: Very vocal; its drawn-out cooing **call**, *who-cooks-for-you,* has many variations.

RANGE Southwestern and Texas species. Inhabits mesquite woodlands, riparian woodlands, citrus groves, cactus-paloverde desert, and wooded residential areas. Present year-round in its southern range, but western birds are strongly migratory (wintering in Mexico). Spring **migration** peaks in March–April, fall migration in early August–mid-September.

FOOD Seeds, nuts, and fruits. Forages on the ground, perched in trees and cacti (an important pollinator of giant saguaro cactus), or clinging to seed stalks.
crescent-shaped white patch
Feeding: Common feeder bird. Comes to seed scattered on the ground or to an elevated feeder. Occasionally wanders far to the north, and many of those rare sightings have occurred at bird feeders.

NESTING *Location:* In a medium-height tree, shrub, or cactus. Nests singly or in large colonies. *Nest:* Flimsy platform of twigs. *Eggs:* Usually 2; incubated by both parents for 14–20 days. *Fledging:* Leaves nest at 13–18 days. *Broods:* 2–3 per year.

Mourning Dove
Zenaida macroura, L 12" (31 cm)

One of the most abundant land birds in North America, with a population of about 350 million. Its mournful cooing (hence its name) is recognized by many people, although some mistake it for an owl.

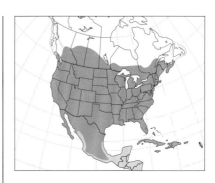

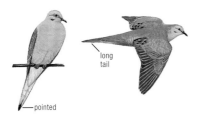

long
tail

pointed

tapered tail with
white tips

♂   **juvenile**

scaly

black spotting

year-round in most of the U.S., but northern breeders are **migratory**. In winter, large flocks congregate around abundant food sources, such as stubble fields or feed lots.

IDENTIFICATION Common to abundant. Medium-size dove; long slender body, tiny head, and long pointed tail. Bursts into flight, the wind whistling through its wings and its tail spread (showing large amounts of white). **Plumage:** Brown with tan head and underparts (slightly pinkish). Black-and-white tail pattern is hidden on perched birds. Male has purplish iridescence on neck. Juvenile is darker with pale feather fringes that give it a scaly look.
Similar species: Larger, heavier White-winged Dove (opposite) has a shorter, square-tipped tail and white wing patches (partially hidden when perched). See also Eurasian Collared-Dove (page 58). "Scaly" juvenile can be confused with Inca Dove (page 59).
Voice: Slow, mournful **call** *oowoo-woo-woo-woo*. Wings make a loud whistling sound in flight, especially during takeoff.

FOOD Seeds of cultivated and wild plants. Feeds on the ground. **Feeding:** Very common feeder bird. Can land on a hanging feeder, but normally feeds on seed scattered below or at a platform feeder.

NESTING *Location:* In a tree or shrub, 10–25 feet up; rarely on a building ledge. *Nest:* Flimsy platform of sticks and twigs. *Eggs:* 2; incubated by both parents for 14–15 days. *Fledging:* Leaves nest at 13–15 days. *Broods:* Up to 6 per year in southern areas.

RANGE Widespread species. Prefers open locations, including rural and residential areas, deserts, and weedy fields; avoids thick forests. Present

SIGHTINGS   JAN   FEB   MAR   APR   MAY   JUN   JUL   AUG   SEP   OCT   NOV   DEC

CUCKOOS　Family Cuculidae

A large family with more than 140 species worldwide, but only six species breed in North America. The anis and roadrunners are included in this family.

Yellow-billed Cuckoo
Coccyzus americanus, L 12" (31 cm)

The Yellow-billed Cuckoo is a summer resident in most of the East, but rare in the West. Local numbers fluctuate in response to insect populations.

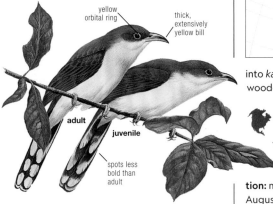

yellow orbital ring

thick, extensively yellow bill

adult

juvenile

spots less bold than adult

into *kakakowlp-kowlp;* sounds hollow and wooden, but carries long distances.

IDENTIFICATION Fairly common. Medium in size, with a slender body and long tail. Tends to stay hidden in thickets and leafy treetops, where its presence is most often revealed by its loud vocalizations.
Plumage: The wings have reddish primaries, most noticeable in flight; black-and-white tail pattern is best seen from below. Yellow color on the bill is usually easy to see. Juvenile has muted tail pattern and buff undertail coverts.
Similar species: Much less common Black-billed Cuckoo (not illustrated) has an all-dark bill, less white in the tail, and lacks reddish color in the wings.
Voice: Calls include a rapid staccato *kuk-kuk-kuk* that usually slows and descends

RANGE Widespread species; summer resident. Favors deciduous woodland with clearings or bordering rivers and streams. Winters in South America. Spring **migration:** mid-April–mid-June; fall migration: August–October.

FOOD Large insects, especially caterpillars. Forages in treetops and shrubbery, where it moves slowly and deliberately.

NESTING *Location:* At low to medium height in a tree, shrub, or vines. *Nest:* Loose platform of twigs. *Eggs:* Usually 2–3; incubated by both parents for 9–11 days. *Fledging:* Leaves nest at 7–19 days.

adult

rufous primaries striking in flight

GOATSUCKERS   Family Caprimulgidae

A family of insect-eaters, active mainly at dusk and night, that includes nighthawks, nightjars, and others. They capture their food in flight with gaping mouths.

Common Nighthawk
Chordeiles minor, L 9½" (24 cm)

Despite its name, the Common Nighthawk is often seen in flight during the day and is not related to hawks. Nighttime foragers seek insects over brightly lit playing fields and parking lots, but most backyard birders will see them flying overhead on warm summer evenings. Its population appears to be declining.

During courtship flight—a U-shaped swooping dive—the male's vibrating primary feathers produce a booming sound.

white throat

♂ speckled above and barred below

juvenile

IDENTIFICATION Fairly common. In flight, its long pointed wings and tail recall those of a falcon. Flight is graceful, but with a bouncy, bat-like quality (a folksy name is "Bullbat"). Roosts on the ground or lengthwise on a branch, where its cryptic plumage makes it difficult to spot. Also perches in the open on fence posts.
Plumage: Mottled and speckled upperparts; tightly barred underparts. Only the adult male has a white throat and tail band, but all birds have a prominent white wing bar visible in flight. Varies geographically—eastern birds are the darkest.
Similar species: Lesser Nighthawk (next page) of the Southwest, which overlaps a bit in range, is very similar, distinguished by the white wing bar closer to the wing-tip, buff underparts, and its trilling call.
Voice: Call is a nasal *peent* given in flight.

RANGE Widespread species; summer resident. No strong habitat preferences, as long as food and nesting habitat are available. **Migrates** to South America for winter. Spring migration: April–early June; fall migration: late August–mid-September.

FOOD Captures insects— moths, mayflies, flying ants, beetles—in flight, mostly at dusk and dawn. Feeds from low to high in the sky, sometimes in loose flocks of up to 100 birds. Drinks on the wing as well, by skimming the water's surface.

bold white bar

♂

NESTING Location: On the ground or flat gravel roofs in urban areas. *Nest:* None. *Eggs:* 2; incubated by female for 16–20 days. *Fledging:* Able to fly at 17–18 days.

male with white bar on tail

SIGHTINGS

| JAN | FEB | MAR | APR | MAY | JUN | JUL | AUG | SEP | OCT | NOV | DEC |

Lesser Nighthawk
Chordeiles acutipennis, L 8½" (22 cm)

The Lesser Nighthawk's trilling twilight call is a familiar spring sound of the desert Southwest. They often congregate near a water source at dusk and are rarely active during midday.

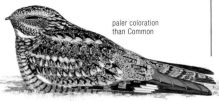

paler coloration than Common

rich buff bars at base of folded primaries

IDENTIFICATION Fairly common. Resembles the Common Nighthawk in lifestyle and plumage, but the two species are rarely seen together. **Plumage:** Mottled and speckled upperparts; buff underparts with faint barring. The **adult male** has a prominent white wing bar (buff in female), white throat (buff in **female**), and white tail band (lacking in female). **Juvenile male**'s wing bar is small; juvenile female's is indistinct. **Similar species:** Common Nighthawk (previous page) is very similar, but habitats of the two species have little overlap: its white wing bar is closer to the body, wings more pointed, underparts whiter, and *peent* call very different. Lesser Nighthawk flies with a looser, fluttery wingbeat and closer to the ground. **Voice:** Distinctive **call** is a rapid, tremulous trill.

RANGE Southwestern species; summer resident. Found in dry, open country, scrubland, and desert, but also frequents lush suburban areas, cities, and open areas with nighttime lighting. Where its range overlaps with Common Nighthawk in the Southwest, Common Nighthawk is found at higher elevations. Vacates the U.S. in winter, moving as far south as Colombia. Spring **migration:** early March–early May; fall migration: early August–October.

FOOD Captures insects—flying ants, swarming termites, mosquitoes—in flight, mostly at dusk and dawn, though sometimes at midday on overcast days. Roams far and wide in search of food, often attracted to insects gathered over bodies of water or around outdoor lighting.

NESTING *Location:* On the ground, sometimes shaded by a shrub, but often fully exposed. Also nests on flat gravel roofs in urban areas. *Nest:* None. *Eggs:* 2; incubated by female for 18–19 days. *Fledging:* Able to fly at about 21 days.

rounder wing tip than Common in all plumages

white bar closer to wing tip than on Common Nighthawk

♂

SWIFTS Family Apodidae

A family of superb aerialists almost always seen roaming the sky in search of insects. They are unable to perch, but can cling to vertical surfaces with tiny, sharp-clawed feet.

Chimney Swift
Chaetura pelagica, L 5¼" (13 cm)

The only swift in the East. In many residential and city locations, they are seen coursing overhead and often nest in chimneys. Tiny spine-like projections at the tips of the tail feathers help it cling to a vertical surface. If you suspect your chimney has nesting swifts, don't light a fire during the nesting season!

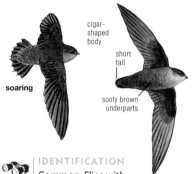

cigar-shaped body

short tail

soaring

sooty brown underparts

IDENTIFICATION Common. Flies with stiff, fluttering wing beats; when soaring, the wings look more rounded and the tail is often spread. Displaying pairs glide in tandem with their wings held in a V. **Plumage:** Often described as "a cigar with wings." The plumage is dark overall, slightly paler (grayish brown) on the throat. **Similar species:** Sometimes mistaken for a martin or swallow. By comparison, Chimney Swift has longer, more pointed, and swept-back wings and flies faster with stiffer ("twinkling") wing beats. See Purple Martin (pages 132–133). Vaux's Swift (not illustrated) is a very similar swift—smaller and slightly paler on the throat and rump—that is fairly common in the Pacific region. If you see a look-alike swift

in that region, chances are it's a Vaux's. **Voice:** Quite vocal in flight. **Call** is a series of chippering notes, sometimes run together into a rapid twitter.

RANGE Eastern species; summer resident. Most abundant around cities and towns. Migrating birds assemble at dusk in large flocks to roost for the night in building shafts, church steeples, and large chimneys. At high speed, hundreds of swirling birds disappear one by one into a dark shaft—a memorable sight. Winters in South America. Spring **migration:** late March–mid-May; fall migration: late September–mid-October.

FOOD Captures small insects in flight. Usually forages high and descends to drink, skimming the water's surface with its bill.

NESTING *Location:* In a chimney or building shaft. *Nest:* Half cup of short twigs, adhered to a vertical surface with sticky saliva. *Eggs:* Usually 4–5; incubated by both parents for 19–20 days. *Fledging:* Able to fly at about 30 days.

HUMMINGBIRDS   Family Trochilidae

Hummingbirds are the smallest of birds. Their glittering plumage, remarkable powers of flight, and attraction to hummingbird feeders offer endless entertainment.

Ruby-throated Hummingbird

Archilochus colubris, L 3¾" (10 cm)

The only hummingbird seen regularly in the East, where it is common at sugar water feeders.

white throat
♀
throat often looks blackish
♂
white tips
forked tail

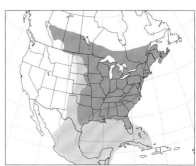

IDENTIFICATION Common. The Ruby-throated has a feisty personality and aggressively defends its nectar source from others.
Plumage: Metallic green above. Only the **adult male** has an iridescent ruby red gorget (throat) with small black chin and blackish, forked tail. **Adult female** and **juvenile** have a whitish throat, rarely with a few red spots, and a tail with large white tips.
Similar species: None in the East. Any hummer that shows up at an eastern feeder after early October should be scrutinized; it could be a Rufous Hummingbird (page 71) or another rarity.
Voice: Slightly twangy chips—*tchew* or *chih*. Chase notes given in rapid series.

RANGE Eastern species; summer resident. Inhabits open woodlands, woodland edges, and flowering gardens. Despite tiny size, most fly nonstop across the Gulf of Mexico to winter in Mexico and Central America. Spring **migration:** March–May; fall migration: August–September.

FOOD Hover-feeds on flower nectar or at feeders; also captures small insects and spiders, the main foods fed to nestlings.
Feeding: Hummingbird feeders and backyard flower gardens.

NESTING *Location:* In a tree or shrub, usually 10–20 feet up. *Nest:* Tiny cuplike bowl of plant down and spiderweb, the exterior decorated with lichen and dead leaves. *Eggs:* 2; incubated by female for 11–16 days. *Fledging:* Leaves nest at 18–20 days.

ruby throat
black under bill and eye
♂

The Anna's Hummingbird builds a nest smaller than a teacup.

A Ruby-throated Hummingbird checks out a petunia.

MINI-TURBOS

Hummingbirds live at warp speed—besides insects, they have the highest metabolism of any animal. A hummer's heart may beat 1,000 times each minute while its lungs inhale 250 breaths. In flight, a hummingbird's muscles consume oxygen 10 times more efficiently than elite human athletes.

To maintain such an active lifestyle, hummingbirds often take in more than their own body weight each day. Sugar water is like rocket fuel for the miniature turbos in your backyard. (For tips on attracting and feeding hummers, see Bird Feeding, pages 22–23.) These tiny birds also eat lots of small insects, which supply necessary fats and proteins.

FLIGHT STYLE

To hover in place, zoom backward, and even fly upside down, hummingbirds twist their wings 180 degrees on each flap. This helps them generate lift on both the upstrokes and downstrokes—a unique ability among birds. Smaller species can beat their wings 80 times a second, generating their namesake hum.

AT REST

Hummingbirds eat every 15 minutes or so during the day, but they can't keep this up while asleep. To cope with the demands of their extreme metabolism, hummers enter a state of torpor at night that slows their heart rate and breathing by more than 90 percent, and lowers internal body temperature close to the point of hypothermia. A sleeping hummingbird may use 50 times less energy than when awake.

NESTING

Male hummingbirds are perennial bachelors. After mating, they zoom off to the next flower while females must build a nest, lay eggs, and raise their chicks on their own. Flashy looks and aerobatic stunts have their allure, but a male hummer just isn't interested in a long-term commitment.

Black-chinned Hummingbird

Archilochus alexandri, L 3¾" (10 cm)

The Black-chinned is one of the most widespread hummers in the West, ranging north to British Columbia and particularly common at low elevations in the Southwest.

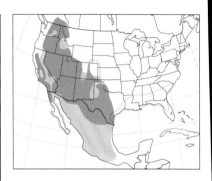

crown with a dusky cast

long, slightly downcurved bill

♀

white tips

extensive white chest cut off sharply and evenly by dark throat

♂

IDENTIFICATION Common. Slender with a medium-to-long bill. When feeding, habitually wags its tail. The male's wings create a dry buzzing in flight, softer in females and juveniles. **Plumage:** Metallic green above. **Adult male**'s gorget is matte black above and violet below (often appears all black); it has a white breast band below the gorget and a black, slightly forked tail. **Adult female** has grayish white face, throat, and underparts; a longer bill; and a shorter tail with white tips. Immature male is similar to female, usually with a few violet feathers on its throat. **Similar species:** Larger female Anna's Hummingbird (opposite) has a shorter bill, is duskier below with green on the flanks, and usually has some red feathers on the throat. **Voice:** Slightly twangy or nasal chips—*tchew* or *chih*—nearly identical to the Ruby-throated.

RANGE Western species; summer resident. Found in open woodlands, streamside groves, shady canyons, suburban gardens, and parks—it's partial to sycamores and oaks. Winters primarily in western Mexico. Spring **migration:** March–mid-May; fall migration: August–late September.

FOOD Hover-feeds on flower nectar or at feeders; also captures small insects and spiders, the main foods fed to nestlings. **Feeding:** Hummingbird feeders and backyard flower gardens.

NESTING *Location:* In a shrub or tree, usually 4–10 feet up. *Nest:* Distinctive, straw-colored cup often built of fuzz from sycamore leaves (looks like felt). *Eggs:* 2; incubated by female for 11–16 days. *Fledging:* Leaves nest at about 21 days.

black chin with violet purple throat band

♂

Anna's Hummingbird
Calypte anna, L 4" (10 cm)

Unlike other North American humming-birds, Anna's is nonmigratory. It is a familiar and welcome resident of West Coast backyards from southern California to southern British Columbia.

IDENTIFICATION Common. Medium-size hummer with a chunky look. Male "sings" a wiry, scratchy song, often for prolonged periods. **Plumage:** Metallic green upperparts; dingy grayish white and green below. Flashy **adult male** has brilliant rose red gorget *and* crown ("helmeted") and a blackish tail. **Adult female** has a white throat with green spots and blotched with red in center; tail has white tips. Immature

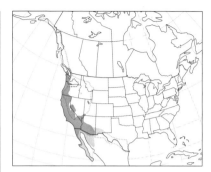

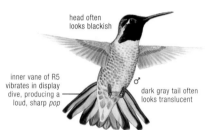

head often looks blackish

inner vane of R5 vibrates in display dive, producing a loud, sharp *pop*

♂

dark gray tail often looks translucent

short bill

usually with some rose red in center of throat

shining rose red crown and gorget

♀

dingy gray below with extensive green flanks

♂

male similar to adult female, but with more red on throat and a few red feathers on crown; immature female lacks any red and is paler below.
Similar species: Compare female and immature Anna's to female Black-chinned (opposite), a slender hummer with paler underparts that never has red on throat.
Voice: Common **call** is a sharp *tewk*, chase call a scratchy twittering *chicka-chicka-chicka* series, and male's song a rhythmic series of scratchy notes. The male's

breakneck, 100-foot display dive creates an explosive pop as it pulls up just short of the perched female.

RANGE West Coast species; year-round resident. Originally lived in riparian thickets, chaparral, and coastal scrub, but now abundant in back-yard gardens and city parks. Colonized southern Arizona and southern Nevada in the mid-20th century.

FOOD Hover-feeds on flower nectar or at feeders; also captures small insects and spiders.
Feeding: Hummingbird feeders and back-yard flower gardens.

NESTING *Location:* In a tree or shrub, 4–30 feet up. *Nest:* Neat cup of plant down and spiderweb. *Eggs:* 2; incubated by female for 14–19 days. *Fledging:* Leaves nest at 18–23 days.

Broad-tailed Hummingbird

Selasphorus platycercus, L 4" (10 cm)

The Broad-tailed is a hummingbird of western mountains, where the adult male's cricket-like wing trill is a signature sound of summer. Separating a female Broad-tailed from a female Rufous Hummingbird is challenging even for experts.

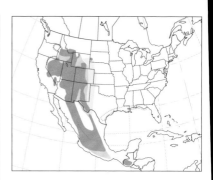

bluish tint to green upperparts

whitish eye ring

♂

thin rufous edges show on folded tail

evenly spotted throat

♀

blended buffy underparts and usually buffy collar

long tail extends beyond wing tips

IDENTIFICATION Common. Average in size and structure, but the tail is impressively large. The narrow tips of the male's outer primary feathers produce a trilling noise in flight, often the first indication of its presence.

Plumage: Metallic green above. **Adult male**'s gorget is rose red with a thin white stripe under the bill, extending around and behind the eye; white breast band contrasts with green flanks and a black tail with thin rufous edging. **Adult female** has a white throat with tiny green spots, sometimes rose red feathers at center, underparts washed with cinnamon, and a broad tail with rufous base and white tips.

Similar species: Female and immature birds can be confused with female Rufous (opposite).

rose red gorget with narrow white line extending under bill

♂

Here are the basics: the female Rufous is smaller, is more intensely rufous on its flanks and smaller tail, and has a whiter forecollar. The Rufous's call—a hard, sharp *tewk*—is very different from the Broad-tailed's metallic *chip*.

Voice: Calls include a metallic *chip*, often doubled as *ch-chip* or repeated in a series. Males' impressive courtship dives are accompanied by loud wing trilling.

RANGE Western species; summer resident. From foothill canyons to high mountain meadows of southern and central Rockies (but not in Canada). Winters mainly in Mexico. Spring **migration:** March–mid-May; fall migration: August–late September.

FOOD Hover-feeds on flower nectar or at feeders; also captures small insects and spiders, the main foods fed to nestlings.

Feeding: Hummingbird feeders and backyard flower gardens.

NESTING *Location:* In a tree or shrub, usually 4–20 feet up. *Nest:* Neat cup of plant down and spiderweb, decorated on the outside with lichen, moss, and bits of bark. *Eggs:* 2; incubated by female for 16–19 days. *Fledging:* Leaves nest at 21–26 days.

Rufous Hummingbird
Selasphorus rufus, L 3¾" (10 cm)

The Rufous Hummingbird is a pugnacious species that breeds farther north than any other hummer. In migration, it is common at feeders throughout the West.

 IDENTIFICATION Common. Small in size but large in personality, it often chases off other hummers at feeding locations.
Plumage: Adult male is bright, coppery rufous on the upperparts, flanks, and spiky tail; sometimes with green flecks on the back; the gorget is red with orange highlights. **Adult female** has metallic

golden green back

reddish center to throat

♀

♂

on most adult males, back all-rufous

gorget often appears dark

triangular white collar borders rufous underparts

green upperparts; a white throat with bronzy green spots, usually with red at the center; white underparts with rufous flanks; and a tail with rufous base and white tips. Immature male is similar to female, but with red spots on its white throat, and more rufous on the back. Immature female has a white throat.
Similar species: Male Allen's Hummingbird (not illustrated) along the West Coast has a solid green back, but is very similar to male Rufous (some male Rufous have green-flecked backs); female Allen's is almost identical to female Rufous. Female and immature Rufous Hummingbirds have more rufous on the flanks and tail than other species detailed in this book.

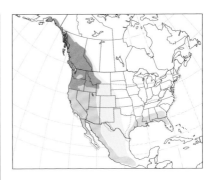

Voice: Hard, sharp **call** *tewk;* chase note *zee-chuppity-chuppity.*

 RANGE Western species; summer resident. Breeds in open forests, clearings, and streamside groves. Winters in Mexico; small numbers along Gulf Coast, strays to East. Spring **migration** (mainly through Pacific lowlands): early February–May; fall migration (mainly through Rockies): late June–mid-October.

FOOD Hover-feeds on flower nectar or at feeders; also captures small insects and spiders.
Feeding: Hummingbird feeders and flower gardens.

NESTING *Location:* In a tree or shrub, 4–30 feet up. *Nest:* Neat cup of plant down and spiderweb. *Eggs:* 2; incubated by female for 15–17 days. *Fledging:* Leaves nest at about 21 days.

flame red gorget

♂

mostly rufous tail

♀

white tips to tail

| | JAN | FEB | MAR | APR | MAY | JUN | JUL | AUG | SEP | OCT | NOV | DEC |

PLOVERS   Family Charadriidae

This family is part of a much larger assemblage of birds collectively known as shorebirds, which includes stilts, avocets, sandpipers, curlews, godwits, dowitchers, and snipes, among others. Many of these species occur in coastal and freshwater locations but are beyond the scope of this book.

Killdeer
Charadrius vociferous, L 10½" (27 cm)

The Killdeer—a type of plover—is a conspicuous shorebird that doesn't require a watery location for breeding or feeding. It prefers open, often human-altered habitats. In fact, few native birds have benefited more from the fragmentation of the American landscape.

moves with a run-stop-run cadence while feeding

two breast bands

IDENTIFICATION Common. Easily recognizable by its shape—slender and horizontal—and distinctive plumage. While feeding, it moves with a jerky, run-stop-run cadence. Its noisy call is often the first signal of its presence. Migrating and wintering birds sometimes form loose flocks of 20 or more birds.
Plumage: Two prominent black bands on chest and black bar on forehead. Brown upperparts, white underparts, and a reddish orange rump, most noticeable in flight or during a broken-wing display (see opposite). Flightless **downy young** have single breast bands and leave the nest shortly after hatching.
Similar species: None. Downy young with a single breast band could be mistaken for

a different species of plover, but an adult Killdeer is usually nearby and probably making a fuss.
Voice: Loud and piercing *kill-dee* (for which it is named) or *dee-dee-dee* **call** is easy to recognize. The Killdeer is often active at night—look for it on lighted playing fields and parking lots—and can be heard calling in the darkness, especially in spring and summer.

RANGE Widespread species. Although often seen around ponds and puddles, the Killdeer prefers

A downy young Killdeer has a single breast band; the adult has two breast bands.

to breed in heavily grazed meadows, large lawns, golf courses, sod farms, airports, and parking lots, among other unnatural landscapes. Northern breeders are migratory, retreating southward for the winter months. Spring **migration** is early, with birds showing up in the middle latitudes with the first bit of warmth after mid-February; fall migration peaks in August–September. Many birds linger in the north until November or later, if warm weather persists.

 FOOD Diet consists mostly of invertebrates, especially earthworms, grasshoppers, beetles, and snails picked from the ground or mud.

NESTING *Location:* Open ground (gravelly areas are favored). *Nest:* Shallow scraped indentation, lined with pebbles and nearby debris—especially white objects, including shells, plastic items, even cigarette filters—and well camouflaged. *Eggs:* Usually 4; incubated by both parents for 22–28 days. *Fledging:* Downy young leave the nest almost immediately and can feed themselves, accompanied by parents; able to fly at 30–40 days.

Displays When protecting its nest or flightless young, the feisty Killdeer has evolved some effective and easily

The Killdeer's ostentatious "broken-wing" display serves to lead a predator away from its nest.

observed tactics. During a **"broken-wing" display**, it drags a partially open wing on the ground, spreads its long tail, and exposes its bright, reddish-orange rump, leading a potential predator away from the area before suddenly flying off. The **"ungulate" display**, another theatrical performance, seems designed to divert a large grazing animal (or person) from trampling its nest: The loudly screaming bird rushes toward the animal; if that doesn't work, it lowers its breast, raises its long tail, and beats the ground with its wings, continuing to give high-pitched calls. Bravo!

long tail and reddish orange rump

The "ungulate" display probably evolved to divert large animals from trampling the Killdeer's nest.

GROWN-UP CHICKS

In the human world, calling someone "precocious" is considered a compliment. It means that a person is ahead of the game, shrewder or more mature than others of the same age.

In the avian world, a similar word applies to birds that develop quickly: They are said to be *precocial*.

LEAVING THE NEST

Most birds are naked and helpless when they hatch, but a few standouts emerge from the egg practically ready to fly. These precocial chicks are already covered with downy feathers, their eyes are open, and they can leave the nest within hours.

Killdeer are a classic example. When a young Killdeer hatches, it starts to walk as soon as its feathers are dry. Though it depends on parents to protect it for a while, the chick can find its own food and run from predators right out of the gate.

This is a good strategy if, like the Killdeer, your nest is an open scrape on bare ground. Any movement might give away the nest's location, so chicks must be born to run.

Downy feathers protect Killdeer chicks from cold and damp.

NAKED AND AFRAID

Compare the Killdeer's strategy to that of, say, an American Robin—which weighs about the same (three ounces). When a robin's egg hatches, the chick is featherless and blind, utterly reliant on its parents for warmth and food.

But here's a big difference: The robin hatches twice as fast. When a Killdeer is one day old, it is actually *two weeks* older than the day-old robin, because it takes so long to develop inside the egg.

A robin chick spends that extra time inside the nest, carefully tended by its parents as it matures. Its brain keeps growing, along with the rest of its body. Out in the open, the young Killdeer is already on the run, having hatched with a developmental head start.

American Robin chicks are hatched featherless and blind.

GULLS   Family Laridae

Identifying gulls can be complicated. Some species take more than three years to reach adult plumage, and the intervening immature plumages are often quite different.

Ring-billed Gull
Larus delawarensis, L 17½" (45 cm)

The Ring-billed Gull is the most widespread and familiar gull over much of North America. Its population probably exceeds four million birds.

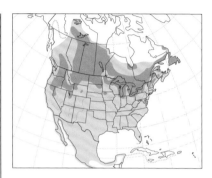

IDENTIFICATION Common to abundant. Ring-billed are the typical gull at inland locations in winter. They notoriously hang out around shopping centers, parks, and garbage dumps, as well as the standard watery locations. **Plumage:** Takes just over two years to reach adult plumage. **Winter adult** is pale gray above, white below; bill is yellow with a prominent black ring, and legs and eyes are yellow. **First-winter** bird has a pale gray back, pinkish legs, mottled brown head and underparts, pink bill with a black tip, and variable, brown tail band. **Similar species:** Discernible from California and Herring Gulls (following pages) by its smaller size. Adult Herring Gull has pink legs and a yellow bill with a red spot. Adult California Gull is darker gray above and has greenish legs, a yellow bill with black and red spots, and dark eyes. First-winter Herring and California Gulls are overall much browner. **Voice: Calls** include a plaintive, mewing *kee-ew* and a sharper *kyow*.

RANGE Widespread species. Most backyard birders see these gulls in winter, but small numbers of immature birds remain in southern locations during the summer. Spring **migration:** February–April; fall migration: September–October.

FOOD In winter, scavenges along beaches, harbors, lakeshores, and garbage dumps for refuse but also catches fish and consumes insects, earthworms, and grain.

NESTING *Location:* Ring-billed Gulls breed in colonies, mostly on low, sparsely vegetated islands in lakes—not typical backyard locations. Seventy percent of the world population breeds in Canada.

pale eye

black subterminal band

breeding adult

pale gray

dark eye

1st winter

pinkish legs

variable width tail band

California Gull
Larus californicus, L 21" (53 cm)

The California Gull is increasing its numbers along the Pacific coast, where it is the most common gull on the coastal slope. State bird of Utah.

IDENTIFICATION Common. Intermediate in size between the smaller Ring-billed Gull and larger Herring Gull, and with a fairly long, straight-sided bill and a lanky look.

Plumage: Takes almost four years to reach adult plumage. **Winter adult** is medium gray above; importantly, its bill is yellow with red and black spots near the tip and it has dark eyes and greenish yellow legs. In flight from below, note the smoky gray secondaries. **First-winter** bird has mottled, brownish-gray plumage, a pinkish bill with a black tip, and pink legs.

Similar species: Resembles Ring-billed and Herring Gulls (previous and opposite pages). Adult Ring-billed is lighter gray above and has pale eyes and a yellow bill with a prominent black ring, while the adult Herring is bigger with pink legs and has no black on its bill. First-winter Herring and California Gulls both have mottled brown backs (not pale gray, like first-winter Ring-billed); the Herring Gull's bill is heavier and blacker, and its head is usually paler.

Voice: Calls include a throaty *kyow* and a higher pitched *kier*.

RANGE Western species. Breeds mainly in the arid interior West, and migrates primarily to the Pacific coast in winter. In spring, adults **migrate** away

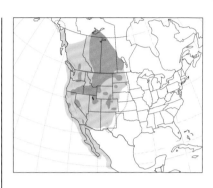

from coastal areas as early as late February; fall migrants leave breeding colonies in July.

FOOD Summer diet consists mainly of insects, supplemented with worms, small rodents, and carrion. Along the coast in winter, they eat marine life and scavenge around harbors and garbage dumps.

NESTING *Location:* Breeds in colonies on islands in rivers and lakes, areas located well away from most backyards.

slender pinkish bill with blackish tip

dark eye

heavy brownish wash

black and red spots

darker gray than Ring-billed or Herring

pinkish legs

1st winter

winter adult

yellowish green legs

dark secondaries

no obvious pale window

Herring Gull
Larus argentatus, L 25" (64 cm)

Distributed around the Northern Hemisphere. Extremely adaptable, the Herring Gull is an opportunistic feeder around human activities and is able to survive in almost any climate.

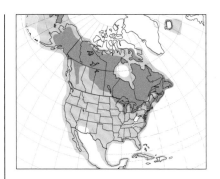

 IDENTIFICATION Common. A large gull with pink legs at all ages and a fairly stout bill.
Plumage: Takes almost four years to reach adult plumage. **Winter adult** is pale gray above, white below; white head is flecked with brown (pure white in summer); and it has a yellow bill with a red spot near the tip, pale yellow eyes, and pink legs. **First-winter** is a mottled brown overall, often looking pale headed by midwinter; bill is dark with variable pink at base.
Similar species: See Ring-billed (page 75) and California Gulls (opposite page). Gray mantle colors of adult Herring and Ring-billed Gulls are almost identical; the California Gull is noticeably darker gray.
Voice: Variety of **calls**, including a trumpeting *keeyow, kyow-kyow-kyow.*

RANGE Widespread species. Breeds along the Atlantic coast of the U.S. and Canada, throughout the Great Lakes region, and in the far north. It is especially abundant in the Northeast, where it both breeds and winters. Herring and Ring-billed Gulls winter together across large sections of the U.S. Usually arrives in wintering areas by October and departs by May.

FOOD Generalist predator. Feeds on fish, marine invertebrates (shellfish, sea urchins, crabs, etc.), insects, other birds (and their eggs and young) and is an opportunistic scavenger of dead fish, carrion, and human refuse.

NESTING *Location:* On the ground; prefers to breed on islands. *Nest:* Scraped indentation. *Eggs:* Usually 3; incubated by both parents for 27–30 days. *Fledging:* Leaves nest in a day or two, but remains nearby; able to fly at about 6 weeks.

pale window

dark tail

1st winter

often pale headed

striking pale eye

extensive streaking

pale gray upperparts

pink legs

winter adult

NEW WORLD VULTURES **Family Cathartidae**

A small family of large soaring birds that primarily eats carrion. All have small, unfeathered heads and hooked bills. Inaccurately, vultures are often referred to as buzzards.

Black Vulture
Coragyps atratus, L 25" (64 cm)

Appropriately dressed in funereal black, this efficient and successful carrion scavenger has a huge hemispheric range extending from southern New England to southern South America.

soars on flat wings, wing flaps are rapid and shallow

adults

pale grayish legs

short tail

extensive white base to outer primaries

IDENTIFICATION Common. In flight, short tail barely extends behind the broad wings and feet almost reach tip of tail. Soars high on steady wings held flat. Usually seen in groups, especially when roosting.
Plumage: Appears all black when perched, with bare head of wrinkled gray skin; whitish legs. In flight, underwings show large whitish patches on outer wing.
Similar species: Turkey Vulture (opposite) has narrower, two-tone wings (not white patches) and a much longer tail, usually flies with up-tilted wings, and almost never flaps rapidly. Adult Turkey Vultures have browner plumage and red facial skin and legs. Immature ones have gray head and legs (like Black Vulture); on perched bird, look for Turkey Vulture's longer wings, more slender body, and smaller head.
Voice: Essentially silent; nesting birds utter hisses and grunts.

RANGE Mainly southeastern species; year-round resident. Abundant in the Southeast, but avoids mountainous country and open plains. Range is expanding into southern New England.

FOOD Feeds on animal carcasses, including roadkill; scavenges at garbage dumps. Soars to great heights, locating its food by sight and also by spying on Turkey Vultures that more efficiently locate food by smell. Dominant at feeding sites.

NESTING *Location:* On the ground in a concealing thicket or hollow log; occasionally in an abandoned building. *Nest:* None. *Eggs:* Usually 2; incubated by both parents for 37–41 days. *Fledging*: Leaves nest at 75–80 days; usually accompanied by parents for many months.

SIGHTINGS

| JAN | FEB | MAR | APR | MAY | JUN | JUL | AUG | SEP | OCT | NOV | DEC |

Turkey Vulture
Cathartes aura, L 27" (69 cm)

The most common vulture across most of North America. Unique among vultures, it locates the carrion it feeds on by using its sense of smell, in addition to visual clues.

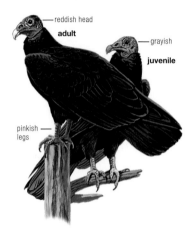

reddish head
adult

grayish
juvenile

pinkish legs

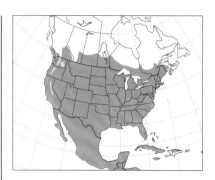

Since birds range far and wide, backyard birders often see them soaring overhead or roosting together in a tree. Northern breeding birds migrate south in fall. Spring **migration** peaks in March–early April; fall migration: September–October.

FOOD Feeds on animal carcasses, specializing in small food items that it can eat quickly. Its keen sense of smell allows it to locate carcasses concealed beneath the forest canopy.

IDENTIFICATION Common. A consummate soaring bird that rarely flaps, seeming to catch the slightest updraft by tilting its long wings from side to side. In flight, note its long, narrow wings, long tail, and tiny head; soaring birds fly with wings in a noticeable dihedral V.
Plumage: Appears blackish brown when perched. In flight, underwings are two-toned—silvery and black. **Adult** has reddish head of bare skin and pinkish legs. **Juvenile** has grayish head and legs.
Similar species: See Black Vulture (opposite), which has a more limited distribution—compare the range maps.
Voice: Essentially silent; nesting birds utter hisses and grunts.

RANGE Widespread species. Favors wooded regions (for breeding) with open areas (for foraging).

soars on slight dihedral, wing flaps are slow and deep

two-toned underwings

long tail

NESTING *Location:* On the ground in an isolated rocky crevice or hollow log; occasionally in an abandoned building. *Nest:* None. *Eggs:* Usually 2; incubated by both parents for 38–41 days. *Fledging:* Leaves nest at 75–80 days. Young birds soon join a nearby communal roost and fend for themselves.

APPRECIATING VULTURES

The best way to show appreciation for vultures is to avoid calling them buzzards, which is technically a name for certain Old World hawks. Vultures are a whole different animal.

These scavengers are amazing creatures. In North America, we have three species of vultures, the California Condor, the Turkey Vulture, and the Black Vulture, and all are worthy of appreciation.

FOLLOW THE NOSE

An adult Turkey Vulture is exquisitely elegant in flight, soaring to lofty heights on a hot thermal of rising air. It holds each wing in a distinctive, upswept profile, which helps separate this species at a distance from most hawks, which usually keep their wings flat.

Despite their cartoonish reputation, Turkey Vultures do not stalk animals they think are about to expire. Instead, they track down carcasses that are already good and dead, releasing certain decomposition gases that Turkey Vultures, with their ultra-sensitive nostrils, can smell from miles away.

The Turkey Vulture has a cast-iron, acidic stomach, as one might expect from its delectable diet. Surprisingly, a Turkey Vulture's excrement is generally sterile, even if it has ingested spores of anthrax or other noxious pathogens. This helps explain why Turkey Vultures habitually poop down their own legs. Doing so helps cool off and sterilize their feet after walking around bacteria-filled carcasses.

With distinctive reddish heads, Turkey Vultures range as far north as southern Canada.

NATURE'S GARBAGE DISPOSAL

Black Vultures and California Condors do not have a well-developed sense of smell, but they make up for this deficiency with situational awareness. Condors rely on their eyesight to find food. Black Vultures look for congregating Turkey Vultures, and will happily join them at the feast.

Up close, Black Vultures and California Condors are perhaps even uglier than their Turkey Vulture cousins, but of course they might disagree. After all, who are we to judge? At least they help clean up our world, one nasty scrap at a time.

Black Vultures live in the southeastern United States and in Latin America.

HAWKS, KITES, & EAGLES   Family Accipitridae

Worldwide family of diurnal birds of prey with hooked bills and strong talons. On flying birds focus on any wing and tail patterns.

Mississippi Kite
Ictinia mississippiensis, L 14½" (37 cm)

The Mississippi Kite is the most common of the fives species of kite that nest in North America.

juvenile

pale gray head

pale bands on tail

black tail

adult ♂

RANGE Southern Great Plains and southeastern species; summer resident. Very common around shelterbelt tree plantings, towns, and backyards in Kansas, Oklahoma, and north-central Texas. Its aggressive nest defense sometimes results in diving attacks on people. Migrates to southern South America for the winter. Spring migration: early April–mid-May; fall migration: late August–mid-October.

IDENTIFICATION Locally common. Buoyant flier with pointed wings. In areas of abundance, these gregarious, crow-size birds often hunt in groups and form loose breeding colonies. **Plumage:** In flight, upper wing has a whitish secondary patch. Adult male is dark gray overall with whitish head and red eyes; female has darker head. Juvenile has heavily streaked underparts and banded tail. **Similar species:** Unlike most common hawks (buteos) that have heavier bodies and broad, rounded wings, the Mississippi Kite looks more like a gray falcon. **Voice:** The two-syllable, high-pitched **call** is whistled: *phee-phew.*

FOOD Nimbly captures and consumes large flying insects in flight; also hunts frogs, lizards, snakes, and a variety of small birds and mammals.

never hovers

adult ♂

whitish secondary patch

NESTING *Location:* In a tree, often at the edge of a woodlot. *Nest:* Loose construction of twigs lined with green leaves. *Eggs:* Usually 2; incubated by both parents for 29–32 days. *Fledging:* Young moves to nearby limbs at 25–30 days; able to fly at 30–35 days.

Sharp-shinned Hawk

Accipiter striatus, L 10–14" (25–36 cm)

This is one of the accipiters—bird-eating woodland hawks. Winter bird feeders are favorite hunting locations. Although some bird-feeding enthusiasts vilify the feisty "Sharpie," our advice is to marvel at the drama of the hunt. These predators serve a needed function by keeping wild bird populations healthy and wary.

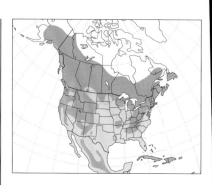

small head — adult ♂

juvenile ♀

thin legs

Cooper's has thinner, darker streaks below. Sharpies are about the size of a grackle; Cooper's are closer to crow size. In direct flight, Sharpies have fast, flicking wing beats; Cooper's have noticeably slower, stiffer wing beats.
Voice: A high, chattering *kew-kew-kew* **call** heard around the nest.

 | RANGE Widespread. Breeds in northern and western forests, but thinly distributed and declining. More widespread and commonly seen in winter, particularly around bird feeders. Northern breeders migrate south in fall. Spring **migration:** mid-April–early May; fall migration: September for juveniles, October for adults.

 | IDENTIFICATION Fairly common. Small hawk with short, rounded wings and long tail that allows it to maneuver rapidly around tree trunks and branches.
Plumage: Adult is bluish gray above and rufous below; dark cap blends into nape. **Female** is larger than male (close to size of male Cooper's Hawk). **Juvenile** is brownish above with coarse brown streaks below.
Similar species: Cooper's Hawk (opposite) has longer round-tipped tail, heavier legs, larger head, and longer neck. Juvenile

 | FOOD Preys mainly on small woodland songbirds. Attacks from a perch or cruises low, using shrubs or even buildings for cover.

| NESTING
Location: Most often concealed high in a conifer. *Nest:* Platform of sticks. *Eggs:* Usually 4–5; incubated mostly by female for 30–35 days. *Fledging:* Leaves nest at about 23 days.

curved leading edge

shorter square tipped tail

juvenile

Cooper's Hawk

Accipiter cooperii, L 15–18" (38–46 cm)

Cooper's Hawk and the similar Sharp-shinned are swift and effective bird ambushers that patrol bird feeders and woodlands in search of a meal.

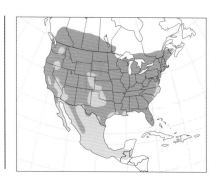

 IDENTIFICATION Fairly common. Cooper's and Sharp-shinned Hawks hunt in a similar fashion, but the larger Cooper's favors larger prey—doves, jays, and robins rather than chickadees, titmice, and sparrows. **Plumage: Adult** is bluish gray above with rusty bars below; blackish cap contrasts with paler nape (more blended in Sharp-shinned). **Juvenile** is brownish above, often with orangish highlights on the head, and thin, dark streaks below. **Similar species:** See Sharp-shinned Hawk (opposite) and Red-shouldered Hawk (next page). **Voice:** Chattering, strident **call** *kak-kak-kak,* reminiscent of Sharp-shinned Hawk but lower pitched.

straight leading edge

head projects

juvenile

long round-tipped tail

NESTING *Location:* In a tree. *Nest:* Bulky platform of sticks. *Eggs:* Usually 3–5; incubated mostly by female for 30–36 days. *Fledging:* Leaves nest at 30–35 days. Young learn to hunt in about 3 weeks.

RANGE Widespread species. Inhabits forests and forest edges, even around urban locations. Year-round resident throughout much of North America, but northern populations migrate south in fall. Spring migration: mainly in April; fall **migration:** September–October.

FOOD Preys primarily on birds up to the size of a flicker, and small mammals up to the size of a squirrel. Hunts much like a Sharp-shinned, but often perches more openly, even on telephone poles.

larger head, longer neck, and tawny nape

juvenile ♀

female larger than male

blackish cap

adult ♂

SIGHTINGS

JAN	FEB	MAR	APR	MAY	JUN	JUL	AUG	SEP	OCT	NOV	DEC

Red-shouldered Hawk

Buteo lineatus, L 17" (43 cm)

The colorful Red-shouldered Hawk is a vocal bird with a loud voice. Backyard birders often hear them calling in flight from high overhead.

 IDENTIFICATION Fairly common. Medium-to-large hawk. Soaring bird holds wings cupped forward and has rounded wingtips.
Plumage: In flight, there is a pale crescent ("window") visible at the base of the primaries. West Coast birds are more richly colored and checkered; those in south Florida, paler with whitish head. **Adult** has rufous upperwing coverts ("red shoulders") and densely barred rufous underparts. Wings and tail are dramatically barred in black and white. **Juvenile** has brown-streaked underparts and a dark tail with numerous pale bands.

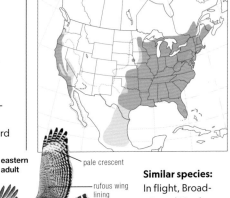

eastern adult

pale crescent

rufous wing lining

banded tail

streaked underparts

pale crescent

Similar species: In flight, Broad-winged Hawk (next page) has pointed wingtips and much paler underwings without pale wing crescent. Also compare to juvenile Cooper's (previous page) and Red-tailed Hawks (pages 86–87).

Voice: The loud, screaming **call** *KEE-ahh* is often given in a series; beware of imitations by Blue Jays or Steller's Jays.

RANGE Widespread species. Inhabits well-watered woodlands, suburban areas with nearby woodlots, and oak and eucalyptus groves in the West. Year-round resident in many areas, but northern breeders in the East are migratory. Spring **migration:** February–early April; fall migration: mid-October–late December.

FOOD A perch-hunter of the forest understory, it feeds on frogs, snakes, lizards, and small mammals.

NESTING *Location:* In a high tree crotch. *Nest:* Bulky platform of sticks. *Eggs:* Usually 3–4; incubated mostly by female for about 33 days. *Fledging:* Leaves nest at about 6 weeks.

eastern juvenile

reddish shoulders

rufous underparts

eastern adult

Broad-winged Hawk
Buteo platypterus, L 16" (41 cm)

The smallest North American buteo hawk, and a rather nondescript bird. It is spectacular in migration, entirely vacating North America and traveling in large "kettles"—spiraling clusters of birds that ride upward on warm air currents and then glide gradually downward in their desired direction.

juvenile

adult

dark malar stripe

rufous-brown barred underparts

black wing tips; more pointed than Red-shouldered

IDENTIFICATION Fairly common. This small woodland hawk has a chunky, compact shape, short tail, and broad-based wings with pointed tips. When breeding, it is inconspicuous and would often go unnoticed if not for its loud whistled call.

Plumage: Dark malar stripe (moustache). In flight, has pale underwings with a dark border. **Adult** is dark brown above and has rufous-brown barred underparts and a blackish tail with two white bands. **Juvenile** has breast variably streaked with brown and indistinct bands on tail.

variable whitish underwing

juvenile

black trailing edge

adult

Similar species: Compare juvenile to juvenile Red-shouldered (opposite), Cooper's (page 83), and Red-tailed Hawks (pages 86–87).

Voice: Call is a thin, shrill, slightly descending whistle *pee-heeeee* that carries well; imitated by Blue Jays.

RANGE Central and eastern species; summer resident. Inhabits forested areas and migrates to Central and South America for the winter. Migrating kettles often pass over suburban and urban locations. Spring **migration:** mid-March–mid-May; fall migration: early September–early October.

FOOD A patient, perch-hunter specialist of the forest understory, often near watery edges. It feeds on frogs, snakes, lizards, small birds, small mammals, and insects.

NESTING *Location:* At mid-level in a large tree. *Nest:* Small platform of sticks. *Eggs:* Usually 2–3; incubated mostly by female for 28–31 days. *Fledging:* Leaves nest at 5–6 weeks.

Red-tailed Hawk

Buteo jamaicensis, L 22" (56 cm)

The Red-tailed Hawk's extensive breeding range makes it the "default" raptor in most of the U.S. and Canada. Juveniles lack the adults' trademark reddish-orange tail feathers.

IDENTIFICATION Common. This bulky, broad-winged, broad-tailed hawk is built for effortless, languid soaring over open country. It perches in the open and is often seen sitting atop roadside utility poles or fence posts. Get to know the Red-tailed's shape, silhouette, and posture and you'll be able to identify many birds without inspecting their plumage. If you are enthusiastic about raptors, purchase a specialized hawk guide and take a trip to a popular hawk-watching location, where scores of hawks can be seen in a single fall day and there are usually experienced birders on hand to help out.

Plumage: Eastern adult is brown above, with white patches on the scapulars that form a broad V across its back. The pale underparts are crossed by a dark belly

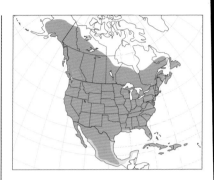

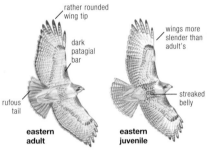

rather rounded wing tip

dark patagial bar

rufous tail

eastern adult

wings more slender than adult's

streaked belly

eastern juvenile

juvenile

heavy bill

white chest with heavily mottled belly

adult

pale rufous tail with narrow or no dark subterminal band

band. The Great Plains **"Krider's Red-tailed"** is much paler above and below (no belly band); its tail has a pale reddish wash. Farther west, **rufous morph** or **dark morph** birds are often encountered, or even the uncommon, blackish **"Harlan's Hawk."** All of this can be a bit confusing, but almost all adults have at least some reddish orange color on the tail. In flight, the best field mark is the distinct dark patch on the leading edge of the underwings; this dark patagial bar is visible on all ages and morphs, except for the very darkest birds. **Juveniles** have gray-brown tails with many blackish bands, and most show some white on the chest and dark mottling on the belly. **Similar species:** In the East, a juvenile Red-tailed might be mistaken for a smaller Red-shouldered juvenile (page 84), but that species lacks the patagial bar and has a rangier body and longer tail. Farther west, Red-taileds are more variable, but the dark patagial bar is a good mark on most birds.

Voice: Distinctive **call**—a harsh, descending *keee-eerrrrrr*—is often given by flying birds.

Broad wings and powerful muscles are required to get a Red-tailed Hawk's 2½-pound body aloft.

RANGE Widespread species. Lives in various habitats, from mountains and woodlands to prairies and deserts, as well as suburban and urban locations with trees and open space. Year-round resident in much of its range. Breeders from Alaska and Canada move south in the fall, so there are more Red-tailed in the Lower 48 during the winter months. Spring migration begins as early as February, but the northernmost breeding areas may not be occupied until early June; peak fall migration is from mid-October to late November.

western dark-morph adult

FOOD Most hunting is done from an elevated perch that allows a visual search of the surrounding area, but Red-tailed also hunt by cruising over open areas or soaring at higher altitudes. Prey includes small mammals (ground squirrels are a favorite in the West), reptiles, and larger birds. Most prey is captured and dispatched on the ground, then taken to a feeding perch to be eaten.

NESTING *Location:* Usually high up in a large tree, but cliff ledges, saguaro cacti, power-line towers, and building ledges are also utilized. *Nest:* Bulky platform of sticks. *Eggs:* Usually 2–3; incubated by both parents for 28–35 days. *Fledging:* Young birds move out of the nest at about 6–7 weeks, but are not strong fliers until about 9 weeks. They continue to receive food from their parents for a month or more, while they hone their flying and hunting skills.

As opportunistic feeders, Red-tailed Hawks will occasionally dine on large insects.

extensive pale above

pale head

adult "Krider's"

pale underparts

TYPICAL OWLS   **Family Strigidae**

A large family with more than 180 species worldwide—18 of which breed in North America. Most owls hunt at night and roost by day. Some species give familiar hooting calls, others do not.

Great Horned Owl
Bubo virginianus, L 22" (56 cm)

This powerful nighttime predator can take prey larger than itself. Roosts during the day. Provincial bird of Alberta.

prominent broad ear tufts on side of head

large yellow eyes

bulky body shape

barred below

Voice: Deep, muffled **hoots** given in rhythmic sets of three to eight (often five) syllables: *hoo hoo-HOO hoooo hoo.*

RANGE Widespread species; year-round resident. Lives just about everywhere but prefers woodlands with open areas and edge habitat.

FOOD Preys on mammals (up to the size of a large hare) and lesser numbers of large birds, snakes, and large insects. City and suburban birds catch large numbers of rats. Small prey are swallowed whole. Occasionally hunts during the day, but most active after sunset and just before dawn.

NESTING Begins as early as January. *Location:* Often reuses the nest of another large bird; other locations include broken-off tree trunks, cliff ledges, deserted buildings, and artificial platforms. *Nest:* Material already present. *Eggs:* Usually 2–3; incubated mostly by female for 30–37 days. *Fledging:* Leaves nest at 30–45 days; able to fly well at 60–70 days.

IDENTIFICATION Fairly common. At dusk or dawn, can be identified by its silhouette: a large, barrel-shaped body with prominent, wide-set ear tufts (ornamental feathers, not ears). **Plumage:** Mostly brown with a multitude of bars and speckling, white throat, and large yellow eyes. Overall plumage varies regionally—dark along the Pacific coast, paler and grayer in the interior West. **Similar species:** Only the rarer Long-eared Owl (not illustrated) also has large ear tufts, but it is a smaller and much more slender bird with close-set ear tufts.

SIGHTINGS

	JAN	FEB	MAR	APR	MAY	JUN	JUL	AUG	SEP	OCT	NOV	DEC

NIGHT OWLS

To hunt at night, owls boast special superpowers—mostly relating to vision, hearing, and silent flight in the darkness.

SEEING IN THE DARK

Owls' eyes, like humans' eyes, face forward, allowing them a large area of binocular vision. This helps them perceive depth, and gauge exact distance to potential prey.

Binocular vision comes with some limitations, though. Owls don't have good peripheral eyesight, and they cannot see behind them at all. In response, they have developed super-flexible necks with twice as many bones as people have. An owl can twist its head 270 degrees—a three-quarter turn.

Owls' large eyes are packed with rod cells, sensitive to dim light, a big advantage after dark. But they have few cones, which perceive color, and so an owl lives in a relatively monochromatic world.

STEALTH AND SOUND

The prominent "ear" tufts of some owls, like the Great Horned Owl and screech-owls, are not ears at all—those upright feathers help camouflage the birds while roosting in dense thickets.

Owls' ears are placed lower down, on each side of the bird's head, invisible beneath its feathers. In many species, the ear openings are symmetrically offset on the edges of a face that is shaped like a parabolic dish. With one ear higher than the other, an owl can more accurately pinpoint a sound and is able to pick up low-frequency noises, such as the hushed rustling of a rodent's feet. An owl is able to pounce on prey in complete darkness or through several inches of snow.

An owl's wing feathers are softened by special comblike structures that dampen airflow and soundproof its movements. Silent flight is a deadly weapon. By flying so quietly, owls can hear better, and they can approach their prey without being suspected.

A dark old barn is an excellent place to look for Great Horned Owls by day.

Barred Owl

Strix varia, L 21" (53 cm)

This woodland owl dozes by day on a well-hidden perch. It flies off when disturbed, seldom tolerating close approach except where accustomed to heavy foot traffic.

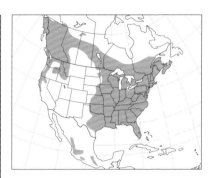

dark eyes

barred breast

vertical streaks

birds. More likely than most other owls to be heard in the daytime. Responds to imitations of its call.

RANGE Widespread species; year-round resident. Lives in mature forest; especially common in river bottoms and southern swamps. Also resides in wooded residential areas and large city parks. Range is expanding in Pacific Northwest, where it overlaps with the Spotted Owl.

IDENTIFICATION Fairly common. Large, chunky owl with dark eyes and a large, round head lacking ear tufts.
Plumage: Mostly brown plumage is spotted with white on the upperparts, pale buff below with dark, vertical streaks. Its name refers to the horizontal barring on its breast.
Similar species: The much rarer Spotted Owl (not illustrated) of the West is similar, but has white spots below (not heavy, dark streaks), and the Great Horned Owl (page 88) is larger, with prominent ear tufts.
Voice: Known colloquially as the "eight-hooter" for its most common **call:** *who-cooks-for-you, who-cooks-for-YOU-ALL?* Highly vocal, with a wide range of calls that include a shorter *you-all* and maniacal laughter exchanged between courting

FOOD Mostly a nocturnal hunter, but also active at dusk and dawn. Searches for prey from an elevated perch and then swoops down on it. Preys mostly on small mammals, but also birds, reptiles, amphibians, fish, and large insects.

NESTING *Location:* In a natural tree cavity, the reused nest of another large bird such as a hawk, or an old squirrel nest. *Nest:* Material already present. *Eggs:* Usually 2–3; incubated by female for 28–33 days. Laid as early as December in the South, but typically March–April. *Fledging:* Leaves nest at 28–35 days; able to fly at about 70 days.
Housing: Will use a nest box located at a height of 15–30 feet.

Eastern Screech-Owl
Megascops asio, L 8½" (22 cm)

A small woodland owl with an extensive range. If you learn to whistle the Eastern Screech-Owl's tremolo call, it will attract a host of woodland songbirds that come to investigate the location of their mortal enemy—just don't overdo it.

rufous morph

gray morph juvenile

rufous morph more numerous in Southeast

IDENTIFICATION Fairly common. Robin-size owl with a big head, ear tufts (sometimes flattened), and yellow eyes. Roosting bird often assumes a very cryptic, elongated pose that mimics tree bark or a dead stick.
Plumage: Two color morphs—rufous and gray; mixed pairs not uncommon. Darker above with white spots and fine barring; underparts marked with vertical dark streaks and fainter cross-hatching (like tree bark). **Fledgling** is finely barred overall with tiny ear tufts.
Similar species: If you are in the West and see a very similar bird, it will most likely be a Western Screech-Owl (not illustrated); the ranges of the two species scarcely overlap.
Voice: Two typical **calls:** a long trill or tremolo on one pitch, and a series of quavering

yellow eyes

pale greenish bill

gray morph

whistles that descend in pitch ("horse whinny"). Despite its name, this owl rarely screeches.

RANGE Eastern and Great Plains species; year-round resident. Lives in a variety of wooded habitats: forests, woodlots, suburban backyards, large city parks.

FOOD Nocturnal hunter. Varied diet; preys mostly on songbirds and rodents, but also large insects, earthworms, snakes, lizards, frogs, and crayfish.

NESTING *Location:* In an old woodpecker hole or natural tree cavity. *Nest:* Material already present. *Eggs:* Usually 4–5; incubated by female for 27–30 days. Laid as early as December in the South. *Fledging:* Young leave the nest at about 28 days, clamber to a tree roost, and are able to fly about 2 weeks later.
Housing: Will use a nest box. Since nest cavities can be scarce, a nest box of the correct size may entice a pair of owls to take up residence in a woodsy backyard. Fasten nest box to a sturdy tree at a height of 10–15 feet. Often uses its nest box as a winter roost.

| JAN | FEB | MAR | APR | MAY | JUN | JUL | AUG | SEP | OCT | NOV | DEC |

WOODPECKERS Family Picidae

Sharp claws and stiff tail feathers enable woodpeckers to climb tree trunks; sharp bill is used to chisel out insect food and nest holes and to drum a territorial signal.

Acorn Woodpecker
Melanerpes formicivorus, L 9" (23 cm)

The clown-faced Acorn Woodpecker lives in communal groups that maintain impressive granaries—thousands of acorns are stored in holes drilled in tree trunks (granary trees).

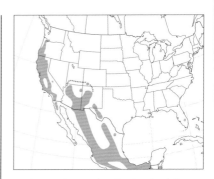

♀ female has black forecrown bar

clown head pattern

♂

wack-a wack-a wack-a that inspired the creator of Woody Woodpecker.

RANGE Western species; year-round resident. Inhabits oak woodlands and mixed oak-conifer or oak-riparian woodlands.

FOOD Despite its name and habit of storing thousands of acorns, nuts make up only about half of its diet (mostly in fall and winter). Their preferred food is insects—particularly ants—supplemented in spring and summer with sugary tree sap.

IDENTIFICATION Fairly common. A sturdy, midsize woodpecker. Often flycatches for insects, but rarely descends to the ground.
Plumage: Boldly patterned: striking head plumage is an ornate combination of red, white, and black. White wing patch and rump are most visible in flight. **Male** has red crown bordering white forehead; female has red crown with black band in front.
Similar species: None.
Voice: Calls given by noisy family groups include *ja-cob ja-cob* and a raucous

NESTING Cooperative breeder—lives in family groups of a dozen or more birds that assist each other. *Location:* Cavity excavated in a large tree and reused for many years. *Nest:* No material added. *Eggs:* Usually 3–7; incubated by both parents for about 11 days. *Fledging:* Leaves nest at about 30 days.

♂

white primary patch

Red-bellied Woodpecker

Melanerpes carolinus, L 9¼" (24 cm)

The Red-bellied is the familiar zebra-striped woodpecker of the East. Its "red belly" amounts to little more than a hard-to-see pinkish blush, but its crown and nape are vibrantly red.

solid red crown and nape

♂

♀

red nape

pink on lower belly

white rump

whitish primary patch

♂

RANGE Eastern species; year-round resident. Inhabits open woodlands, suburbs, and parks. Abundant in the Southeast, particularly along water-courses and in swamp country. Northern range continues to expand, for example, from central Pennsylvania (1960s) to southern Vermont (2000), but it is uncommon in northernmost areas.

FOOD Seldom excavates wood in search of food, but forages opportunistically for insects, nuts, fruits, seeds, and sometimes catches flying insects in the air. Stores food in tree bark crevices. **Feeding:** Suet, peanuts, and sunflower seeds are all relished. Dominates Downy and Hairy Woodpeckers and smaller birds at feeders, about equal with Blue Jay. Usually shy and wary around people, but feeder visitors eventually become more trusting.

IDENTIFICATION Common. A lanky, midsize woodpecker—smaller than a flicker.
Plumage: Only zebra-striped woodpecker in the East. White wing patch and rump are visible only in flight. **Male** has red extending from bill to nape; **female** has red only on nape.
Similar species: Overlaps in Texas with similar Golden-fronted Woodpecker (not illustrated), which has golden orange feathers on the nape and above the bill and black (not barred) tail.
Voice: Song is a loud volley of churring notes. **Call** is a conversational *chiv-chiv*.

NESTING *Location:* Cavity excavated in a dead tree, stump, or telephone pole. *Nest:* No material added. *Eggs:* Usually 4–5; incubated by both parents for 12–14 days. *Fledging:* Leaves nest at 22–27 days. Parents accompany and often feed young birds for about 6 weeks after they leave the nest.
Housing: Will use a nest box mounted on a tree or pole.

Yellow-bellied Sapsucker
Sphyrapicus varius, L 8½" (22 cm)

These woodpeckers drill evenly spaced rows of holes in living trees and then visit these "wells" for the sap and the insects attracted to it. Other birds also feed at these sugary seeps, especially hummingbirds. Two closely related species, with different ranges, are covered on the following pages.

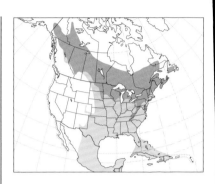

 IDENTIFICATION Fairly common. Medium-size woodpecker. Although often noisy and conspicuous when breeding, most backyard birders will encounter the Yellow-bellied Sapsucker on its migration or in winter when it is quiet and secretive.
Plumage: Striped face pattern and longitudinal white slash on the wing are good field marks. **Male** has red throat and forecrown; **female** has white throat and red forecrown. **Juvenile** differs from adult until about March—head is brownish, body mottled brown, wings like adult.
Similar species: See Red-naped Sapsucker (opposite), a western relative whose range overlaps somewhat.

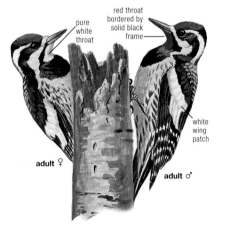

pure white throat

red throat bordered by solid black frame

white wing patch

adult ♀

adult ♂

Voice: Unusual **calls** that are worth learning—a nasal squeal *weeah* and cat-like *meeww*—are often the first indication that a sapsucker is nearby.

RANGE Eastern species. Breeds in open forests in Appalachians, north through New England, and extensively in Canada, then spends October–March throughout the South and Mid-Atlantic. Spring **migration:** mid-April–early May; fall migration: mid-September–October.

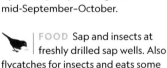

brownish

juvenile

FOOD Sap and insects at freshly drilled sap wells. Also flycatches for insects and eats some fruit and seeds.
Feeding: Irregular at feeders, but will take suet and sunflower seeds.

NESTING *Location:* Cavity excavated in a tree, often an aspen, poplar, or birch. *Nest:* No material added. *Eggs:* Usually 3–7; incubated by both parents for 12–13 days. *Fledging:* Leaves nest at 25–29 days. Parents feed their young for an additional 1–2 weeks and teach them the sapsucking technique.

SIGHTINGS | JAN FEB MAR APR MAY JUN JUL AUG SEP OCT NOV DEC

Red-naped Sapsucker
Sphyrapicus nuchalis, L 8½" (22 cm)

For most of the 20th century, this species was considered a western subspecies of the Yellow-bellied Sapsucker. The two species look almost identical, but there are subtle differences. Read the Yellow-bellied Sapsucker account (opposite) to find out more about the sapsucker's lifestyle.

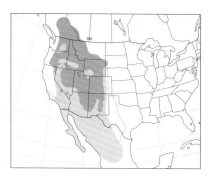

 IDENTIFICATION Fairly common. Medium-size woodpecker that is easy to overlook.
Plumage: Striped face pattern and longitudinal white slash on the wing are good field marks. Named for the spot of red on the nape of both sexes. **Male** and female both have red throat and forecrown, but **female** also has some white feathering under the chin. **Juvenile** resembles Yellow-bellied juvenile (opposite), but unlike Yellow-bellied, Red-naped looks similar to the adult by fall migration.
Similar species: Yellow-bellied Sapsucker (opposite) is a close eastern relative that lacks the red nape spot and has a heavier black border around the throat. Ranges of the two species barely overlap.
Voice: Calls include a nasal squeal *weeah* and catlike *meeww.*

RANGE Interior West species. Breeds in aspen parklands and leafy groves within coniferous forests; favors groves along mountain streams and rivers. Migrates south to winter at lower elevations; often found in shady parks and suburban neighborhoods. Some birds winter in Southern California. Spring **migration:** mid-March–early May; fall migration: late August–October.

FOOD Sap and insects at freshly drilled sap wells—conifers, quaking aspen, alder, and willow are often

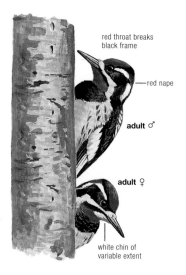

red throat breaks
black frame

red nape

adult ♂

adult ♀

white chin of
variable extent

tapped. Also flycatches for insects and eats some seeds and fruit.
Feeding: Irregular at feeders, but will take suet and sunflower seeds.

NESTING *Location:* Cavity excavated in a tree, often a quaking aspen. *Nest:* No material added. *Eggs:* Usually 4–7; incubated by both parents for 11–15 days. *Fledging:* Leaves nest at 23–32 days. Parents feed their young for an additional 1–2 weeks and teach them the sapsucking technique.

SIGHTINGS

| JAN | FEB | MAR | APR | MAY | JUN | JUL | AUG | SEP | OCT | NOV | DEC |

Red-breasted Sapsucker

Sphyrapicus ruber, L 8½" (22 cm)

The Red-breasted Sapsucker is a more colorful West Coast version of the closely related Red-naped Sapsucker. Where the ranges of the two species come into contact, they frequently interbreed.

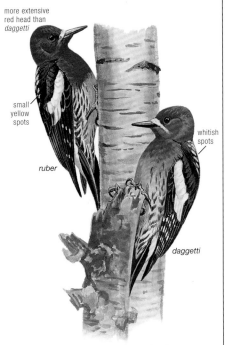

more extensive red head than *daggetti*

small yellow spots

ruber

whitish spots

daggetti

IDENTIFICATION Fairly common. Medium-size woodpecker, often quiet and retiring. The northern breeding subspecies (*ruber*, from southern Oregon northward) is deeper red above and more solidly yellow below; the paler, but still colorful, *daggetti* subspecies occupies the rest of the range. **Plumage:** Vivid red head and breast, and white wing patch like other sapsuckers. **Male** and **female** are alike. **Juvenile** (see illustration of similar, but paler, Yellow-bellied juvenile on page 94) differs from adult until about September.
Similar species: None. Full red head of adult makes it easy to identify.
Voice: Calls include a nasal squeal *weeah* and catlike *meeww*.

RANGE West Coast species. Breeds in a variety of habitats, from moist coniferous forests to streamside woodlands and from near sea level up to 8,000 feet. Some birds are resident; others migrate south or move to lower elevations for the winter. Wintering birds can be found in shady parks and suburban neighborhoods as far south as Southern California (where it is more numerous than Red-naped). Spring **migration:** not apparent; fall migration: late September–early October.

FOOD Sap and insects at freshly drilled sap wells. Also flycatches for insects and eats some fruit and seeds. **Feeding** Irregular at feeders, but will take suet and sunflower seeds.

NESTING *Location:* Cavity excavated in a tree, often dead or dying. *Nest:* No material added. *Eggs:* Usually 4–7; incubated by both parents for 11–15 days. *Fledging:* Leaves nest at 23–32 days. Parents feed their young for an additional 1–2 weeks and teach them the sapsucking technique.

Ladder-backed Woodpecker

Picoides scalaris, L 7¼" (18 cm)

The Ladder-backed Woodpecker scratches out a living in desert areas across a wide swath of the Southwest. An alternate name was "Cactus Woodpecker."

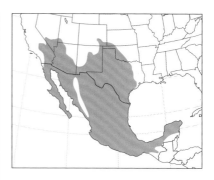

IDENTIFICATION Fairly common. A small, active woodpecker that presents a somewhat disheveled appearance. Fairly tame and often quite vocal.

Plumage: Black-and-white, ladder-like bars evenly spaced on the back and similar pattern on wings; underparts buff with small dark spots; pale face with black stripes. Male has red crown with black and white speckles near the bill; female has black crown, and juvenile's crown is red with white flecking.

Similar species: Nuttall's Woodpecker (next page) is blacker above, with a heavy black bar on the upper back, and whiter below; their ranges meet only on the western fringes of the Mojave Desert. Downy and Hairy Woodpeckers—not often seen in the desert Southwest—have a white stripe (not bars) up the back.

Voice: Most common call is a fairly high, sharp pik (like the Downy's); also has a descending whinny.

RANGE Southwestern species; year-round resident. Inhabits desert scrub, mesquite woodlands, and arroyos; piñon-juniper woodlands and oaks are favored in Texas. Often seen in residential areas near desert habitat.

FOOD Seldom drills into wood, but probes and gleans insects (especially beetle larvae) from trees, cacti, agaves, yuccas, and weed stems. Also eats cactus fruit and some seeds.

Feeding: Suet, peanuts, and sunflower seeds; able to cling to hanging feeders. Visits birdbaths.

NESTING *Location:* Cavity excavated in a desert tree, large agave, or yucca (Joshua tree). *Nest:* No material added. *Eggs:* Usually 4–7; incubated by both parents for 12–14 days. *Fledging:* Age at first flight unknown.

Housing: Will use a nest box mounted on a tree or pole.

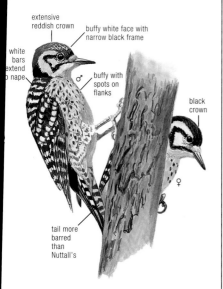

extensive reddish crown

buffy white face with narrow black frame

white bars extend to nape

♂

buffy with spots on flanks

black crown

♀

tail more barred than Nuttall's

Nuttall's Woodpecker
Picoides nuttalli, L 7½" (19 cm)

Nuttall's Woodpecker is found only California and nearby Baja California. It occurs over a large portion of the state, but shuns the desert habitat favored by the similar-looking Ladder-backed Woodpecker.

IDENTIFICATION Common. This moderately small, chunky woodpecker forages actively, but can be hard to spot. Its loud calls often announce its presence before it is seen.
Plumage: Crisp black-and-white plumage; mostly black back with narrow white bars and a wide black bar at base of the neck; underparts white with black spots and bars on the sides; black face with white stripes. **Male** has a red patch at rear of crown; **female** has black crown.

Similar species: Downy (smaller; page 100) and Hairy (larger; page 101) Woodpeckers look similar from a distance, but have a white stripe up the back, not horizontal bars. Also see Ladder-backed Woodpecker (previous page).
Voice: Most common **call** is a short, staccato *p-r-r-t*; also makes a longer rattle and loud *kweek-kweek-kweek* when birds interact.

RANGE California species; year-round resident. Favors oak groves and riparian forests, but also occurs in residential suburbs and wooded parks. Sometimes wanders after the nesting season is over.

FOOD Seldom drills into wood, but scales off bark, probes, and gleans insects from tree trunks and branches. Occasionally eats acorns, seeds, and fruit.
Feeding: Suet and sunflower seeds.

NESTING *Location:* Cavity excavated in a tree, or sometimes a fence post or utility pole. *Nest:* No material added. *Eggs:* Usually 3–6; incubated by both parents for about 14 days. *Fledging:* Leaves nest at about 14 days.
Housing: Will use a nest box mounted on a tree or pole.

red restricted to rear crown

black face with white borders

black bar at base of neck

♂

white underparts

black crown

♀

outer tail feathers with fewer bars than Ladder-backed

WHY DON'T WOODPECKERS GET HEADACHES?

Woodpeckers are so called due to their headbanging behavior against immovable objects. Woodpeckers "drum" and peck to find insect prey, to make cavities for nesting and roosting, and to communicate with other woodpeckers. During the courtship season, when males drum against resonant trees or rain gutters to attract mates, a healthy woodpecker may peck thousands of times a day (females may also drum briefly to announce themselves in a male's territory). The thought of it makes one's head hurt. How do the birds avoid constant concussion?

EXTRA PADDING

Strong muscles in a woodpecker's head and neck help cushion against impact while preventing whiplash. The birds' anatomy has been studied for inspiration in football helmet designs, which aim to do the same thing.

But these peckers have some other tricks up their beaks. Their upper nostril connects to a thin bone called the hyoid, which in woodpeckers has elongated so that it wraps all the way between the eyes, over the top of the skull, and around the back of the head. At the base of the skull, the tongue attaches to the end of this bone.

The hyoid acts like a seat belt, contracting and tightening around the brain to dampen force. It also diverts shock vibrations away from the cranium: Because a woodpecker's upper beak is slightly longer than the lower, the forces of impact travel first through the upper nostril into the hyoid, which helps dissipate energy into other muscles, including the tongue.

BRAIN
The brain fits tightly into the skull with practically no cushioning fluid.

SKULL
The thick skull is made of strong yet spongy bone.

BEAK
The beak is straight and strong, and strengthened with horn.

THIRD EYELID
A third inner eyelid works like a seat belt to keep eyeballs from popping out.

HYOID APPARATUS
Inside the tongue, the hyoid apparatus acts like an accordion to make the tongue stick out farther.

Woodpeckers have physical features and behaviors to help them prevent concussions.

EYES CLOSED

A millisecond before striking, a woodpecker blinks its third eyelid, called the nictitating membrane, which shuts from front to back. This eyelid, present in most bird species, helps protect and moisturize. For a woodpecker, the benefits are obvious: With the eyelids closed, a woodpecker doesn't get flying wood chips in its eyeballs, and its eyes don't pop out on impact. And because this membrane is translucent, the bird can still see where it's pecking.

Downy Woodpecker
Picoides pubescens, L 6¾" (17 cm)

The Downy is the smallest and the best known woodpecker in North America. It seems content to live anywhere there are trees, except in the arid Southwest.

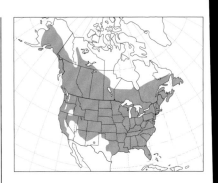

 IDENTIFICATION Very common. The Downy, with its petite bill and tubular body, has a toylike quality, enhanced by its jerky, stop-and-go movements. At feeders, it gives way to the larger, look-alike Hairy Woodpecker.
Plumage: Crisp black-and-white plumage; black back with white stripe up the middle; underparts unmarked white; white outer tail feathers barred. **Male** has a small red patch at rear of crown; **female's** crown is black, and **juvenile's** has patchy red at the front.
Similar species: Only the larger Hairy Woodpecker (opposite) also has a white stripe up the back. Size can be difficult to judge on a lone bird, so focus on proportions: the Hairy's bill is nearly as long as its head; the Downy's is about half as long as its head. Also useful: Hairy has pure white outer tail feathers; Downy has black bars on those feathers. Hairy is less common and more restricted to forested areas, and has a louder, slightly longer, more emphatic call.
Voice: Call is a sharp, high-pitched *pik!* Rattle call descends in pitch and trails off.

male has red hindcrown spot

white back stripe

short, stubby bill

♂

barred outer tail feathers

♀

♂

RANGE Widespread species; year-round resident. Inhabits most types of woodland, including backyards and city parks; avoids desert areas.

FOOD Actively probes, gleans, and drills into wood for insects. Forages on branches and sometimes descends to large weed stalks; female is more likely to forage on tree trunks.
Feeding: Favors suet, but also consumes peanuts, peanut butter, sunflower seeds.

NESTING *Location:* Cavity excavated in a tree trunk or limb. *Nest:* No material added. *Eggs:* Usually 3–6; incubated by both parents for about 12 days. *Fledging:* Leaves nest at 20–25 days.
Housing: Will use a nest box mounted on a tree or pole.

Hairy Woodpecker
Picoides villosus, L 9¼" (24 cm)

The Hairy Woodpecker inhabits forested areas from coast to coast. Its name derives from the "hairy" quality of the white feathers in the middle of its back.

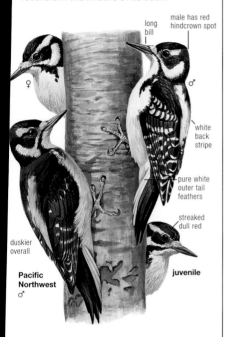

long bill

male has red hindcrown spot

♀

♂

white back stripe

pure white outer tail feathers

streaked dull red

duskier overall

Pacific Northwest ♂

juvenile

IDENTIFICATION Fairly common. The Hairy is a typical, well-proportioned, medium-size woodpecker. Its longish bill gives the head a wedge-shaped look that differs from the round-headed look of the smaller Downy Woodpecker.
Plumage: Crisp black-and-white plumage; black back with white stripe up the middle; pure white outer tail feathers. **Male** has a small red patch at rear of crown, **female** has black crown, and **juvenile** has patchy red on top of crown. Birds in the Pacific Northwest have smoky brown underparts and less white on the wings.

Similar species: Downy Woodpecker is much smaller, but almost identical in plumage (see "similar species" section opposite).
Voice: Call is a loud, emphatic, high-pitched *PEEK!* Rattle call is a loud series of *peek* calls.

RANGE Widespread species; year-round resident. Inhabits a variety of forests and woodlands, but prefers mature forest with large trees. Also resides in well-wooded suburbs and urban parks.

FOOD Actively probes, scales off bark, and drills into wood for insects. Works over tree trunks and larger limbs, chiseling out chunks of dead or diseased wood to get to insect larvae. Also eats some fruits and seeds.
Feeding: Visits suet feeders; shier around people than Downy Woodpecker. Also consumes peanuts, peanut butter, and sunflower seeds.

NESTING *Location:* Cavity excavated in a tree. *Nest:* No material added. *Eggs:* Usually 3–6; incubated by both parents for about 14 days. *Fledging:* Leaves nest at 28–30 days.
Housing: Will use a nest box mounted on a tree or pole.

Northern Flicker
Colaptes auratus, L 12½" (32 cm)

The Northern Flicker breaks the wood-pecker mold—it is mostly brown and spends much of its time on the ground. There are two different color groups: "Yellow-shafted" in the East and far north and "Red-shafted" in the West, with interbreeding on the Great Plains where the two ranges overlap. The two groups were considered two separate species until 1973, when scientists "lumped" them (classified them as a single species). Even so, most birders continue to use their more colorful group names. State bird of Alabama (referred to as the Yellowhammer).

all North American flickers have white rumps

"Yellow-shafted" ♀

female lacks whisker

yellow underwing

red nape and pale brown face

male has black whisker

"Yellow-shafted" ♂

underparts. In flight, the white rump is very conspicuous. The "Yellow-shafted" has bright yellow underwings and under-tail, tan face, and gray crown with red patch on nape; male has a black whisker mark on the face, absent in female. The "Red-shafted" has salmon pink under-wings and undertail, gray face, and brown crown and nape (no red nape patch); male has a red whisker mark on the face, lacking in female. Intergrades between the two

IDENTIFICATION Common. Large woodpecker. When forag-ing on the ground, hops from place to place. It also spends time in trees, cling-ing vertically to tree trunks (like a normal woodpecker) or perched high up on small branches looking very alert with lots of head jerking and bowing.
Plumage: All Northern Flickers have a brown back with black bars, a bold black crescent on the chest, and spotted

The golden yellow underwings of the "Yellow-shafted" Flicker are completely hidden when the wings are closed.

Unlike other woodpeckers, the flicker is often seen on the ground. Its stout bill is used to dig in the soil while searching for ants, a favorite food.

subtypes show a mix of characteristics.
Similar species: Similar Gilded Flicker (not illustrated) is restricted to desert areas of southern Arizona and near the Colorado River—not typical backyard habitat.
Voice: Highly vocal. Single, piercing *klee-yer!* or *keeew!* **call** is given year-round. Long, loud *wick-a-wick-a-wick-a* call is heard in breeding season (can be confused with Pileated Woodpecker's call).

RANGE Widespread species. Found in open woodlands, forest edges, woodlots, shelterbelts, suburban areas, and city parks. Avoids deep forest with thick undergrowth, but needs trees for nesting. Overall population is declining, possibly due to nest hole competition with European Starlings, fewer available dead trees (overmanaged forests), or pesticide application to agricultural fields and suburban lawns. Conserving the flicker is important because it's a keystone forest species, providing nest holes and roosting sites for many animals that can't excavate their own. Northern breeders migrate south in fall. Spring **migration:** late March–April; fall migration: late September–October.

FOOD Specializes in foraging on the ground for ants, picking them from the surface or vigorously digging out their underground nests ("ground-pecker"). Rarely forages on tree trunks or branches. Many birds shift to berries and other fruits in late fall and winter.
Feeding: Visits suet feeders, where it is usually the dominant woodpecker. Also consumes peanuts, peanut butter, and sunflower seeds.

NESTING *Location:* Cavity excavated in a tree, usually dead or diseased. *Nest:* No material added. *Eggs:* Usually 5–8; incubated by both parents for 11–13 days. *Fledging:* Leaves nest at 24–27 days.
Housing: Will use a nest box mounted on a tree or pole at least 6 feet off the ground.

"Red-shafted" ♂

male has red whisker

brown nape and gray face

salmon pink underwing

"Red-shafted" ♀

Pileated Woodpecker
Dryocopus pileatus, L 16½" (42 cm)

Spectacular, crow-size woodpecker with a flaming crimson crest. Pairs defend a large forested territory (100+ acres) year-round. Its numerous excavations are crucial assets of the forest ecosystem, used for shelter and nesting by a diverse array of animals.

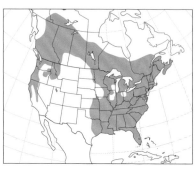

female has black forecrown and whisker

♀

♂ —white wing patch

♀ extensive white underwing

♂

Similar species: None.
Voice: Loud, echoing series of *kuk* notes with a laughing quality, similar to a Northern Flicker, or a loud *wuck* note or series of notes. Often calls in flight.

RANGE Widespread species; year-round resident. Prefers mature forest with large trees, but is also found in woodlots, wooded suburbs, and large wooded parks. Uncommon in its western range; most common in the South.

FOOD Chisels vigorously into dead, diseased, or live trees for insects, primarily carpenter ants and beetle larvae, making unique large oval or rectangular excavations. Often descends to forage on fallen logs. Also eats fruits, nuts, and berries.
Feeding: Occasionally visits suet feeders.

IDENTIFICATION Fairly common. Big, rangy woodpecker with a long neck and tail. For such a dramatic species, it is surprisingly inconspicuous and shy. Its presence is most often revealed as it flies from tree to tree or by its loud, ringing call.
Plumage: Mostly black. Head has a red crest and black-and-white pattern. In flight, wings flash black and white. **Male** has complete red crest and red whisker; **female** has red crest with black forecrown and black whisker.

NESTING *Location:* Cavity excavated in a tree; also excavates night-roosting cavities with multiple entrances. *Nest:* No material added. *Eggs:* Usually 4; incubated by both parents for 15–18 days. *Fledging:* Leaves nest at 24–31 days, but dependent on parents for several months (until fall).
Housing: Will use a nest box mounted on a tree.

SIGHTINGS

JAN	FEB	MAR	APR	MAY	JUN	JUL	AUG	SEP	OCT	NOV	DEC

FALCONS Family Falconidae

Falcons are distinguished from hawks by their long wings, which are narrow, pointed, and bent back at the "wrist." Females are larger than males.

American Kestrel
Falco sparverius, L 10½" (27 cm)

This petite and colorful raptor lives in open habitats from coast to coast and is North America's most common falcon. Its north–south range extends from Alaska to the southern tip of South America.

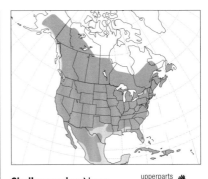

frequently hovers

all with two dark facial stripes

adult ♂

male has bluish gray wings

adult ♂

upperparts uniformly rufous

adult ♀

lacks white primary marks of male

adult ♂

Similar species: None.
Voice: Distinctive **call** is a shrill, rapid *killy-killy-killy*.

RANGE Widespread species. Lives in rural and suburban areas with open fields; often seen hunting along roadways. Declining in the East. Spring **migration:** April–mid-May; fall migration: August–September.

FOOD Prey consists of large insects, lizards, rodents, and small birds. Most prey is attacked on the ground and carried off to a feeding perch.

IDENTIFICATION Fairly common. The American Kestrel is a buoyant flier with slender pointed wings and a long tail. It is capable of hovering on rapidly beating wings while searching for prey.
Plumage: Two black facial stripes. **Adult male** has blue-gray wings, chestnut back with black bars, chestnut tail with a black bar near the tip, and apricot underparts with dark spots. **Juvenile males** are similar, but with paler underparts, more dark bars on the back, and streaked breast. **Adult female** has reddish brown upperparts and tail with dark bars; reddish streaks on underparts.

adult ♀

uniformly rufous brown

rufous tail with dark bars

NESTING *Location:* In an old woodpecker hole or natural cavity. *Nest:* No material added. *Eggs:* Usually 4–5; incubated mostly by female for 29–30 days. *Fledging:* Leaves nest at 28–31 days.
Housing: Will use a nest box fastened to a tree or pole 10–20 feet off the ground.

JAN	FEB	MAR	APR	MAY	JUN	JUL	AUG	SEP	OCT	NOV	DEC

TYRANT FLYCATCHERS   Family Tyrannidae

A family of small to medium-size birds that specialize in capturing insects in flight. Most species sit upright on exposed perches from where they launch their attacks. In general, they have drab plumage, large heads with broad-based bills, tiny legs and feet, and simple songs.

Western Wood-Pewee
Contopus sordidulus, L 6¼" (16 cm)

The name pewee derives from the song of the closely related Eastern Wood-Pewee, not the "peewee" size of these birds.

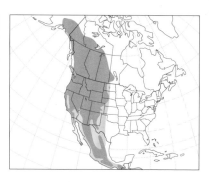

averages darker than Eastern, but identification safely done only by voice

long wings

paler adult

darker adult

IDENTIFICATION Fairly common. Small, drab flycatcher with a large head and a distinctive voice.
Plumage: Dark, grayish olive above, with two thin wing bars; olive color washes across the breast (like a vest). Base of bill is yellow or orange.
Similar species: Different range and voice than the almost identical Eastern Wood-Pewee (opposite). Easily mistaken for an *Empidonax* flycatcher, a confusing group of small greenish flycatchers that also have two wing bars (their specific identification is beyond the scope of this book); in general, "empids" are smaller, often flick their longer tails (something pewees don't do), and have whitish eye rings.
Voice: Most common **song** is a harsh, burry, descending whistle *PEEeeer* given throughout the day. **Calls** include a clear, descending peer.

RANGE Western species; summer resident. Common in open western woodlands, forest edges, and riparian groves. In suburban backyards, most often seen during migration. Winters mostly in South America. Spring **migration:** late April–mid-June; fall migration: August–September.

FOOD Captures insects in flight. Flies out (sallies) from an exposed perch to capture flies, flying ants, bees, and wasps. An audible snap of the bill usually signifies a miss. Often returns to the same perch.

NESTING *Location:* Straddling a tree branch, usually 15–30 feet up. *Nest:* Neat cup of fine fibers and plant down, bound together with spiderweb; outside decorated with moss or lichen. *Eggs:* Usually 3; incubated by female for 12–15 days. *Fledging:* Leaves nest at 14–18 days.

SIGHTINGS

JAN   FEB   MAR   APR   MAY   JUN   JUL   AUG   SEP   OCT   NOV   DEC

Eastern Wood-Pewee
Contopus virens, L 6¼" (16 cm)

The wing length of many birds is tied to the length of their migrations—long wings for long-distance migrants. On pewees (which winter in South America), the wing tip is prominent; on Eastern Phoebe (next page), a short-distance migrant, it is mostly hidden.

 IDENTIFICATION Fairly common. Small, drab flycatcher with a large head and a distinctive voice. It perches quietly, often for an extended period—then suddenly darts out to snatch an airborne insect, sometimes in a lengthy, twisting pursuit. It usually returns to the same perch and starts the process over.
Plumage: Dark, grayish olive above with two thin wing bars; olive color washes onto sides of breast (like a vest). Base of bill is yellow or orange.
Similar species: Eastern Phoebe (next page) is darker above, somewhat bulkier, lacks wing bars, has shorter wings, and—importantly—constantly pumps its tail (pewees never do). Easily mistaken for an *Empidonax* flycatcher (see the "similar species" section opposite). Different range and voice than the almost-identical Western Wood-Pewee.
Voice: Most common **song** is a slow, plaintive, whistled *pee-a-WEE,* with the second note lower; this phrase often alternates with a down-slurred *PEE-yeer.* **Call** is an up-slurred *pewee.*

 RANGE Eastern species; summer resident. Common in a variety of woodland habitats; frequents forest edges and clearings. In suburban backyards, it is most often seen and heard during migration. Winters mostly in South America. Long wings—notice the prominent wing tip that extends well beyond the white-edged tertials—are usually a feature of species that have long migrations. Spring **migration:** mid-April–May; fall migration: mid-September–October.

 FOOD See Western Wood-Pewee (opposite).

 NESTING See Western Wood-Pewee (opposite).

slightly paler nape than Western

usually adults have orange lower mandible

fresh spring adult

worn late-summer adult

juveniles can have all-dark bill

juvenile

long primary projection

JAN FEB MAR APR MAY JUN JUL AUG SEP OCT NOV DEC

Eastern Phoebe
Sayornis phoebe, L 7" (18 cm)

The Eastern Phoebe is a flycatcher with a penchant for nesting under bridges and around outbuildings and homes—often constructing a nest and raising a family under a porch roof near a busy door. Although drably colored and unobtrusive, its endearing acceptance of people has made it one of the most familiar summer birds in eastern North America.

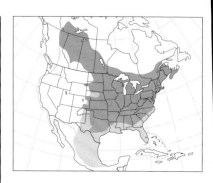

IDENTIFICATION Common. Medium-size flycatcher (bigger than a pewee) with the habit of constantly pumping—rapidly down and slowly up—and spreading its long tail. Usually perches at low to middle levels around open areas or near the forest edge.
Plumage: Brownish gray above, darker on the wings (no wing bars or one faint one) and tail. White throat contrasts strongly with the dark, almost blackish head. Underparts are mostly white, with pale olive wash on sides and breast. Molts in the fall before migrating. The fresh fall feathers on the underparts are tinted pale yellow, and the wing feathers have noticeable, pale edges that can form a faint lower wing bar. **Juvenile** is very similar to the adult but has two cinnamon wing bars and cinnamon tips to the feathers of the upperparts.

Similar species: Eastern Wood-Pewee (previous page) has greenish olive plumage, two white wing bars, and longer wings but is most easily separated from phoebe by the phoebe's distinctive tail wagging. Pewees are shier forest birds that usually select a higher perch and have a different song. An *Empidonax* flycatcher (or empid) is smaller, has two strong wing bars and a white eye ring, and usually flicks its tail upward (not up and down).
Voice: Distinctive **song** is a harsh, emphatic *fee-bee,* often alternated with a longer *fee-b-be-bee.* Both songs are given throughout the day by the male. Typical **call** is a sharp *chip,* given by both sexes.

RANGE Eastern species. Common around homes, but needs some wooded habitat nearby and prefers

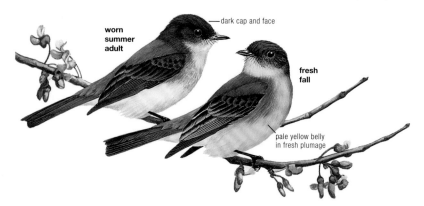

worn summer adult

dark cap and face

fresh fall

pale yellow belly in fresh plumage

Eastern Phoebes are one of the first spring migrants to arrive in many parts of the East.

locations in the vicinity of water. More common in rural backyards than suburban ones. One of the earliest migrants to arrive in spring. Northern breeders move south in fall, and most spend the winter months in the southeastern U.S., although some continue on to Mexico. Spring **migration:** March–late April; fall migration: October–November.

FOOD Captures flying insects, including many wasps and bees, occasionally descending to the ground while in pursuit. Sallies from an exposed perch and frequently moves from perch to perch. Small fruits are an important food source from fall to early spring.

NESTING *Location:* In a sheltered niche on a building, bridge, culvert, or, rarely, rock crevice. *Nest:* Cup of mud pellets, grass, moss, and other fibers. *Eggs:* Usually 5; incubated by female for 14–16 days. *Fledging:* Leaves nest at 15–17 days, but fed by parents for an additional 2–3 weeks.

Housing: Phoebes adapt to many artificial sites, but you can encourage them by adding a nest shelf to a sheltered location such as a porch or under a deck.

A fledgling Eastern Phoebe waits patiently for food. The colorful, fleshy gape of its mouth is a feature of many young birds.

SIGHTINGS

JAN FEB MAR APR MAY JUN JUL AUG SEP OCT NOV DEC

Black Phoebe
Sayornis nigricans, L 6¾" (17 cm)

The only black-and-white flycatcher in North America, elegantly attired in "black topcoat and white pants." This charming bird goes about its business—invariably in the vicinity of water—paying scant attention to anyone nearby.

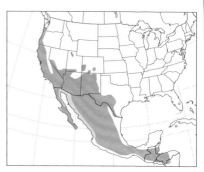

blackish

sharply contrasting white belly

phoebes drop their tail down

rusty wing bars

juvenile

IDENTIFICATION Common. Medium-size flycatcher with a large, slightly crested head and a rather long tail that give it a front-heavy appearance. This active bird's energy extends to its tail, which is pumped up and down, especially after alighting.
Plumage: Black and white. Matte black above, with thin silvery edges on the wings and outer tail feathers; black breast, flanks, and tail contrast abruptly with the snow white belly. Dark eyes and bill blend into the black head. **Juvenile** has rusty wing bars.
Similar species: None. Sometimes seen with Say's Phoebe (opposite), mostly in winter.
Voice: Song alternates between two high, thin, whistled phases: *pi-tsee* and *pi-tsew*. **Call** is a sharp, high *tsip*.

RANGE West Coast and southwestern species; year-round resident. Strongly associated with water: rivers, creeks, ponds, seaside cliffs—even backyard pools, park fountains, and cattle troughs. Prime habitat is a stream with overhanging branches and a nearby bridge or sheltered structure for nesting. Most birds are permanent residents, but in winter vacate highest breeding locations and northern edge of range in Southwest.

FOOD Insects captured during darting flights from a low branch or creekside rock. Occasionally descends to the ground or snatches prey from the water's surface; known to catch small minnows.

NESTING *Location:* Attached to a sheltered vertical wall or in a niche; often uses a man-made structure such as a bridge, culvert, or building eave. Pairs often return to the same nest site year after year. *Nest:* Mud-and-grass cup lined with plant fiber. *Eggs:* Usually 4–5; incubated by female for 15–17 days. *Fledging:* Leaves nest at about 18 days.
Housing: Will use a nesting shelf placed in a sheltered location, for example, under a porch roof or eave. The female constructs the nest.

SIGHTINGS

JAN	FEB	MAR	APR	MAY	JUN	JUL	AUG	SEP	OCT	NOV	DEC

Say's Phoebe
Sayornis saya, L 7½" (19 cm)

Say's Phoebe is the northernmost breeding flycatcher in the world—almost reaching the Arctic Ocean. Needless to say, it is highly migratory there. Its population center is in the arid interior West.

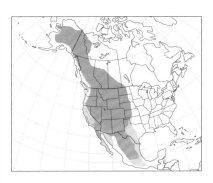

 IDENTIFICATION Common. Medium-size flycatcher with large head, but well proportioned overall. Like other phoebes, often pumps and fans its tail. Buoyant flight, with noticeably dark tail and pale underwings.
Plumage: Dusty grayish brown above, with slightly paler throat and breast. Cinnamon underparts and blackish tail are eye-catching field marks. **Juvenile** is paler with buff wing bars.
Similar species: Slightly overlaps in range with Eastern Phoebe (pages 108–109), which is about the same size and shape but has white (not cinnamon) belly and white throat.
Voice: Song is a fast *pit-tsee-eur*, often given in fluttering flight. Typical **call** is a plaintive, down-slurred whistle: *pee-ee.*

RANGE Western species; mostly a summer resident. Favors arid country of all kinds—dry grasslands, parched foothills, rocky canyons, sagebrush flats, ranchlands, rimrock country, and tundra (in northern Alaska). Unlike other phoebes, avoids forested areas and well-watered land. Migrates south in fall, except in the southernmost part of its breeding range, where it is present year-round. Spring **migration:** late February–mid-May; fall migration: late September–October.

FOOD Mostly flying insects— often bees and wasps—captured during darting flights from a low perch on a boulder, bush, or fence post. In cold weather or when flying insects are scarce, hovers overhead to spot prey on the ground.

NESTING *Location:* In a sheltered rocky niche or cliff overhang; often uses a man-made structure such as a porch, abandoned farm building, or mine shaft. *Nest:* Grass-and-fiber cup. *Eggs:* Usually 4–5; incubated by female for 12–18 days. *Fledging:* Leaves nest at 17–21 days.
Housing: Will use a nest shelf placed in a sheltered location like a porch or house eave.

grayish back

tawny belly

blackish tail

Ash-throated Flycatcher
Myiarchus cinerascens, L 7¾" (19 cm)

The Ash-throated Flycatcher is a common summer resident across a large swath of western North America.

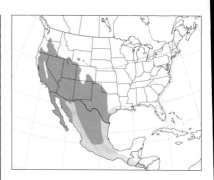

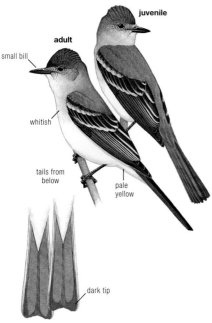

juvenile

adult

small bill

whitish

tails from below

pale yellow

dark tip

juvenile   adult

IDENTIFICATION Common. Medium-large, slender, bushy-crested flycatcher. Usually perches within the tree canopy, but territorial birds sing from more open perches. Does not pump its tail.
Plumage: Grayish brown upperparts, with pale gray throat and breast that blends into pale yellow belly. Wings have rufous primaries, most visible in flight; tail has rufous inner webs, best seen from below.
Similar species: Brown-crested Flycatcher (page 115) is larger, with brighter yellow underparts that are more sharply con-

trasted and a different undertail pattern. Say's Phoebe (page 111) lacks rufous color in wings and tail, has cinnamon (not yellow) underparts, and frequently pumps its tail.
Voice: Song is a series of *ka-brick* notes. Distinctive **call** is a rough *prrrt.*

RANGE Western species; summer resident. A habitat generalist that is found from sea level to about 8,000 feet in a variety of open woodlands and arid scrub—but avoids humid, densely forested areas. Winters from extreme southwestern U.S. to Central America. Spring **migration:** mid-March–mid-May; fall migration: August–mid-September.

FOOD Mostly insects. Hunts by moving from perch to perch, then hovering briefly to pick an insect off a leaf or branch; aerial pursuits are uncommon. Supplements its diet with wild fruits and small reptiles.

NESTING *Location:* In a natural cavity or old woodpecker hole in a tree or cactus. *Nest:* Bulky cup of weeds, fur, and other found objects. *Eggs:* Usually 4–5; incubated by female for 14–16 days. *Fledging:* Leaves nest at 13–17 days.
Housing: Will use a nest box—or even a tin can nailed to a fence post.

Red-winged Blackbirds chase and harass raptors like this Red-shouldered Hawk.

THE MOB

Listen: Do you hear a lot of angry birds? Then it's likely that a predator, maybe a snake, cat, or hawk, is nearby—and has been spotted.

You might think that a bird's reaction to a dangerous predator in its neighborhood is to flee, or at least go quiet, but often the opposite is true. Small birds like chickadees, blackbirds, and hummingbirds "mob" the predator, flying straight toward it while screaming alarm calls at full volume.

This behavior employs two strategies. First, there is safety in numbers—if birds group together, then the predator may become disoriented. And second, removing the element of surprise means that a predator has little chance of catching any bird that mobs it.

WORKING TOGETHER

Different species of birds can recognize each other's alarm calls, interpreting what kind of predator has been spotted and even how far away it is. They perch nearby, strafe, and peck the intruder until it leaves the area.

It's hard not to feel sorry for a passing Red-tailed Hawk that attracts this kind of attention from a horde of crows, which caw and dive-bomb so aggressively that the poor hawk has to perform evasive maneuvers. But crows themselves may be mercilessly mobbed by Red-winged Blackbirds, which recognize crows as a danger to their eggs and chicks.

Birds don't always restrict their harassment to predators, especially near nests. Relatively peaceful large birds, such as Great Blue Herons and Turkey Vultures, are occasionally targeted by fierce mobs—better to be safe than sorry. People may find themselves on the receiving end, too; if you get mobbed, retreat slowly.

Great Crested Flycatcher
Myiarchus crinitus, L 8½" (21 cm)

The Great Crested Flycatcher's penchant for adding a shed snakeskin to its nest was noted by early naturalists. The assumption was that it scared away potential predators. Nowadays, these flycatchers are as likely to substitute a piece of crinkly cellophane or plastic wrap—possibly seeking a decorative effect rather than protective one.

IDENTIFICATION Common. Medium-large, lanky flycatcher with a moderate crest and a heavy bill. Much of its time is spent high up in leafy trees, where it would go unnoticed except for its loud and regular vocalizing.
Plumage: Dark olive brown upperparts; gray throat and breast; and bright lemon yellow belly. Wings have rufous primaries, most visible in flight; tail has rufous inner webs, best seen from below.
Similar species: None in the East.
Voice: Distinctive call is a loud, hoarse, ascending *wheep!*

RANGE Eastern species; summer resident. Inhabits open deciduous forest, including woodlots, second-growth woodlands, and suburban and urban areas with numerous large shade trees. It has probably benefited from forest fragmentation. Winters in Central and South America and in southern Florida. Spring **migration:** mid-March–May; fall migration: late August–October.

FOOD Mostly insects. Hunts from a perch, sallying out to capture insects in flight, sometimes involving a lengthy pursuit, or hovering briefly to pick insects off a leaf or branch; occasionally pursues insects on the ground. Supplements diet with small wild fruits.

NESTING *Location:* In an old woodpecker hole or natural cavity. *Nest:* Bulky cup of leaves, fur, and other found objects, including snakeskins and plastic wrap. *Eggs:* Usually 4–5; incubated by female for 13–15 days. *Fledging:* Leaves nest at 14–15 days.
Housing: Will use a nest box.

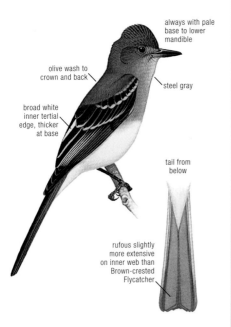

always with pale base to lower mandible

olive wash to crown and back

steel gray

broad white inner tertial edge, thicker at base

tail from below

rufous slightly more extensive on inner web than Brown-crested Flycatcher

SIGHTINGS

JAN   FEB   MAR   APR   MAY   JUN   JUL   AUG   SEP   OCT   NOV   DEC

Brown-crested Flycatcher

Myiarchus tyrannulus, L 8¾" (22 cm)

The Brown-crested Flycatcher has a much smaller North American range than the Ash-throated, but the two species occur together and are difficult to tell apart.

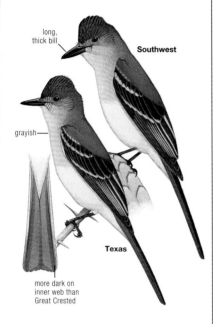

long, thick bill

Southwest

grayish

Texas

more dark on inner web than Great Crested

the similar-size Great Crested Flycatcher (opposite).

Voice: Song is a clear musical whistle, a rolling *whit-will-do*. **Call** is a sharp, emphatic *whit*.

RANGE Southwestern and South Texas species; summer resident. Inhabits riverside groves of sycamore, cottonwood, and willow in the Southwest or mesquite, hackberry, and ash in Texas, as well as towns and suburbs with large shade trees; also common around saguaro cacti of southwestern deserts. Seldom seen on migration, but is present in the U.S. from late April to mid-August, wintering in Mexico and Central America.

FOOD Mostly insects. Hunts by hovering briefly to pick an insect off a leaf or branch; aerial pursuits are less common. Supplements its diet with wild fruits (including cactus fruit) and small reptiles.

NESTING *Location:* In a natural cavity or old woodpecker hole in a tree or cactus. *Nest:* Bulky cup of weeds, fur, and other found objects. *Eggs:* Usually 4–5; incubated by female for 14–15 days. *Fledging:* Leaves nest at 12–18 days.

Housing: Will use a nest box or even an open pipe of a suitable dimension.

IDENTIFICATION Fairly common. Large, robust, bushy-crested flycatcher with a large bill. The subspecies in Texas is smaller. Does not pump its tail.

Plumage: Grayish-brown upperparts; gray throat and breast contrast with yellow belly. Wings have rufous primaries, most visible in flight; tail has rufous inner webs, best seen from below.

Similar species: Ash-throated Flycatcher (page 112) is a smaller, lankier bird with paler yellow underparts that blend into the pale gray breast and with a different undertail pattern and voice. In southern Texas (during migration), compare to

Eastern Kingbird
Tyrannus tyrannus, L 8½" (22 cm)

The kingbirds—this species and the following two—are flycatchers found in open or broken country. The group name refers both to their brazen behavior of chasing off larger birds and their hidden "crowns" of red feathers, seen only when a bird is highly agitated.

 IDENTIFICATION Common. Moderately large, white-bellied flycatcher. Like other kingbirds, often perches high up on dead branches and power lines, or much lower on fences and shrubs.
Plumage: Slate gray above, head almost black, and wings edged with white; underparts are snow white with a pale gray wash across the breast. Black tail with white tip. **Juvenile** is browner above with an indistinct pale tip to the tail.
Similar species: Gray Kingbird (not illustrated) of coastal Florida, which is larger, paler, larger billed, and has a forked tail without a white tip.

Voice: Call is single buzzy *dzeet*. Also gives a stuttering series of notes: *kip-kip-kipper-kipper* or *dzee-dzee-dzee*.

RANGE Widespread species; summer resident. The only kingbird in most of the East, it overlaps with the Western Kingbird in many midwestern and western locales (see range maps). Favors open country with scattered trees and is common around farms, along roadsides, and in streamside thickets, suburban parks, golf courses, and athletic fields. Winters in South America. Spring **migration:** late March–mid-June; fall migration: late July–late September.

FOOD Mostly flying insects. Prey is captured during sallying flight from a perch, but also glides to the ground, gleans insects from bushes, and hovers over fields. Diet also includes wild fruits and berries, especially during fall migration and in winter.

NESTING *Location:* In a tree away from the trunk; occasionally on a utility tower or other man-made structure. *Nest:* Disheveled but sturdy cup of small twigs and weed stems. *Eggs:* Usually 3–4; incubated by female for 14–17 days. *Fledging:* Leaves nest at 16–17 days.

blackish head

small bill

black tail with white tip

snow white underparts

SIGHTINGS

JAN　FEB　MAR　APR　MAY　JUN　JUL　AUG　SEP　OCT　NOV　DEC

Western Kingbird
Tyrannus verticalis, L 8¾" (22 cm)

The Western Kingbird is a conspicuous summer bird over large areas of the Great Plains and West. Pairs don't tolerate larger birds getting too close to their nest tree—passing predators are chased and briskly escorted out of the area.

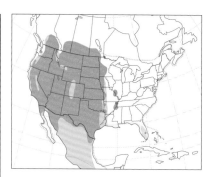

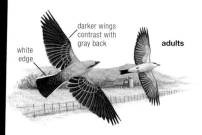

white edge
darker wings contrast with gray back
adults

 IDENTIFICATION Common. Moderately large, yellow-bellied flycatcher. Perches high or low. Buoyant flight; sometimes hovers briefly.
Plumage: Soft, pale gray above and on chest (slightly olive on back). White throat blends into gray chest, which blends into yellow belly. Faint, dark face mask. Black tail contrasts sharply with pale gray back; the tail has white edges, which can wear off by fall.
Similar species: Cassin's Kingbird (next page) is darker gray above and on chest,

has a white chin surrounded by dark gray, and has a pale tip (not white edges) to the tail. Also compare to Say's Phoebe (page 111).
Voice: Song is a fast *pik pik peek PEEK-a-loo*. Common **call** is a sharp *kip*, given singly or in a stuttering series.

RANGE Great Plains and western species; summer resident. Favors dry country interspersed with trees as well as towns and urban parks. Winters in Mexico and Central America, with small numbers in southern Florida. Spring **migration:** mid-March–mid-May; fall migration: late July–September.

adult ♂

FOOD Insects. Most prey are captured during sallying flights from a perch, but also from the ground or gleaned from bushes.

NESTING *Location:* On the outer branches of a tree or shrub, or on man-made structures such as a building, a utility pole, or even a city lamppost. *Nest:* Untidy cup mostly of grasses and weed stems. *Eggs:* Usually 4; incubated by female for 12–18 days. *Fledging:* Leaves nest at 16–17 days.

pale gray head and back

spring adult ♂

black tail with white edge

Cassin's Kingbird
Tyrannus vociferans, L 9" (23 cm)

Cassin's Kingbird is a loud, boisterous summer bird of western North America. Not as widespread or common as the Western Kingbird (the "default" yellow-bellied kingbird), but the two species overlap in range and habitat. They sometimes even nest in the same tree.

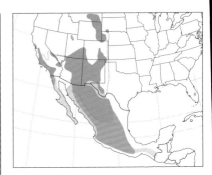

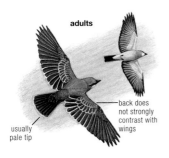

adults

back does not strongly contrast with wings

usually pale tip

IDENTIFICATION Fairly common. Moderately large, stocky, yellow-bellied flycatcher.
Plumage: Dark gray above and on chest. White chin contrasts with dark gray throat; wings barely contrast with the upperparts. Dark tail is tipped in buff, with faint, pale edges.
Similar species: Western

adult ♂

Kingbird (previous page) is paler overall, but its darker wings contrast with its pale gray body; its white throat blends into a paler gray breast and black tail is edged in white. Also compare to Say's Phoebe (page 111).
Voice: Very vocal. **Call** is a strident, burry *chi-BEER* or *CHE-brrr*, given singly or run into a stuttering series.

RANGE Western species; summer resident. Most common in the Southwest and Southern California.

Favors parklike areas interspersed with trees—cottonwood, juniper, eucalyptus. Some winter in Southern California (sometimes in small flocks), but most move to Mexico. Spring **migration:** mid-March–May; fall migration: late July–October.

FOOD Mostly flying insects. Most prey are captured during sallying flights from a perch; also glides to the ground or gleans insects from bushes. Winter diet includes wild fruits and berries.

NESTING *Location:* Outer branches of a tall tree. *Nest:* Substantial cup of small twigs and weed stems. *Eggs:* Usually 3–4; incubated by female for 12–14 days. *Fledging:* Leaves nest at 16–17 days.

dark gray head, back, and breast

white chin

adult ♂

pale tip

Scissor-tailed Flycatcher
Tyrannus forficatus, L 13" (33 cm)

If you live in the southern Great Plains, you may have the "Prairie Kingbird" as a summer neighbor. State bird of Oklahoma.

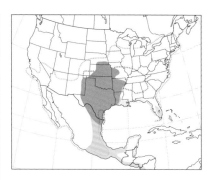

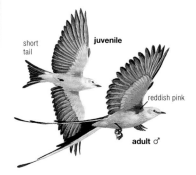

short tail

juvenile

reddish pink

adult ♂

 IDENTIFICATION Common. Medium-large, long-tailed flycatcher. The Scissortail is a common roadside bird, often seen perched on a barbed-wire fence or low shrub.
Plumage: Very pale gray upperparts; dark wings edged in white; salmon pink belly and underwings; scarlet red where the wings meet the body; and a very long, black-and-white tail. **Males** have a longer tail than females; **juvenile** has an even shorter tail and is yellowish pink on belly.
Similar species: Western Kingbird (page 117) resembles juvenile Scissortail, but has a pure yellow belly and an even shorter, unforked tail.
Voice: Song is similar to Western Kingbird's. Common **call** is a sharp *kip* or *pup* given singly or in a stuttering series.

RANGE Texas and southern Great Plains species; summer resident. Favors prairies, savannas, and open country with scattered trees; common around farms and along roadsides, but also near urban shelterbelts and golf courses. Most winter in Mexico or Central America, with small numbers in southern Florida. Spring **migration:** mid-March–early May; fall migration: late September–early November.

FOOD Insects, especially grasshoppers, crickets, and beetles.

NESTING *Location:* In an isolated tree or shrub. *Nest:* Sturdy cup of small twigs and weed stems. *Eggs:* Usually 4–5; incubated by female for 13–16 days. *Fledging:* Leaves nest at 14–17 days.

juvenile

pale gray head and back

adult ♂

orange buff

long forked tail with extensive white; female has shorter tail

VIREOS   Family Vireonidae

The vireos are a family of small songbirds with short, sturdy bills slightly hooked at the tip. They are generally chunkier and less active than warblers.

Red-eyed Vireo
Vireo olivaceus, L 6" (15 cm)

This vireo is probably the most common summer bird in eastern woods, and its range extends far to the west. Its persistent singing earned it the nickname "preacher bird" in the 19th century.

olive above, white below

black lateral crown stripe

breeding

pale yellow

1st fall

cheer-o-wit ("Here I am, over here, see me, where are you?"). **Call** is a nasal, whiny *queee*.

IDENTIFICATION
Very common. This small songbird moves sluggishly through the leafy treetops and would be hard to detect if not for its incessant singing—heard throughout the summer, from dawn till dusk. Its signature red eyes are revealed only with a very close look.

Plumage: Boldly striped head pattern with white eyebrows, bordered above and below with black, and a gray crown. Olive green upperparts; white underparts. No wing bars. **First-fall** has dark eyes; extensive yellowish wash on undertail coverts and flanks, which may extend up to the bend of the wing.

Similar species: Warbling Vireo (next page) lacks dark stripes on face.

Voice: Song is a series of sweet, singsong phrases: *chit-a-wit, de-o, cher-ee,*

RANGE Widespread species; summer resident. Most common in mature deciduous forests, but also lives in mixed pine-hardwood forests and in residential areas and urban parks with large trees. Winters in South America. Spring **migration:** April–May; fall migration: late August–mid-October.

FOOD Gleans insects, particularly caterpillars, from leaves and twigs, or plucks them from leaves while hovering. Active, but methodical, as it moves about the canopy or mid-levels of the forest. Also eats small fruits, mostly in late summer and fall.

NESTING *Location:* In a shrub or low tree, usually 5–10 feet up. *Nest:* Open cup of papery bark, grasses, and rootlets, suspended from a forked branch. *Eggs:* Usually 3–5; incubated by both parents for 11–14 days. *Fledging:* Leaves nest at 10–12 days.

SIGHTINGS

JAN	FEB	MAR	APR	MAY	JUN	JUL	AUG	SEP	OCT	NOV	DEC

Warbling Vireo
Vireo gilvus, L 5½" (14 cm)

Plain and pale, the Warbling Vireo is most appreciated for its rapid, warbling song that emanates from the forest canopy in spring and summer.

 IDENTIFICATION Common. Compact and nicely proportioned, with a relatively slender bill. Its dark eye stands out on a pale face. Recent research has shown that there are likely two species of Warbling Vireo—an eastern one and a considerably smaller western one.

Plumage: There are not many field marks on this plain bird: brownish olive upperparts, whitish underparts, no wing bars. Face pattern is ill defined: pale eyebrow and dusky line through the eye. In fall, birds have a yellow wash on the underparts.

Similar species: Red-eyed Vireo (opposite), discernible by its boldly striped face pattern.

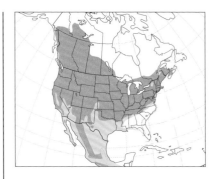

Voice: Persistent singer. **Song** is a complex series of rambling warbles; as a memory aid, try this ode to a caterpillar that approximates the song's cadence: "If I sees you, I will squeeze you, and I'll squeeze you till you squirt." **Call** is a nasal *eahh*.

 RANGE Widespread species; summer resident. Most common in mature deciduous forests, especially near water; also lives in residential areas and urban parks with large trees. Winters in Mexico and Central America. Spring **migration:** mid-April–early May in the East, early March–late May in the West; fall migration: mid-August–early September in East, late July–mid-October in West.

FOOD Gleans insects, particularly caterpillars, from leaves and twigs, or plucks them from leaves while hovering. Active, but methodical, as it moves about the canopy or mid-levels of the forest.

NESTING *Location:* In a tree, usually 20–60 feet up. *Nest:* Open cup of bark strips, grasses, hair, rootlets, and so forth, woven into the crotch of a forked twig. *Eggs:* Usually 3–4; incubated by both parents for 12–14 days. *Fledging:* Leaves nest at about 14 days.

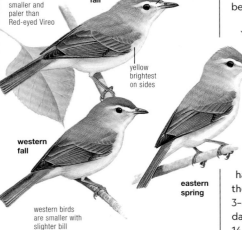

smaller and paler than Red-eyed Vireo

eastern fall

pale lores

yellow brightest on sides

western fall

eastern spring

western birds are smaller with slighter bill

Yellow-throated Vireo
Vireo flavifrons, L 5½" (14 cm)

The Yellow-throated Vireo is a colorful species, but its combination of yellow, olive, white, and gray is very good camouflage in the leafy treetops it frequents. The first clue to its presence is usually its distinctive song.

IDENTIFICATION Uncommon. Large vireo with a stocky body, heavy bill, short tail, and typical, sluggish vireo movements as it forages methodically through the forest canopy. Often cocks its head as it surveys its surroundings.
Plumage: Clean, bright colors. Yellow spectacles, throat, and breast are distinctive. Olive green upperparts, bold white wing bars, gray rump, and white belly.
Similar species: Pine Warbler (page 227) has similar pattern and color, but has a yellowish rump, streaked sides that look dingy, a thinner bill, a more active lifestyle, and different vocalizations.
Voice: Persistent singer throughout the breeding season. **Song** is series of lazy, slurred phrases separated by fairly long

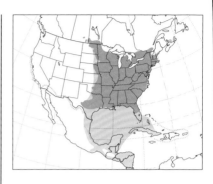

pauses: *de-a-ree, three-eight*. **Calls** include a rapid, harsh series of *cheh* notes.

RANGE Eastern species; summer resident. Breeds in open deciduous forests with mature trees (oaks and maples are favorites), preferring wooded edges with water nearby; also lives in old orchards, woodsy suburbs, and urban parks with tall shade trees. Unevenly distributed and may be scarce in large areas of its mapped breeding range. Winters from southern Mexico to northern South America, and in the Caribbean. Spring **migration:** mid-March–May; fall migration: September–mid-October.

FOOD Methodically gleans insects—caterpillars, moths, butterflies, and a variety of small bugs—from leaves and twigs; sometimes hovers briefly. Supplements its diet with small fruits, mostly in fall.

NESTING *Location:* In a tree, usually 20–60 feet up. *Nest:* Deep, rounded cup of plant fibers and spiderweb, with flakes of lichen covering the outside, woven into the crotch of a forked twig. *Eggs:* Usually 4; incubated by both parents for about 13 days. *Fledging:* Leaves nest at about 13 days.

white wing bars

yellow spectacles

thick bill

yellow throat and breast

white belly

gray rump

| JAN | FEB | MAR | APR | MAY | JUN | JUL | AUG | SEP | OCT | NOV | DEC |

CLEVER CORVIDS

Of all the world's birds, two groups stand out for remarkable intelligence. The first group includes parrots and their relatives, which excel in language, puzzles, and solving problems. The other group is called Corvidae, better known as the corvids.

Crows, ravens, jays, and magpies are all members of the corvid family. Collectively, these birds have redefined our understanding of animal intelligence, and of what it means to be a bird.

BIRD BRAINS

Calling someone a "birdbrain"—once considered an insult—could, these days, be construed as a compliment. The more we study corvids, the more the gap narrows between their brains and our own. Behaviors that were once thought to be hallmarks of humanity have been increasingly documented in this family of birds: tool use, self-image, recognition of individuals (both avian and human), grief, cunning, spatial and temporal memory, and complex problem solving.

The brains of corvids are large relative to body size, on par with great apes and nearly proportional to humans. And a corvid's brain is more densely packed with neurons than our mammalian brains, especially the forebrain—the part responsible for higher cognition.

Corvids are gregarious and omnivorous, which requires them to navigate complicated social and physical environments. For them, like people, the energetic cost of a large brain is outweighed by survival benefits.

In other words, it's no surprise that a crow might learn to solve a multistep puzzle, or that a magpie could glance in a mirror and recognize itself, or that videos of these birds regularly go viral. Because these clever behaviors overlap our own ideals of intelligence, we enjoy seeing a little of ourselves in the lives of corvids.

A Common Raven plays with a plastic ball containing treats.

CROWS & JAYS   Family Corvidae

Harsh voices and an aggressive manner draw attention to these large, often gregarious birds. Their powerful, all-purpose bills efficiently handle a varied diet. The jays are long-tailed and colorful; crows and ravens are entirely black.

Blue Jay
Cyanocitta cristata, L 11" (28 cm)

Blue Jays have personality to spare. A partial list of descriptive adjectives would include: conspicuous, colorful, brassy, loud, domineering, raucous, adaptable, intelligent, inquisitive, thieving, handsome, and unmistakable. They are the only blue colored jay in the East (except in Florida), and one of the most well-known backyard birds. Provincial bird of Prince Edward Island.

long, wedge-shaped tail fringed with white

bluish crest

white trailing edge to secondaries and elsewhere on wing

blackish throat band

extensive white in wings

white tail tips

IDENTIFICATION Common. Large, easily recognized, crested jay. Hops from limb to limb or on the ground when foraging, and often perches up high when less active. Lands at feeders with an assertive flourish of wings, but also glides quietly through the forest. Loose flocks of migrating jays fly with steady wing beats well above the treetops. Jays are shy and secretive when nesting, except when mobbing a predator such as an owl, hawk, snake, or cat.

Plumage: Bright blue upperparts, crest (sometimes flattened), wings, and tail; wings with a bold, white wing bar and spots; tail with a broad white tip; white face encircled with a black necklace; and white underparts, often shaded buff gray on the breast and flanks.

Similar species: None. Range barely overlaps with two other species of western "blue jays": crested Steller's Jay (page 126), which is much darker and has no white in its wings or tail; and California Scrub-Jay (page 127), which lacks a crest and has a dark face. The Florida Scrub-Jay (very similar to the California Scrub-Jay) is restricted to central Florida, lacks a crest, has no white in its wings and tail, and has a dark face.

Voice: Wonderfully diverse array of **calls:** piercing *jay, jay, jay;* musical *wheedle-wheedle;* liquid, whistled *tooli;* and quiet, low-pitched rattle, as well as a very convincing mimic of Red-shouldered and Red-tailed Hawk calls.

RANGE Eastern and midwestern species. Inhabits a variety of forested areas and mixed woodlands (especially with oaks). Locally abundant in suburbs and urban areas, probably as a result of bird-feeding activity. A permanent resident in many locations, but northern breeders (and others?) move south in fall and many spend the winter months in the Southeast. Large numbers of Blue Jays are sometimes seen migrating in loose flocks, but numbers vary from year to year. Spring **migration:** late April–late May; fall migration: mid-September–late October.

FOOD Omnivorous—a varied diet including acorns and other nuts, fruits, seeds, insects, bird eggs and nestlings (infrequently), and other small animals. Feeds in trees, on the ground, and at bird feeders. Caches acorns and other seeds by burying them in the ground. Since many nuts are not retrieved, this activity disperses acorns throughout the forest and results in the propagation of many new oak trees. **Feeding:** Very common at feeders. Whole peanuts, sunflower seeds, and cracked

During aggressive confrontations, most birds, like these Blue Jays, try to look as large as possible.

corn are favorites. Dominates smaller birds; feeders that restrict the access of jays and other large birds are available.

NESTING *Location:* On a horizontal tree branch, usually 5–50 feet up. *Nest:* Bulky, open cup of twigs, grass, and bark, sometimes cemented with mud. *Eggs:* Usually 4–5; incubated by female for 16–18 days. *Fledging:* Leaves nest at 17–21 days.

The Blue Jay's crest is often held flattened against the top of its head.

Steller's Jay
Cyanocitta stelleri, L 11½" (29 cm)

Steller's Jays are raucous, inquisitive jays of western forests. They frequently interact with people in backyards, campgrounds, picnic areas, and anywhere else they can expect (or demand) a handout. Provincial bird of British Columbia.

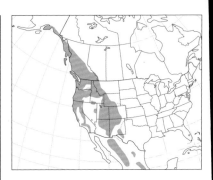

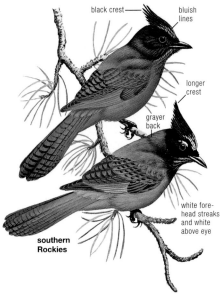

black crest

bluish lines

longer crest

grayer back

white forehead streaks and white above eye

southern Rockies

North America is both all dark and crested. **Voice:** Diverse array of **calls:** piercing *SHECK, SHECK, SHECK;* harsh, descending *SHHHHKK!;* and a variety of rattles and whistles. Frequently mimics hawks.

RANGE Western species; year-round resident. Inhabits coniferous and mixed coniferous-deciduous forests, from sea level to high elevations. Very common in the Pacific Northwest and in areas, including suburban backyards, where it is accustomed to being fed. Though nonmigratory, may move to lower elevations in winter.

FOOD Omnivorous, with a varied diet of nuts, seeds, fruits, insects, bird eggs and nestlings, and other small animals. Feeds in trees, on the ground, and at bird feeders.
Feeding: Common at feeders. Whole peanuts, sunflower seeds, and suet are favorites.

IDENTIFICATION Common. Large, dark, shaggy-crested jay. Flies on broad wings; a descent to the ground from a high perch is often accomplished with a series of undulating glides. Although bold and aggressive around campgrounds and picnic areas, it is often shy in wilder places. When not breeding, mated pairs band together in small flocks. **Plumage:** Blackish head and crest. Birds from the central and southern Rockies have white lines on the crown and a white arc over the eye; birds from the rest of the range have bluish lines just on the crown. **Juveniles** are browner with a short crest. **Similar species:** None. No other jay in

NESTING *Location:* Typically, high in a conifer, but often much lower when nesting near houses. *Nest:* Bulky, open cup of twigs, grass, and bark, sometimes cemented with mud. *Eggs:* Usually 4–5; incubated by female for 16–18 days. *Fledging:* Able to fly well at about 30 days.

California Scrub-Jay
Aphelocoma californica, L 11" (28 cm)

The most familiar "blue jay" along the West Coast, the California Scrub-Jay has successfully adapted to a variety of suburban and urban habitats, where it is a frequent and conspicuous backyard bird. Very similar-looking birds of the interior West (eastern California to central Texas) were recently recognized as a separate species, Woodhouse's Scrub-Jay.

IDENTIFICATION Common. Large, but slender, long-tailed jay without a crest. Hops from branch to branch and frequently descends to the ground. In flight, it swoops and glides across open spaces, often calling harshly and loudly, as if protesting. Birds of the interior West (Woodhouse's Scrub-Jay) are less common and rather shy compared with their boisterous coastal cousins.

grayish brown back

deep blue upperparts

blue breast band

whitish underparts

Plumage: Deep blue upperparts, a brownish patch on the back, a partial blue collar, and whitish underparts. **Juvenile** is mostly grayish brown on head.
Similar species: Woodhouse's Scrub-Jay (not illustrated) has paler upperparts, grayer underparts, and a more blended breast band; the ranges of the two species barely overlap along the California-Nevada border. Steller's Jay (opposite page) has a crest and all-dark plumage. Blue Jay (page 124) has a crest and conspicuous white areas in its wings and tail.
Voice: Its most common **calls** are a harsh, up-slurred *jaaay?* or *jreeee?* and a rapid series of raspy *shreep* notes.

RANGE Western species; year-round resident. Inhabits chaparral and brushy areas, scrubby woodlands, and suburban and city backyards.

FOOD Omnivorous—nuts, seeds, fruits, insects, bird eggs and nestlings, and other small animals. Feeds on the ground and in trees. As with the Blue Jay in the East, the Scrub-Jay's habit of caching acorns plays an important role in the propagation of oaks; both jays have excellent spatial memory, but many acorns are never retrieved and some end up sprouting.
Feeding: Common at feeders. Whole peanuts, sunflower seeds, and suet are favorites.

NESTING *Location:* In a tree or bush, usually 3–10 feet up. *Nest:* Bulky, open cup of twigs, grass, bark, and hair. *Eggs:* Usually 2–3; incubated by female for 15–17 days. *Fledging:* Leaves nest at 18-23 days.

Fish Crow
Corvus ossifragus, L 15½" (39 cm)

If you live in Fish Crow country, you're faced with an identification challenge—telling it apart from the ubiquitous American Crow. The two species look almost identical, but thankfully, they sound completely different. If you're wondering about a silent crow, simply wait until it calls.

wings more pointed than American Crow

smaller than American Crow

shorter legs than American Crow

IDENTIFICATION Common. Structure is very similar to the American Crow, but Fish Crow is a bit smaller, has slightly shorter legs, and more pointed wings.
Plumage: All black. **Juvenile** has duller, sooty plumage.
Similar species: American Crow (opposite) is slightly larger, less glossy, and longer legged, but looks almost identical—the two are best separated by voice. Grackles (pages 221–223) are smaller, slender birds with much longer tails.
Voice: Distinctive, nasal **call** of *kah-uhh* or *uh-uhh* is very different from American Crow's cawing.

RANGE Eastern and southern species. Inhabits coastal and tidewater areas, as well as inland areas, mostly along main river valleys; also common in suburbs and cities throughout its range. Forms large flocks in fall and winter that congregate around dependable food sources such as garbage dumps and shopping centers. Flocks disperse and individuals return (migrate) to their breeding areas in mid-March–April.

FOOD Omnivorous. Insects, shrimp, crayfish, crabs, bird eggs, nestling birds, carrion, garbage, grain, seeds, and fruit are the main items.

NESTING *Location:* In a tree, usually 20–80 feet up. *Nest:* Bulky basket of sticks, twigs, grass, and sometimes mud. *Eggs:* Usually 4–5; incubated by female for 16–19 days. *Fledging:* Leaves nest at 32–40 days.

To confirm the identity of a Fish Crow, listen for its distinctive *uh-uhh* call, very different from the cawing of an American Crow.

American Crow
Corvus brachyrhynchos, L 17½" (45 cm)

There are other black birds, even other crows, but the abundant and widespread American Crow is the one that everybody knows. Crows are bold, inquisitive birds that are also very intelligent and surprisingly well organized. Cohesive family groups include immature and adult helpers that act as sentinels or scouts, help feed nestlings, and can communicate among themselves with a large vocabulary of sounds.

IDENTIFICATION Common to abundant. The American Crow is a large, sturdy bird with a heavy bill and strong legs for walking (strutting, really) and hopping on the ground. Its flight is strong and direct ("as the crow flies") on broad wings and a slightly rounded tail. **Plumage:** All black, including legs, feet, bill, and eyes. **Juvenile** has duller, sooty plumage; **just fledged young** has pink skin at the base of the bill.
Similar species: Fish Crow (opposite) is almost identical and best

wing tip more rounded than Fish Crow

larger and heavier and bigger billed than Fish Crow

separated by voice. Common Raven (page 130) is larger; has a heavier bill, shaggy throat feathers, a wedge-shaped tail, and deeper call; and often soars (crows never soar). Male Great-tailed Grackle (page 221) has a much longer tail and pale eyes. **Voice:** Familiar *caw, caw, caw* that changes depending on its context.

RANGE Widespread species. Inhabits a variety of habitats, particularly open areas with scattered trees. Northern breeders migrate south in fall, and family groups band together into large, noisy flocks. Nighttime roosts at favored locations can number in the thousands. Spring **migration:** mid-February–early April; fall migration: late October–December.

FOOD Omnivorous and opportunistic—insects, earthworms, bird eggs and young, rodents, snakes, carrion, garbage, grain, seeds (including birdseed), fruit, and more.

NESTING *Location:* In a tree or large bush, 10–70 feet up. *Nest:* Large, bulky basket of sticks, twigs, grass, and sometimes mud. *Eggs:* Usually 4–6; incubated by female for about 18 days. *Fledging:* Leaves nest at about 35 days.

Common Raven
Corvus corax, L 24" (61 cm)

The majestic Common Raven is distributed around the globe in the Northern Hemisphere and has entered the folklore of many cultures. If you live in the West, chances are good that these intelligent and opportunistic birds are somewhere nearby. Provincial bird of Yukon Territory.

IDENTIFICATION Common to uncommon. Weighing about 2½ pounds, the Common Raven is heavier than a Red-tailed Hawk. When perched, the raven's feathers often look shaggy or ruffled, and the long, thin throat feathers (hackles) flare out when it croaks. The raven is a consummate flier, with long wings and a wedge-shaped tail, soaring with ease and even engaging in aerial acrobatics.
Plumage: All black (glossy, in some light), including legs, feet, bill, and eyes.
Similar species: American Crow (previous page) is much smaller and lighter. A crow never soars and has shorter, more rounded wings and a slightly rounded (rather than wedge-shaped) tail.
Voice: Extremely varied. Most common call is a low, drawn-out, croaked *kraaah;* another is a deep, nasal, and hollow *broooonk.*

RANGE Widespread species. Most abundant in the West, uncommon in the East (south through the Appalachians), and largely absent from the Midwest (except in the northern states) and Southeast. Lives in a multitude of habitats, including mountains, seacoasts, tundra, deserts, farmland, towns, and suburbs.

long wings

long, wedge-shaped tail

heavy bill and shaggy throat feathers

FOOD Omnivorous. The majority of its diet is animal matter, either from scavenged carrion and human garbage or from animals caught and killed—rodents, reptiles, large insects, adult and fledgling birds, bird eggs. Also consumes grain and fruit. Does most of its feeding on the ground.

NESTING *Location:* On a sheltered rock ledge or large fork of a tree. *Nest:* Large construction of sticks and twigs, often lined with animal hair. *Eggs:* Usually 4–6; incubated by female for 18–21 days. *Fledging:* Leaves nest at 4–7 weeks.

very large, about the size of a Red-tailed Hawk

SIGHTINGS

| JAN | FEB | MAR | APR | MAY | JUN | JUL | AUG | SEP | OCT | NOV | DEC |

Black-billed Magpie
Pica hudsonia, L 19" (48 cm)

The striking, long-tailed magpie graces many of the open spaces of the West. Some of the magpie's fascinating behaviors include following coyotes and foxes to steal food from them and conducting "funerals"—poorly understood, noisy gatherings of up to 40 birds around a dead magpie that last for 10–15 minutes before they all fly off in silence.

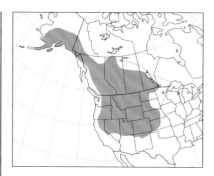

large white wing patch

IDENTIFICATION Fairly common. Relatively tame and inquisitive. Magpies hop and walk on the ground with a confident, swaggering gait, perch conspicuously on fence posts and tall shrubs, and fly with steady, rowing wing beats often ending with a swooping glide to a perch. Sometimes gather in large flocks.

Plumage: Showy black-and-white plumage with glossy blue, green, and violet highlights on the wings and an extremely long tail.

Similar species: Yellow-billed Magpie (not illustrated) is found primarily in California's Central Valley, where the Black-billed does not occur.

Voice: Quite varied **calls** include a quick series *mag, mag, mag* (like a Steller's Jay, but less piercing) and a whining, rising *mee-aaah.*

RANGE Western species; year-round resident. Inhabits open woodlands, forest edges, scrublands, and rangelands, often near watercourses; is also at home in suburbs, towns, and urban parks.

FOOD Omnivorous and opportunistic. Eats animal matter, either from scavenged carrion and human garbage or from animals caught and killed—rodents, reptiles, insects, ticks (from live deer and moose), fledgling birds, bird eggs. Also consumes quantities of grain and fruit. Foraging takes place on the ground, rarely in trees. Magpies often cache food in scattered locations.

NESTING *Location:* In a tree or tall shrub; nests are often quite noticeable. *Nest:* Bulky, ball-shaped construction of sticks with an interior cup lined with mud, dung, and animal hair. *Eggs:* Usually 6–7; incubated by female for about 18 days. *Fledging:* Leaves nest at 22–29 days.

glossy blue

black-and-white coloration

long tail

SIGHTINGS

JAN   FEB   MAR   APR   MAY   JUN   JUL   AUG   SEP   OCT   NOV   DEC

SWALLOWS   Family Hirundinidae

Adept aerialists, swallows dart and swoop in pursuit of flying insects. They all have very similar shapes, with slender bodies and long wings. North American species are highly migratory, some flying as far as southern South America for the winter.

Purple Martin
Progne subis, L 8" (20 cm)

In late winter, male martins leave their winter home in the Amazon and head north for the coming breeding season, arriving as early as January on the Gulf Coast and early March in the Mid-Atlantic. Competition is fierce at their colonial nest sites. Females follow several weeks later, and pair with males that have been successful in staking a claim to a favorable nest hole. In the East, their nests are almost exclusively located in housing provided by people—large martin apartment houses are typical, but suspended hollow gourds are also used. Martins are much less numerous in the West, where they nest primarily in tree or cactus cavities.

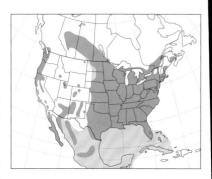

eastern ♀

eastern females are darker than western females

dark purple overall

adult ♂

IDENTIFICATION Common to uncommon. North America's largest, most popular swallow, the colonial-nesting Purple Martin is noticeably larger when seen perched next to other swallows. In flight, which includes more soaring and gliding than other swallows do, note the triangular wings and relatively short, forked tail.

Plumage: Distinctive **adult male** is all dark, with a purplish blue gloss. **Female** and **juvenile** are streaky or grayish below; **first-spring male** has some purple feathering on the underparts.

Similar species: All other swallows are smaller and have paler, cleaner underparts. Compare the adult male martin to the Chimney Swift (page 65) and European Starling (page 176): the swift has narrow wings and flickering wing beats; the starling doesn't swoop through the air and spends most of its time on or near the ground.

Voice: Common **call** is a sharp *churr*. **Song**, alternating between rough and liquid phrases, is composed of chortles, warbles, twitters, and croaks.

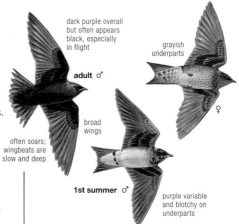

dark purple overall but often appears black, especially in flight

grayish underparts

adult ♂

♀

broad wings

often soars; wingbeats are slow and deep

1st summer ♂

purple variable and blotchy on underparts

RANGE Widespread species; summer resident. In the East, inhabits open areas in rural, suburban, and urban locations, always in the vicinity of nest boxes offered by people. Avoids dense forest and wooded residential areas without surrounding fields. Absent from many areas of the West. Winters in South America. Spring **migration:** mid-January–early May (early April–mid-May in the West); fall migration: July–early October. After nesting, eastern birds gather (mostly in August) in pre-migration flocks of thousands of birds at favored locations.

FOOD Flying insects, both large (dragonflies, hornets, butterflies) and small (midges, flies), but contrary to popular belief, mosquitoes are rarely captured because they fly too low.

NESTING *Location:* In a hollow gourd or martin apartment; in the West, a cavity (usually a woodpecker hole) in a tree or saguaro cactus. *Nest:* Twigs, plant material, and sometimes mud, filling the available space. *Eggs:* Usually 3–6; incubated by female for 15–18 days. *Fledging:* Leaves nest at 28–29 days. **Housing:** Apartment houses come in many sizes and designs, but hanging gourds painted white (or plastic alternatives) seem to be favored by the martins and are less attractive to starlings and House Sparrows. If you're considering becoming a Purple Martin landlord, check the Purple Martin Conservation Association website (*purplemartin.org*) for detailed information.

Although Purple Martins nest colonially, they are even more sociable after breeding, when they gather in large flocks for their fall migration to South America.

Tree Swallow
Tachycineta bicolor, L 5¾" (15 cm)

Tree Swallows nest in cavities—which are scarce commodities, and competition for them is intense. Starlings and House Sparrows take control of many sites.

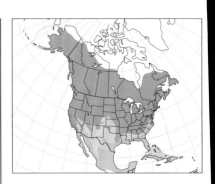

1st spring ♀

adult

bluish patches on upperparts

adult

America. Spring **migration:** February–April; fall migration: July–early November.

FOOD Flying insects and small fruits. Tree Swallows can survive on a fruit diet, which allows them to linger in fall and to winter farther north than any other swallow.

NESTING *Location:* In a natural tree cavity or old woodpecker hole. *Nest:* Dry grasses and other plant material. *Eggs:* Usually 4–6; incubated by female for 13–16 days. *Fledging:* Leaves nest at 18–22 days.
Housing: Will use a nest box identical to the ones bluebirds use.

IDENTIFICATION Very common. In flight, adds a graceful glide after a series of energetic flapping. The wing has a triangular shape.
Plumage: Adult plumage is crisply bicolored: dark, metallic blue or blue-green above, snow white below. The **juvenile** is grayish brown above and has a diffuse grayish band across the chest. By October, most juveniles look like adults.
Similar species: Violet-green Swallow (opposite) is smaller, has more white in the face, and has large white patches that almost meet across the lower back.
Voice: Calls include liquid twittering and short chirping notes.

RANGE Widespread species. Needs open habitat—fields, large lawns, marshes—and prefers to nest and forage near water. Winters from the East Coast and southern U.S. to Central

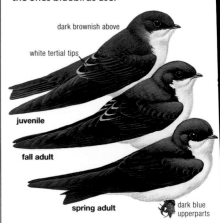

dark brownish above

white tertial tips

juvenile

fall adult

spring adult

dark blue upperparts

Violet-green Swallow
Tachycineta thalassina, L 5¼" (13 cm)

Well before the dawn of a summer day, Violet-green Swallows start their liquid twittering in coniferous forests throughout the West. Later in the heat of the day, they forage high over the pine forests, at a height more typical of swifts and soaring raptors.

adults

♂

small size with fluttery wingbeats

juvenile

♂

white up sides of rump

white around eye

primary tips extend well past short tail

adult ♂

bright olive green upperparts, violet rump, and snowy white underparts

Similar species: Tree Swallow (opposite) has bluish plumage, a longer tail, eyes hidden in a dark face, and lacks big white flank patches.

Voice: Calls include twittering and short chirping notes, like the Tree Swallow's but higher pitched and buzzier.

RANGE Western species; summer resident. Principally found in mountain forests (at lower elevations farther north), where it forages above the forest and over bodies of water. Winters from California (scarce in lowland areas) to Mexico. Early spring migrant: early February–early May; fall **migration:** late September–late October.

FOOD Flying insects. Feeds singly or in small loose flocks, often foraging higher in the sky than other species of swallows.

NESTING *Location:* In an old woodpecker hole or natural cavity in a dead tree, commonly in small colonies of up to 25 nests. *Nest:* Dry grasses and other plant material, lined with feathers (usually white). *Eggs:* Usually 4–6; incubated by female for 14–15 days. *Fledging:* Leaves nest at 23–25 days.

Housing: Will use a nest box located under a building eave or on a tree 10–15 feet up.

IDENTIFICATION Common. Small, compact swallow with a short tail.

Plumage: Colorful **male** is green backed (more bronzy on crown), with a purple rump and snow white underparts. The white extends onto the face and almost encircles the dark eye. Two white flank patches almost meet across the lower back. Adult **female** is duller than male—browner on head, face, and ear coverts. **Juvenile** has a similar pattern, but is brownish above and has less white on the face.

Barn Swallow
Hirundo rustica, L 6¾" (17 cm)

The graceful Barn Swallow swoops over fields and pastures across North America, where it is one of the most popular birds of summer. Its range extends well beyond North America; in fact, it is the most widely distributed and abundant swallow in the world—breeding throughout the Northern Hemisphere and wintering in much of the Southern Hemisphere.

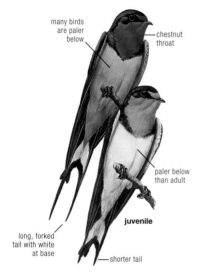

many birds are paler below

chestnut throat

paler below than adult

juvenile

long, forked tail with white at base

shorter tail

IDENTIFICATION Common. Its long, forked tail—it's our only swallow with a "swallowtail"—and slender body present an elegant appearance. In flight, the tail can be either spread (when banking or landing) or, more often, folded in a long point. Like other swallows, it's often seen perched on overhead wires. **Plumage:** Glossy, steel blue above; chestnut forehead and throat; orangish underparts; white spots visible when tail is spread. **Male** has a longer tail and deeper orange underparts than **female** (females

prefer to mate with the males that have the longest and most symmetrical tails). **Juvenile** has a much shorter forked tail and whitish buff underparts.
Similar species: None. The adult's orangish underparts and very long tail are unique. Shorter tailed juveniles resemble Cliff Swallows (page 138) but have a dark rump and a forked tail.
Voice: Song is a long series of scratchy, warbling phrases, interspersed with a grating rattle. Flight **call** is a high-pitched *chee-jit.*

RANGE Widespread species; summer resident. Has three basic habitat requirements: open areas for foraging (fields, pastures, golf courses,

Barn Swallows are sociable birds that often nest in small colonies.

Sticky mud pellets allow the Barn Swallow to adhere its nest directly to a vertical wall.

large yards); a man-made structure to shelter its nest (barn, culvert, bridge, pier, porch); and a body of water that provides mud for nest building. Avoids deserts and dense forest, but as human development continues to spread into new areas, the Barn Swallow will surely follow. Most birds winter in South America. Spring **migration:** late January–mid-May; fall migration: August–early November. After nesting, gathers in large, pre-migration flocks with other swallows.

FOOD Flying insects. Pursues insects lower to the ground than other swallow species. Drinks on the wing by skimming the water's surface with its bill.

NESTING *Location:* Rarely nests anywhere other than in or on a man-made structure. Nests in small colonies where nesting sites are plentiful and good habitat is available. Ancestral Barn Swallows used mostly caves as nesting sites. *Nest:* Cup of mud and dried grass, lined with feathers. *Eggs:* Usually 4–5; incubated by both parents for 12–17 days. *Fledging:* Leaves nest at 15–24 days. **Housing:** Will use a nesting platform added to a porch or open garage.

bluish above

JAN	FEB	MAR	APR	MAY	JUN	JUL	AUG	SEP	OCT	NOV	DEC

Cliff Swallow

Petrochelidon pyrrhonota, L 5½" (14 cm)

Eastward ho! Unlike the westward expansion of modern human settlement across North America, the colonial Cliff Swallow has ventured east. The construction of bridges, culverts, and buildings offered suitable nest sites, and over the past 150 years Cliff Swallows have pushed across the Great Plains and into New England.

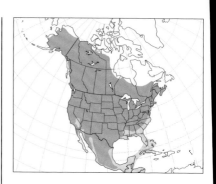

in Southwest has cinnamon forehead like Cave

Southwest

IDENTIFICATION Common. The compact Cliff Swallow has a chunky body; a short, square-tipped tail; and broad, relatively short wings. Being a colonial nester, it is often found in flocks. **Plumage:** Most have a white forehead, chestnut cheeks and throat, and significantly, a buff rump patch. **Juvenile** has a darker, less patterned face, but paler throat.
Similar species: Cave Swallow (not illustrated), found mostly in Texas, has dark chestnut forehead and much paler throat and face.
Voice: Song is a series of squeaking and grating notes. **Calls** include rough *chrrr* and more musical *veeew* notes.

RANGE Widespread species; summer resident. Common to abundant in the West, scarcer and local in the East. Needs open habitat for foraging, overhanging cliffs or man-made structures for nesting, and a supply of mud for nest construction. Winters in South America. Spring **migration:** late February–mid-May; fall migration: July–late September.

FOOD Flying insects. Aerial flocks often gather around swarming insects.

NESTING *Location:* Plastered to a sheltered rock wall or building (typically under the eaves); often in large colonies with tightly packed nests touching each other. *Nest:* Gourd-shaped with a tubular entrance, built completely of mud pellets. *Eggs:* Usually 4–6; incubated by both parents for 12–16 days. *Fledging:* Leaves nest at 20–26 days.

white forehead

dark throat

dusky throat and forehead on juvenile, often with some whitish feathers

juvenile

buffy rump

RETURN OF THE SWALLOW

More than 2,000 years ago, before bird migration was well understood, the Greek philosopher Aristotle wrote that swallows hibernate in crevices—in rocks, trees, and mud—during the winter. It was such a plausible explanation for the birds' seasonal disappearances that ornithologists were still citing hibernating swallows into the 1800s.

The truth, that these half-ounce birds travel thousands of miles each year to reach their wintering grounds in the tropics, is even more incredible. Only recently, with miniature tracking devices, have we really begun to appreciate the epic journeys of these long-distance migrants.

Cliff Swallows build their elaborate colonies from mud.

FAIR-WEATHER FRIENDS

In most of North America, swallows are a sign of summer. They arrive in spring and depart in fall, winging across continents to follow food and warmth.

Not all of them leave entirely; some hardy Tree Swallows winter along the Pacific coast and the Gulf Coast, surviving on berries during cold snaps.

But most swallows fly much farther south. The Cliff Swallow, which famously returned to Mission San Juan Capistrano near Los Angeles each March until a mission remodel in the 1990s removed nests and habitat, spends its nonbreeding season in South America, below the Equator—which means it never experiences true winter. Some of these Cliff Swallows migrate to central Argentina and back, 12,000 miles round-trip.

FLIGHT TRACKERS

In 2008, researchers deployed tiny devices called geolocators on several Purple Martins nesting in Pennsylvania. For the first time, the martins' migration was documented remotely: The birds flew to central Brazil, "wintering" within the Amazon Basin.

Amazingly, one martin made the return trip in just 13 days, coming back to the same site in Pennsylvania by mid-May. The speedy journey stunned scientists—this small bird had covered more than 300 miles a day!—and showed how technology can illuminate the natural world in new and surprising ways.

CHICKADEES & TITMICE   Family Paridae

Grays and blacks predominate in this small family of small birds: chickadees have dark caps and throats; titmice are crested. What they lack in color and size, they make up for with their endearing acceptance of people, bird feeders, and nest boxes.

Black-capped Chickadee
Poecile atricapillus, L 5¼" (13 cm)

Active and energetic, the Black-capped Chickadee seems immune to the harshest winter weather—no small feat for a bird weighing less than half an ounce. It copes by eating high-calorie foods (like black-oil sunflower seeds), roosting in a tree cavity at night (sometimes in small groups), fluffing out its insulating body feathers, and even lowering its body temperature. State bird of Maine and Massachusetts; provincial bird of New Brunswick.

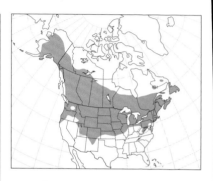

IDENTIFICATION Common. Like all chickadees, the Black-capped is small and "cute," with a big, "no-neck" head. Acrobatic and restless, it is able to cling upside down using its strong feet. Joins roaming flocks of other small woodland birds in fall and winter.

Plumage: Has a black cap and throat and white cheek; otherwise, grayish olive above and white below with buff flanks. The wing coverts and tertials are brightly edged in white, but these edges are usually worn off by late summer.

Similar species: Carolina Chickadee (page 142) is very similar and its range overlaps in a narrow zone (see the range map). In fall and winter, the Black-capped has broad white edges on its wing coverts; these are dull, grayish white on the Carolina. The Black-capped *chick-a-dee* calls are slower and lower pitched. The two species sometimes interbreed (hybridize).

Voice: Less vocal in summer, when nesting. **Song** is a clear, whistled *fee-bee* or *fee-bee-ee,* the first note higher. **Call** is a slow, harsh *chick-a-dee-dee-dee.*

RANGE Widespread species; year-round resident. Inhabits woodlands and wooded edges, suburbs, towns, and tree-filled urban parks. In some winters, numbers of Black-capped

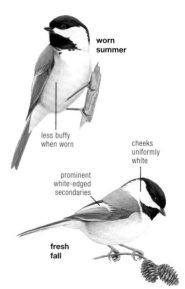

worn summer

less buffy when worn

cheeks uniformly white

prominent white-edged secondaries

fresh fall

birds move south into the northern part of the Carolina Chickadee's range.

FOOD Insects, spiders, seeds, and small fruits. In breeding season, about 90 percent of its diet is animal (mostly caterpillars); in winter, that changes to about half animal (insects and spiders, often their eggs and pupae) and half seeds and berries.

Feeding: Very common at feeders. Black-oil sunflower seeds and suet are preferred. Makes back-and-forth trips throughout the day. Large quantities of seeds are cached in bark crevices for later consumption (chickadees have excellent spatial memory); others are taken to a perch, hammered open, and eaten.

NESTING *Location:* An existing cavity in rotted wood or some-times an old woodpecker hole in a tree. *Nest:* Cavity is enlarged and lined with moss, weed stems, and animal fur. *Eggs:*

The short, rounded wings of the Black-capped Chickadee allow it to maneuver in tight spaces.

Usually 4–5; incubated by female for 12–13 days. *Fledging:* Leaves nest at about 16 days.

Housing: Will use a nest box, especially if bottom is covered with sawdust. You can encourage chickadees (and some other cavity nesters) to excavate their own nest holes by using a cordless drill to bore a 1⅛" hole into the dead wood of a tree, at least 5 feet off the ground.

The Black-capped Chickadee and a few other species can be hand-tamed, but it usually takes a period of weeks working patiently with the same bird to gain its trust.

SIGHTINGS | | | | | | | | | | | |
JAN FEB MAR APR MAY JUN JUL AUG SEP OCT NOV DEC

Carolina Chickadee
Poecile carolinensis, L 4¾" (12 cm)

The Carolina Chickadee looks almost identical to the Black-capped Chickadee (pages 140–141), but has a more southern distribution. Chickadees of all species have many similarities—see the Black-capped Chickadee description for more information about the behavior, feeding, and housing of chickadees.

grayish tinge to rear cheek

fresh fall

slightly duller flanks than Black-capped

worn summer

slightly shorter tail than Black-capped

IDENTIFICATION Common. Similar to Black-capped Chickadee.
Plumage: Has a black cap and throat and white cheek that becomes grayer toward the back; otherwise, gray above and white below with light buff flanks. The wing coverts and tertials have thin, grayish white edges that are almost completely worn off by late summer.
Similar species: Black-capped Chickadee (previous page), in the narrow zone along the Carolina Chickadee's northern border where the two species overlap. Throughout the South (except in the Appalachians above about 4,000 feet), the Carolina is the only chickadee.

Voice: Less vocal in summer, when nesting. **Song** is a clear, four-note whistle: *fee-bee fee-bay.* **Call** is *chick-a-dee-dee-dee,* higher and faster than the Black-capped's.

RANGE Mid-Atlantic, midwestern, and southern species; year-round resident. Inhabits woodlands and wooded edges, suburbs, towns, and tree-filled urban parks. In winter, flocks roam over a wider area and are concentrated around bird feeders.

FOOD Insects, spiders, seeds, and small fruits. In breeding season, about 90 percent of its diet is animal (mostly caterpillars); in winter, that changes to about half animal (insects and spiders, often their eggs and pupae) and half seeds and berries.
Feeding: Very common at feeders. Black-oil sunflower seeds and suet are preferred.

NESTING *Location:* An existing cavity in rotted wood or sometimes an old woodpecker hole in a tree. *Nest:* Cavity is enlarged and lined with moss, weed stems, and animal fur. *Eggs:* Usually 5–8; incubated by female for 12–15 days. *Fledging:* Leaves nest at 16–19 days.
Housing: Will use a nest box located at least 5 feet above the ground.

Mountain Chickadee
Poecile gambeli, L 5¼" (13 cm)

When an autumn chill is in the air and conifer seeds have ripened in the western mountains, the tiny Mountain Chickadee is hard at work caching and defending stores of seeds. The insects that made up the bulk of its summer diet will soon be much harder to find.

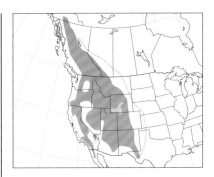

 IDENTIFICATION Common. Chickadees of all species have many similarities.

Plumage: White eyebrow and a slash of black through the eye that resembles a "bandit's mask." Otherwise, quite similar to Black-capped Chickadee (pages 140–141).

Similar species: None; the white eyebrow is unique. Juveniles often have a broken or messy eyebrow stripe, but the white is there if you look closely.

Voice: Less vocal in summer, when nesting. **Song** is a three- or four-note descending whistle: *fee-bee-bay* or *fee-bee fee-bee.* **Call** is a hoarse *chick-adee-adee-adee.*

RANGE Western species; year-round resident. Inhabits montane evergreen and mixed forests, as well as residential areas, towns, and parks with similar wooded habitat. In winter, some birds descend to lower elevations. Exceptionally, many birds may move out of the mountains (irrupt), and some turn up in unexpected places.

FOOD Gleans insects—especially caterpillars and insect eggs and larvae—and spiders from foliage, often involving acrobatic hanging from branch tips. During fall and winter, turns to a diet based on conifer seeds.

Feeding: Attracted to feeders. Black-oil sunflower seeds and suet are preferred.

NESTING *Location:* In an old woodpecker hole or natural cranny; not known to excavate its own cavity. *Nest:* Cavity is lined with moss, weed stems, and animal fur. *Eggs:* Usually 6–12; incubated by female for 12–15 days. *Fledging:* Leaves nest at 17–23 days.

Housing: Will use a nest box located at least 5 feet above the ground.

white eyebrow

California

broader white eyebrow in Rockies

Rockies

warmer colored flanks

Chestnut-backed Chickadee

Poecile rufescens, L 4¾" (12 cm)

From Santa Barbara County to almost as far north as Anchorage, the colorful Chestnut-backed Chickadee's range traces a narrow ribbon up the West Coast and into the Sierra Nevada and Cascades. The chickadees likely expanded north with the advancing forests as the last Pleistocene glaciers retreated between 15,000 and 10,000 years ago.

widespread form

chestnut back

pure white cheeks

chestnut sides

chestnut back

coastal central California

gray sides

IDENTIFICATION Common. Smallest and shortest tailed of the chickadees. Tends to forage in the tops of conifers, but also comes to feeders. Chickadees of all species have many similarities.

Plumage: Back, rump, and flanks are rich chestnut; has a sooty brown cap and black bib. The chestnut plumage may be hard to discern in dark, shadowy forests. Birds on the central California coast show almost no chestnut below.

Similar species None. Separated from all other chickadees by chestnut back and rump.

Voice: Call is a high, scratchy *tseek-a-dee-dee* given rapidly. Does not have a *fee-bee* song like other chickadees.

RANGE Western species; year-round resident. Inhabits humid coastal and interior forests, and riparian habitats; also found in residential areas, towns, and parks with similar wooded areas. During the past half century, the species has colonized the central Sierra Nevada and suburban areas around eastern San Francisco Bay.

FOOD Gleans insects and spiders from foliage. Diet is supplemented with conifer seeds, berries, and other small fruits.

Feeding: Attracted to feeders, mostly in winter. Black-oil sunflower seeds and suet are preferred.

NESTING *Location:* Enlarges a cavity in rotted wood or may use an old woodpecker hole. *Nest:* Cavity is lined with moss, weed stems, and animal fur. *Eggs:* Usually 6–7; incubated by female for 12–14 days. *Fledging:* Leaves nest at 18–21 days.

Housing: Will use a nest box.

SIGHTINGS

| | JAN | FEB | MAR | APR | MAY | JUN | JUL | AUG | SEP | OCT | NOV | DEC |

Resident birds like Black-capped Chickadees may be enjoyed in the backyard year-round.

HOW DO CHICKADEES SURVIVE WINTER?

In the frostiest depths of January, a few birds stick around to keep backyard birders company. If you're lucky, and keep a feeder stocked, these all-weather friends might include chickadees.

Even in parts of North America where the temperature plunges to 40 degrees below zero, chickadees keep a steady presence. How can a bird that weighs less than half an ounce endure such frigid conditions?

Their size is a definite disadvantage. Tiny birds have a high ratio of surface area to volume, which means they lose more heat than bigger birds, for the same reason that small ice cubes melt faster than big ones.

BEARING THE COLD

Chickadees have developed special strategies for the cold. They spend winter nights tucked in narrow cavities, sometimes huddling together for warmth with downy feathers fluffed out. These crevices are typically smaller, and cozier, than a summer nest hole.

Black-capped Chickadees in northern regions enter torpor on chilly nights, cooling their body temperature from about 107°F (42°C)—hotter than a human—to below 90°F (32°C). This saves a significant amount of metabolic energy.

FUELING UP

Chickadees still must eat—a lot—to stay warm. A chickadee can consume 60 percent of its body weight each day in seeds and insects, putting on 10 percent of its weight in fat by dusk. That extra fuel is burned overnight, as if a 150-pound human slept outside and woke up 15 pounds lighter.

For the sake of the chickadees, keep those winter feeders full.

Oak Titmouse

Baeolophus inornatus, L 5" (13 cm)

The Oak Titmouse is a plain-looking bird with a short crest and beady black eyes. Of greater interest, particularly to any out-of-state visitors: the Oak Titmouse is nearly endemic to California and a vocal backyard feeder visitor in many areas.

slight brownish tint above

short grayish crest

worn

fresh

RANGE West Coast species; year-round resident. Prefers live-oak woodlands and where oaks mix with chaparral, streamside groves, and low-elevation conifers. Also found in residential areas, towns, and parks with similar wooded habitat.

FOOD Diet is equal parts animal and plant food. Gleans insects from bark and foliage, often pecking into bark crevices or chipping away bark to reach a beetle or bug; sometimes hangs upside down. Main plant foods are seeds (primarily acorns), leaf buds, berries, and fruits, including cultivated varieties.
Feeding: Common visitor to bird feeders in wooded areas. Prefers larger, striped sunflower seeds to smaller black-oil types; also relishes whole peanuts, peanut butter, and suet.

IDENTIFICATION Common. Larger than a chickadee, but not by much, with a short crest that can be raised and lowered depending on the bird's state of agitation. Pairs mate for life. Often joins mixed-species flocks in winter.
Plumage: Plain grayish brown overall, with slightly paler underparts.
Similar species: Bushtit (page 149) is smaller and has a long tail. Juniper Titmouse (not illustrated) is a look-alike species that lives in relatively unpopulated areas of piñon-juniper woodland east of the Sierra Nevada.
Voice: A variety of simple, cheery **songs**, such as *pee-doo, pee-doo, pee-doo* or *tu-wee, tu-wee, tu-wee.* **Call** is a hoarse *tsicka-dee-dee.*

NESTING *Location:* In an old woodpecker hole or natural cavity; sometimes a pair will enlarge an existing cavity in rotted wood. *Nest:* Cavity is lined with moss, weed stems, and animal fur. *Eggs:* Usually 6–7; incubated by female for 14–16 days. *Fledging:* Leaves nest at 16–21 days.
Housing: Will use a nest box or sheltered building crevice.

Tufted Titmouse
Baeolophus bicolor, L 6¼" (16 cm)

Peter-peter-peter, the simple, cheerful song of the Tufted Titmouse, is often heard in woodsy backyards throughout the East. Pairs are monogamous, and families often stay together through the winter. The following spring, one of the young birds may help the mated pair raise the next generation.

IDENTIFICATION Common. Larger than a chickadee, with an obvious crest that can be raised and lowered. Regularly descends to the ground, unlike chickadees.
Plumage: Crested head with a small black forehead and large, dark eyes. Buff flanks, but otherwise gray above and whitish below. Juvenile lacks the black forehead.
Similar species: Chickadees have black-and-white heads and no crest. Black-crested Titmouse (not illustrated) has a black crest and pale forehead and occurs in the western half of Texas.

Voice: Noisy and vocal, except when nesting. **Song** is a loud, whistled *peter-peter-peter,* repeated over and over. **Call** is a hoarse, chickadee-like *tsicka-dee-dee.*

RANGE Eastern species; year-round resident. Inhabits deciduous woods, generally below 2,000 feet, and is also common in wooded suburbs, orchards, towns, and parks. Over the past 50 years, Tufted Titmice have expanded northward, probably in response to the warming climate and the proliferation of bird feeders.

FOOD Gleans insects from bark and foliage, sometimes pecking into bark crevices or chipping away bark to reach a beetle or bug. Main plant food is seeds (primarily acorns and birdseed); also consumes some wild fruits and berries.
Feeding: Common feeder visitor. Enjoys sunflower seeds, shelled peanuts, peanut butter, and suet. Like chickadees, caches food in winter.

NESTING *Location:* In an old woodpecker hole or natural cavity. *Nest:* Cavity is filled with moss or dried grass, often lined with animal fur. *Eggs:* Usually 5–6; incubated by female for 12–14 days. *Fledging:* Leaves nest at 15–18 days. **Housing:** Will use a nest box.

gray forehead

juvenile

dark forehead

pinkish flank patch

adult

SIGHTINGS

JAN FEB MAR APR MAY JUN JUL AUG SEP OCT NOV DEC

VERDIN   Family Remizidae

The Verdin is the only New World representative of this small Old World family of tiny birds known as penduline tits.

Verdin
Auriparus flaviceps, L 4½" (11 cm)

If you live in the desert Southwest, you may have seen this tiny bird's conspicuous, ball-shaped nest of twigs, even if you've never focused on the bird itself.

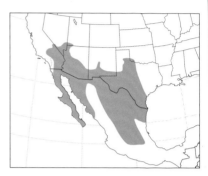

yellow head, black eye line

sharply pointed bill

chestnut lesser coverts

very plain, lacks yellow head

juvenile

IDENTIFICATION Common. Tiny songbird, among the smallest in North America. Restless and nimble as it forages in desert trees and scrub, hanging from small branches or probing into flowers with its short, sharp bill. **Plumage:** Yellow head and throat; chestnut shoulder patch, though often hard to see. The rest of the bird is gray, paler below. Juvenile is confusingly plain; it has brownish plumage and lacks the yellow head and rusty wing patch, but is usually attended by adults.
Similar species: Juvenile resembles a Bushtit (next page), but the Bushtit has a much longer tail and is seen in small flocks.
Voice: Very vocal, even when foraging. **Song** is a three-note whistle: *sweet sweet sweet*. **Calls** include sharp, piercing *tschep* and rapid series of *chip* notes.

RANGE Southwest species; year-round resident. Mainly found in thorny desert scrub—acacia, paloverde, smoketree, mesquite—chiefly around washes; also at the edges of desert riparian corridors and in residential neighborhoods and some urban parks.

FOOD Mostly insects, but also pierces flowers for nectar and sometimes visits hummingbird feeders.

NESTING *Location:* Near the outer edge of a shrub, low tree, or cactus. *Nest:* Unusual ball-shaped nest of thorny twigs about 6–8 inches in diameter; also builds smaller roosting nests that are used year-round. *Eggs:* Usually 4; incubated by female for 14–18 days. *Fledging:* Leaves nest at about 18 days.

SIGHTINGS   JAN   FEB   MAR   APR   MAY   JUN   JUL   AUG   SEP   OCT   NOV   DEC

BUSHTIT   Family Aegithalidae

Members of this small family of tiny, long-tailed birds live in social groups and build hanging nests. The Bushtit's closest relative lives in Eurasia.

Bushtit
Psaltriparus minimus, L 4½" (11 cm)

When not nesting, Bushtits band together in small, noisy flocks that move frenetically through the shrubbery. Sometimes the entire flock emits a shrill, trilling alarm—a good clue that a hawk is flying overhead.

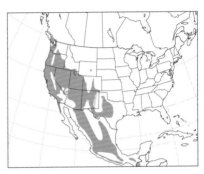

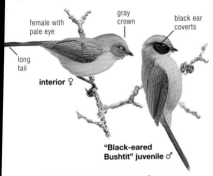

female with pale eye

gray crown

black ear coverts

long tail

interior ♀

"Black-eared Bushtit" juvenile ♂

 IDENTIFICATION Common. Tiny songbird with a plump, loosely feathered body and a long tail. Very tame. Busy flocks of 10–40 birds forage together. They can land on the tiniest branches, and often hang upside down to reach a hidden insect.
Plumage: Drab gray above, paler below. Coastal birds have a brown crown; interior birds, a brown mask and gray crown. **Male** has dark eyes; **female** has pale eyes. **Juvenile males** and some adult males in the Southwest have a black mask (this "Black-eared Bushtit" was formerly considered a separate species). **Similar species:** Blue-gray Gnatcatcher (page 159) has a black-and-white tail and is never in flocks. Also similar to a juvenile Verdin (opposite).
Voice: Very vocal. Flock members call constantly—a rapid, twittering *pit pit pit* or *tsee tsee tsee.* Calls of interior birds are slower and sharper.

RANGE Western species; year-round resident. Found in a variety of habitats, from forested mountains with shrubby undergrowth to arid brush and chaparral; also common in backyard gardens and parks.

FOOD Small insects and spiders gleaned from foliage.

NESTING *Location:* From low in a bush to high in a tree. *Nest:* gourd-shaped, hanging nest woven from vegetation and spiderwebs; entrance near the top. *Eggs:* Usually 5–7; incubated by both parents for 12–13 days. *Fledging:* Leaves nest at about 18 days.

grayish face

coastal ♂

brown crown

NUTHATCHES   Family Sittidae

Short-tailed, acrobatic birds that climb up, down, and around tree trunks and branches. Suet feeders will likely attract any nuthatches living in your neighborhood.

White-breasted Nuthatch
Sitta carolinensis, L 5¾" (15 cm)

When moving head-first down a tree trunk, the nuthatch probably gains a feeding advantage—the different perspective reveals insects hidden in bark crevices that other birds, like woodpeckers, might miss as they move upward. The nuthatch has especially long and strong hind claws that anchor it to a tree trunk.

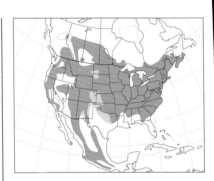

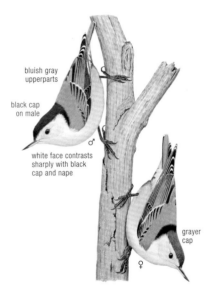

bluish gray
upperparts

black cap
on male

♂

white face contrasts
sharply with black
cap and nape

grayer
cap

♀

IDENTIFICATION Common. Small, but larger than a chickadee, with a stocky, angular body, short tail, and wedge-tipped, dagger-like bill. It clings securely to tree bark with large, sharp-clawed feet that also serve to anchor a seed or nut that needs to be hammered open ("hatched") with its bill.

Joins mixed-species foraging flocks in winter that often include chickadees and titmice.
Plumage: Black cap tops an all-white face and breast, with a variable amount of rust under the tail. **Female** has a crown that is grayish or, in the South, blackish like **male**'s. Western birds (see photograph below) have longer bills.
Similar species: Red-breasted Nuthatch

Western White-breasted Nuthatches (two distinct groups) have longer bills and different calls from eastern birds.

(page 153) has cinnamon underparts and a bold black line through the eye.

Voice: Song is a rapid series of nasal whistles. **Call** is a low-pitched, nasal *yank* in the East and a higher pitched *eehr* on the West Coast, with multiple high-pitched calls in the interior West.

RANGE Widespread species; year-round resident. Inhabits mature deciduous or mixed forests; also common in wooded suburbs, orchards, towns, and parks. Although nonmigratory, in some years numbers move south (irrupt) in fall and winter, but not as conspicuously or as often as Red-breasted Nuthatches.

FOOD Gleans insects from bark and foliage, sometimes pecking into bark crevices or chipping away bark to reach a beetle or bug; feeds nestlings mostly insects. Relies mainly on seeds in winter (acorns, beechnuts, and birdseed are important). Like chickadees and titmice, caches seeds in winter, usually removing their shells beforehand. Individual seeds are cached separately in a bark crevice, or sometimes on the ground. Nuthatches have excellent spatial memory, so most of the seeds are eventually retrieved and eaten.

The white outer tail feathers of the White-breasted Nuthatch are easiest to see on a bird in flight.

Feeding: Common feeder visitor. Likes suet, sunflower seeds, and shelled peanuts.

NESTING *Location:* In an old woodpecker hole or natural cavity. *Nest:* Bedding of bark strips, often lined with animal fur. Known to rub crushed insects around the entrance and on the inside of its nest cavity, possibly to repel predators. *Eggs:* Usually 5–9; incubated by female for 12–14 days. *Fledging:* Leaves nest at about 26 days.

Housing: Will use a nest box.

This eastern White-breasted Nuthatch has a shorter bill than the western subspecies (opposite).

SIGHTINGS

JAN FEB MAR APR MAY JUN JUL AUG SEP OCT NOV DEC

An Acorn Woodpecker inspects its acorn storage.　　Scrub-Jays are experts at caching food.

CACHING FOOD

Nut-eating birds, including some jays and woodpeckers, face a challenge: When nuts ripen in late summer and fall, there is too much food to eat. Then, in winter and spring, no more nuts. What to do?

A few bird species behave like squirrels, hiding nuts to be retrieved later when food is scarce. This is called caching, and it comes with its own challenges—namely, that others might dig up your food before you do or that you won't be able to remember where you hid all those nuts.

DEVIOUS JAYS

Scrub-Jays are particularly adept at storing nuts for later enjoyment, and they tend to hide more than they could ever eat. This is partly because they forget locations and partly because others steal, given the chance. When a scrub-jay buries a nut, it first checks to make sure no other jays are watching, and it will sometimes re-hide a cache to be safe.

Intriguingly, a scrub-jay is much more apt to employ counterespionage tactics if it has itself stolen caches in the past.

It might sound funny, but this behavior hints at intelligence. Recognizing that another individual might steal, especially given personal thieving experience, shows cognitive attribution—that a jay can project certain mental states onto others—which is no mean feat for a bird brain.

WOODPECKER LARDERS

One bird has taken caching to the next level. The Acorn Woodpecker loves acorns, and maintains fortresses of acorn-size storage holes, like latticework, in standing snags. These woodpeckers can even use a telephone pole for the purpose, if it has the right texture.

Acorn Woodpeckers spend their lives carefully conserving their larders, called "granaries," which require constant upkeep.

Red-breasted Nuthatch

Sitta canadensis, L 4½" (11 cm)

The Red-breasted Nuthatch ("Little Yank") is the smaller cousin of the White-breasted Nuthatch ("Big Yank")—the nicknames refer to their calls and different sizes. In many locations, the Red-breasted is seen only in fall and winter.

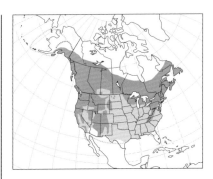

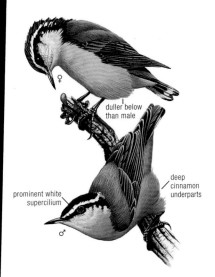

duller below than male

prominent white supercilium

deep cinnamon underparts

♀

♂

Voice: High-pitched, nasal **call** sounds like a toy tin horn: *yank yank* or *ehhnk ehhnk.*

RANGE Widespread species. Inhabits coniferous forests, typically spruce and fir; southern breeders live mostly in mountainous areas. In winter, many birds move south and into lowlands, but how far and how many vary greatly from year to year. In a good "irruption" year, they move deep into the South or into western lowlands; other years, there are none.

FOOD Relies mostly on insects and spiders gleaned from tree bark in summer, and on seeds in winter (acorns, beechnuts, and birdseed are important).
Feeding: Common feeder visitor, but irregular. Eats suet, sunflower seeds, and shelled peanuts. Planting conifers in your yard will provide shelter and foraging locations for them.

NESTING *Location:* Excavates its own hole in a tree; smears resin around the entrance to deter predators. *Nest:* Bedding of bark strips, often lined with animal fur. *Eggs:* Usually 5–6; incubated by female for 12–13 days. *Fledging:* Leaves nest at 18–21 days.
Housing: Rarely uses a nest box.

IDENTIFICATION Common to uncommon. Attractively small and compact, about the size of a chickadee. Foraging behavior similar to the larger White-breasted Nuthatch, but with more restless, jerkier movements. Prefers conifers and often forages with mixed flocks of resident birds in winter.
Plumage: Striped head has a bold black line through the eye, white eyebrows, and a black cap; cinnamon underparts. **Female** and **immature birds** have a duller face pattern and paler underparts.
Similar species: White-breasted Nuthatch (pages 150–151) has a white face and underparts and is larger.

SIGHTINGS

| | JAN | FEB | MAR | APR | MAY | JUN | JUL | AUG | SEP | OCT | NOV | DEC |

WRENS   Family Troglodytidae

Found in most of North America, wrens are chunky with slender, slightly curved bills; tails are often uptilted. Loud and vigorous territorial defense belies the small size of most species.

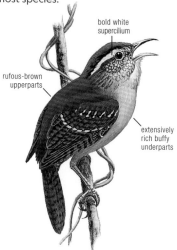

bold white supercilium

rufous-brown upperparts

extensively rich buffy underparts

Carolina Wren
Thryothorus ludovicianus, L 5½" (14 cm)

The loud, rollicking song of the male Carolina Wren reverberates across backyards throughout the East. Pairs remain together throughout the year. State bird of South Carolina.

IDENTIFICATION Common. Chunky wren with a sturdy, down-curved bill. Relatively tame and fearless in backyards, but sticks to cover and almost always stays low. Pairs may mate for life. **Plumage:** Overall ruddy plumage: deep rusty brown above, cinnamon below. Bold white stripe above the eye and white throat. **Similar species:** Slender Bewick's Wren (opposite), very rare in the East, has pale (not cinnamon) underparts and a long, twitchy tail with white bars near the tip. **Voice:** Vocal throughout the year. Male's **song** is a loud, rolling chant of *tea-kettle*

tea-kettle tea-kettle with many variations and inflections. **Calls** include harsh notes and buzzy trills.

RANGE Eastern species; year-round resident. Inhabits brushy woods, clearings, and wooded backyards. Severe winters can devastate northern populations, but they often recover within a few years.

FOOD Gleans insects and spiders from tree trunks, brushy tangles, woodpiles, and building crevices. **Feeding:** The only wren that regularly visits bird feeders; suet feeders are visited most often, but also takes sunflower seeds.

NESTING *Location:* In a vine tangle or open tree cavity, rarely higher than 10 feet up. *Nest:* Bulky, domed cup of dried vegetation. *Eggs:* Usually 4–6; incubated by female for 12–14 days. *Fledging:* Leaves nest at 14–16 days. **Housing:** More likely to nest in a sheltered building nook, open tool shed, or overturned flowerpot than in a nest box.

SIGHTINGS

JAN   FEB   MAR   APR   MAY   JUN   JUL   AUG   SEP   OCT   NOV   DEC

Bewick's Wren
Thryothorus bewickii, L 5¼" (13 cm)

Bewick's Wren is an enigma. The species is common in the West, but east of the Mississippi has declined so dramatically in the past 60 years that it has all but vanished there. The decline in the East is probably due to aggressive, nest-destroying House Wrens, whose numbers have increased with the disappearance of Bewick's Wrens.

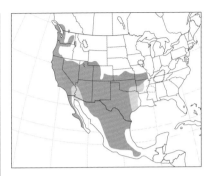

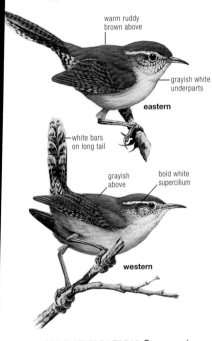

warm ruddy brown above

grayish white underparts

eastern

white bars on long tail

grayish above

bold white supercilium

western

IDENTIFICATION Common in the West. Slender wren with a long tail that is often held cocked upward and twitched from side to side. Usually found near or on the ground.
Plumage Upperparts vary: grayish brown in the Southwest, brown along the Pacific coast, and reddish brown in the East; underparts are pale gray. Has a bold white stripe above the eye and white bars near the tip of the tail.

Similar species: Carolina Wren (opposite) does not occur in the West, has cinnamon underparts and no white in its tail, and is larger. House Wren (next page) lacks the white eye stripe and has no white in its shorter tail.
Voice: Quite vocal. **Song** is complex and varied, starting with short notes and buzzes and ending in a musical trill. **Calls** include a scratchy *jip* and scolding *bzzzzz.*

RANGE Mostly western species, now rare in the East; mostly resident. Small numbers may persist in the Southeast, west of the Appalachians (where it is migratory). Western birds inhabit brushy woodland, coastal and desert scrub, and chaparral and are fairly common in many residential areas and parks.

FOOD Gleans insects and spiders from bark crevices, root tangles, and rocky crevices.

NESTING *Location:* near the ground in a rocky crevice, or sometimes an old woodpecker hole or tree cavity. *Nest:* Cup of dried vegetation. *Eggs:* Usually 5–7; incubated by female for about 14 days. *Fledging:* Leaves nest at 14–16 days.
Housing: Will use a nest box; may also use a sheltered building nook, open shed, and so forth.

SIGHTINGS

JAN FEB MAR APR MAY JUN JUL AUG SEP OCT NOV DEC

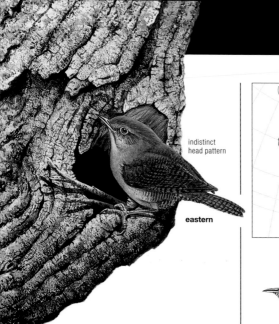

indistinct head pattern

eastern

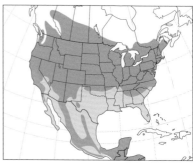

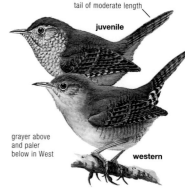

tail of moderate length

juvenile

grayer above and paler below in West

western

House Wren
Troglodytes aedon, L 4¾" (12 cm)

The male House Wren's loud and bubbly song is a familiar summer sound in backyards across North America. The species was not always so common or widely distributed. The shrubby edges and open woods so perfect for House Wrens were scarce commodities in the primeval forests of pre-European North America, but today's fragmented woodlands and woodsy backyards mimic its traditional habitat, and the House Wren has flourished.

IDENTIFICATION Very common. Small wren with a moderately long tail. Fairly tame and approachable. Spends much of its time darting around in thickets and low in trees, occasionally descending to the ground. The male sings his territorial song from an exposed perch with such force that his whole body quivers from the effort.
Plumage: Plain, without strong patterns. Brown upperparts have fine black barring, most noticeable on the wings and tail. The underparts are paler, with more fine barring on the back half. Juvenile has more buff below, often with indistinct scalloping on the breast, and is less barred than the adult.
Similar species: Carolina Wren (page 154) and Bewick's Wren (previous page) both have bold white stripes above the eye. Brown Creeper (page 158) has a bill that resembles the House Wren's, but has streaky upperparts and pure white underparts and climbs up vertical tree trunks.
Voice: Exuberant **song** is a cascade of bubbling whistled notes. **Calls** include a soft *chek* and a harsh scold.

RANGE Widespread species. Lives in open forests, thickets, woodland edges, and wooded towns

This ceramic birdhouse—a style that has been popular since colonial times—makes an attractive nest site for a family of House Wrens.

An old woodpecker hole—a valuable piece of forest real estate—is the perfect home for many cavity-nesting songbirds.

and suburbs. Moves to the southern tier of states and Mexico in winter. Spring **migration:** April–early May; fall migration: September–October.

FOOD Gleans insects and spiders from trees, saplings, shrubs, and the ground.

NESTING *Location:* In an old woodpecker hole, natural cavity, or enclosed crevice. *Nest:* Cup of dried vegetation. *Eggs:* Usually 5–8; incubated by female for about 14 days. *Fledging:* Leaves nest at 15–18 days. *Nest wars:* House Wrens are fierce competitors for nest holes and nest boxes—a limited commodity in most places. They are known to evict larger birds, puncture and remove eggs from nest sites they want, and sometimes kill nestlings and even adult birds. Common species that lose out include Tree Swallows, bluebirds, and chickadees. If you have House Wrens nesting in your backyard (they're otherwise delightful birds), put up multiple nest boxes to ease the pressure on other species. **Housing:** Will use a nest box 4–5 feet up and many other human structures

with nooks and crannies—flowerpots, mailboxes, clothespin bags, discarded boxes, farm equipment. John James Audubon famously painted a pair nesting in an old hat.

Typical wren posture—the chunky body is held low and the tail uptilted.

CREEPERS   Family Certhiidae

A small family of forest birds with highly cryptic plumage. The Brown Creeper is the only member found in the New World.

Brown Creeper
Certhia americana, L 5¼" (13 cm)

This bird is hard to see. Perched vertically on a tree trunk, its back plumage almost perfectly matches the furrowed bark where it finds its food. Its thin, very high-pitched call is often the best clue that one is around.

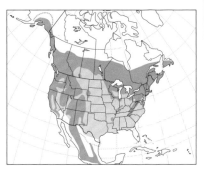

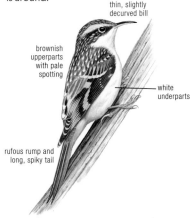

thin, slightly decurved bill

brownish upperparts with pale spotting

white underparts

rufous rump and long, spiky tail

IDENTIFICATION Fairly common. Smaller than a nuthatch, the creeper has a long, spiky-tipped tail, which it uses like a prop when climbing, and a thin, curved bill. It forages in a very predictable way: starting at the base of a large tree, it spirals up the trunk, poking into bark crevices, until it reaches the first large branches, at which point it flies to the base of a nearby tree and starts over. You can often watch the whole process a few times before losing sight of the bird. **Plumage:** Brown, streaky upperparts; whitish below. In flight, the wing has a bold buff stripe.
Similar species: Nuthatches move up and down the trunk (rather than spiraling up like a creeper) and onto branches and are not streaked. Somewhat similar to House Wren (pages 156–157), but shape and behavior very different.
Voice: Thin and very high-pitched. **Song** is a variable *see see see titi see.* **Call** is a soft, sibilant *seee* or buzzier and doubled *tee-see* in the West.

RANGE Widespread. Inhabits woodlands with large trees, mainly conifers or mixed conifer-deciduous when breeding. Widespread and less choosy in winter, when it is as likely to be found in deciduous forest, suburbs, or parks. Spring **migration:** April; fall migration: October.

FOOD Gleans prey—insects and larvae, spiders and their eggs—from bark crevices.

NESTING *Location:* Behind a flap of loose tree bark. *Nest:* Cup of bark strips and twigs, adhered to the vertical bark flap with insect cocoons. *Eggs:* Usually 5–6; incubated by female for 13–17 days. *Fledging:* Leaves nest at 15–18 days.

GNATCATCHERS   Family Polioptilidae

Gnatcatchers are tiny, active birds with long tails. The family also includes the gnatwrens of Central and South America.

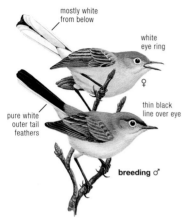

mostly white
from below

white
eye ring

♀

thin black
line over eye

pure white
outer tail
feathers

breeding ♂

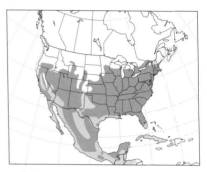

Blue-gray Gnatcatcher
Polioptila caerulea, L 4¼" (11 cm)

The insistent peevish call of the Blue-gray Gnatcatcher announces its early spring arrival in many parts of the country. New arrivals in the East are easy to spot in the budding branches, but later in the season, their treetop activities are often hidden from view. Western birds tend to stay lower down in oaks, piñons, and shrubs.

 IDENTIFICATION Common. Small and slender, with a long tail. The gnatcatcher restlessly flits and hops from twig to twig. Even when perched, it keeps moving—its long tail swishing from side to side.
Plumage: Pale, silvery blue-gray upperparts; white eye ring; whitish underparts; black tail with white outer tail feathers (looks mostly white from below). **Breeding male** has a thin, black eyebrow, absent in the **female** and winter male.
Similar species: The Bushtit (page 149), a western bird, has a gray tail and travels

in flocks (also see juvenile Verdin, page 148). The breeding male Black-tailed Gnatcatcher (not illustrated) of the desert Southwest has a full black cap.
Voice: Song is a series of thin, wheezy notes. **Call** is a querulous *speeeee*.

RANGE Widespread. Breeds mostly in moist deciduous forests in the East; in the West, breeding habitat includes oaks, piñons, and junipers. Winters in the southern tier of states, in coastal scrub, chaparral, and brushy areas as well as forests. Spring **migration:** March–early May; fall migration: mid-August–September.

FOOD Small insects and spiders. Usually gleans prey from foliage, but also in hovering flight or sallying after flushed prey.

 NESTING *Location:* In a tree or shrub, anywhere from 3 to 80 feet up. *Nest:* Neat, high-walled cup of plant fibers, lichen, and bark flakes bound with spiderweb. *Eggs:* Usually 4–5; incubated by both parents for 11–15 days. *Fledging:* Leaves nest at 10–15 days.

KINGLETS Family Regulidae

A small family—just six species worldwide—of tiny, hyperactive birds that eat insects. Two species occur in North America.

Ruby-crowned Kinglet
Regulus calendula, L 4¼" (10 cm)

Backyard birders typically encounter the Ruby-crowned Kinglet in fall and winter. It breeds in mountainous areas and far to the north.

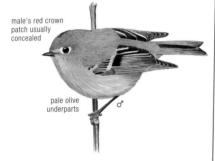

male's red crown patch usually concealed

pale olive underparts

♂

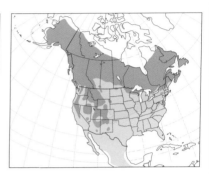

RANGE Widespread. Breeds in coniferous forests in Canada, New England, and the mountainous West. Winters at lower elevations in the southern and western U.S. and into Mexico. Winter habitat is diverse: woodlands of all types, thickets, chaparral, coastal scrub, suburban backyards, and city parks. Spring **migration:** March–early May; fall migration: mid-September–October.

IDENTIFICATION Common. Tiny, somewhat plump songbird with a large head, short tail, and tiny bill. Very active, constantly flitting about and nervously flicking its wings.
Plumage: Plain, mostly olive green, with two white wing bars. Blank face is punctuated with a large black eye and white eye ring (broken above). **Male**'s red crown is hidden except when the bird is agitated.
Similar species: Golden-crowned Kinglet (opposite) has black and white head stripes and a colorful crown. Hutton's Vireo (not illustrated), mainly from the West Coast, is larger, has a thicker bill, and lacks the black panel next to the lower wing bar.
Voice: Song is a loud and complex series of high notes ending in warbled, three-note phrases.
Call is a husky, scolding *je-dit*.

FOOD Gleans small insects and spiders from foliage and bark, often hovering in front of a leaf to pick off an insect or flying out after flushed prey. Eats small amounts of fruit in winter.
Feeding: Will feed on suet. Shrubs and vines with winter fruit attract kinglets to backyard gardens.

slightly broken white eye ring

NESTING *Location:* In a conifer, from 4 to 100 feet up. *Nest:* Deep cup of plant fibers, lichen, moss, and pine needles, bound with spiderweb. *Eggs:* Usually 7–8; incubated by female for 12–14 days. *Fledging:* Leaves nest at about 16 days.

| JAN | FEB | MAR | APR | MAY | JUN | JUL | AUG | SEP | OCT | NOV | DEC |

Golden-crowned Kinglet
Regulus satrapa, L 4" (10 cm)

In winter, the tiny Golden-crowned Kinglet often joins small foraging flocks of insect-eating woodland birds such as Ruby-crowned Kinglets, Brown Creepers, Yellow-rumped Warblers, and chickadees. On cold winter nights, these hardy kinglets may seek shelter in a squirrel nest or tangle of tree roots.

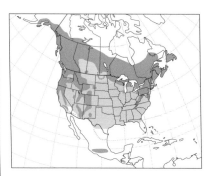

orange-red median crown stripe, bordered by yellow

♂

whitish underparts

yellow median crown stripe

bold whitish supercilium bordered by black

♀

Voice: Song is a series of accelerating *see* notes, ending in a lower pitched, jumbled warble. When flocking, a very high, sibilant jingling *tsii tsii tsii*. **Call** is a similar series of very high, thin notes: *see see see*.

RANGE Widespread. Breeds mainly in coniferous forests, a few in mixed or deciduous forests. In winter, many birds remain in breeding range, but most move south, where they are found in a wide variety of forested habitats, including wooded residential areas, towns, and parks. Spring **migration:** March–April; fall migration: October–November.

IDENTIFICATION Fairly common. Tiny—smaller than the Ruby-crowned Kinglet—with a short tail and thin bill. Behavior is similar to Ruby-crowned: very active, constantly flitting about and nervously flicking its wings.
Plumage: Conspicuously striped head—white eyebrow bordered above and below with black. Mostly grayish olive above, paler below; darker wings with two white wing bars. Center of yellow crown is reddish orange on **male**, all yellow on **female**.
Similar species: Ruby-crowned Kinglet (previous page) is more olive above and yellow below and has a plain head and white eye ring.

FOOD Gleans small insects and spiders from foliage and bark, often hovering in front of a leaf to pick off an insect or sallying out after flushed prey. Eats small amounts of fruit in winter.
Feeding: Suet is the best choice. Shrubs and vines with winter fruit attract kinglets to backyard gardens.

NESTING *Location:* In a conifer, from 6–50 feet up and suspended near the end of a branch. *Nest:* Deep cup of plant fibers, lichen, moss, and pine needles bound with spiderweb. *Eggs:* Usually 8–9; incubated by female for 12–14 days. *Fledging:* Leaves nest at about 16–19 days.

♀

white belly and
undertail coverts

THRUSHES   Family Turdidae

This large family with a worldwide distribution includes many outstanding vocalists. Thrushes feed on insects and fruits, and many species are migratory.

Eastern Bluebird
Sialia sialis, L 7" (18 cm)

Known for their brilliant plumage, endearing behavior, and attraction to nest boxes, Eastern Bluebirds have millions of adoring fans. State bird of Missouri and New York.

 IDENTIFICATION Common. Bluebirds often allow close approach and choose low perches where they are easy to observe.
Plumage: Male has flashy blue upperparts; female's are more subdued. Rusty color on breast and flanks wraps up behind the ear coverts; belly is white. **Juvenile** is heavily spotted, but has blue wings.
Similar species: Western Bluebird (page 164) is very similar, but overlaps little in range.
Voice: Simple musical **song** consists of a rich warble: *chur chur-lee chur-lee*. **Call** is a rising *chur-lee*.

RANGE Eastern species primarily; year-round resident throughout much of its range. Lives in open, rural areas. **Migration** covers short distances, and some bluebirds, even in northern areas, don't migrate. Spring arrival in southern Canada is as early as mid-March.

 FOOD From spring to early fall, bluebirds primarily eat insects.

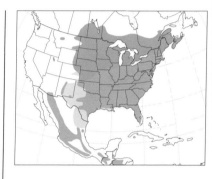

In winter, they rely on small fruits.
Feeding: Offer live mealworms. Fruiting trees and vines provide winter sustenance.

 NESTING *Location:* In a natural cavity or old woodpecker hole. *Nest:* Cavity is filled with grass and other plant material. *Eggs:* Usually 4–5; incubated by female for 11–19 days. *Fledging:* Leaves nest at about 19 days.
Housing: Will use a nest box.

rufous in both sexes
wraps around sides of
neck and includes throat

juvenile

spotted

♂

A female Eastern Bluebird delivers a moth to chicks in her nest box.

BACKYARD BLUEBIRDS

Don't confuse blue birds, like jays and Indigo Buntings, with real bluebirds—small, portly, cheerful members of the thrush family. If your backyard is not too urban, you might host bluebirds. They inhabit a variety of fields, pastures, and open spaces, and are honored guests in any neighborhood.

BLUEBIRD CONSERVATION

Non-native House Sparrows and European Starlings, both introduced to North America in the late 1800s, aggressively compete with bluebirds for nesting cavities. To give bluebirds a helping hand, conservationists encouraged bluebird "trails" in the 1960s: Dozens or even hundreds of birdhouses are placed at intervals along a road, path, or fence line where they can be regularly monitored.

Today, a significant percentage of Eastern Bluebirds nest in man-made birdhouses, and bluebird trails have had a positive impact on their populations. Bluebirds have expanded into the Great Plains, taking advantage of settlements with trees and birdhouses, and many nest along golf courses and parks with open spaces.

Tips about attracting bluebirds may be found in Birdhouses, pages 24–29, and you can find out more about starting a bluebird trail from the North American Bluebird Society (nabluebirdsociety.org).

A word about color: The feathers of bluebirds aren't strictly blue. Their cobalt hue is structural, the same way the sky or water appears blue but has no pigment. Bluebirds look blue because of the way light scatters from tiny air pockets and proteins within each feather. Most other colors in the bird world, like red and yellow, are derived from pigments, but blue is a trick of the light—and that goes for all blue birds, not just bluebirds.

Western Bluebird
Sialia mexicana, L 7" (18 cm)

Because they favor open parklike woods, Western Bluebirds have less contact with backyard birders than Eastern Bluebirds do. Both species are equally stunning and attracted to nest boxes.

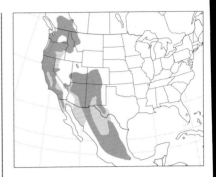

 IDENTIFICATION Common. Similar in structure to the Eastern Bluebird; has a plump body—bigger than a sparrow, smaller than a robin—and a large head.

Plumage: Male's upperparts are deep cobalt blue and can look very dark; breast and back are chestnut. **Female** has a grayish head and back, with a pale chestnut breast. **Juvenile** (not illustrated) is very similar to juvenile Eastern Bluebird. **Similar species:** Eastern Bluebird (page 162) does not overlap much in range. Female Mountain Bluebird (not illustrated), a western species, is grayer, has more uniform coloration, and lacks a rusty breast.

Voice: Simple **song** consists of a series of call notes—*few few fawee*—primarily heard at dawn. **Call** is a simple, mellow *few* or *peurr*.

gray sides to neck

♀

all-blue head

♂

gray undertail coverts

some dark rufous scapulars

RANGE Western species; year-round resident throughout much of its range. Breeds in open woodlands, especially ponderosa pine, piñon, juniper, or oak; also found around orchards, farmland with scattered trees, and golf courses. **Migration** covers relatively short distances, often simply moving to a lower altitude.

FOOD In summer, insects are the primary food. Hunts from a perch, swooping down to the ground to capture an insect; sometimes gleans foliage or catches insects in midair. In winter, feeds mostly on small fruits and berries—mistletoe and juniper berries are favorites. **Feeding:** Use live mealworms; rarely eats birdseed.

NESTING *Location:* In a natural tree cavity or old woodpecker hole. *Nest:* Cavity is filled with dry grass and other plant material. *Eggs:* Usually 4–5; incubated by female for 12–18 days. *Fledging:* Leaves nest at about 20 days. *Broods:* In many areas, 2 per year is normal. **Housing:** Will use a nest box. The North American Bluebird Society (*nabluebird society.org*) has good advice and nest box building plans.

Hermit Thrush
Catharus guttatus, L 6¾" (17 cm)

The Hermit Thrush's song has inspired poets and writers. Frank Chapman, the inventor of the field guide, didn't curb his enthusiasm when in 1897 he wrote, "The Hermit's hymn echoes through the woods like the swelling tones of an organ in some vast cathedral." State bird of Vermont.

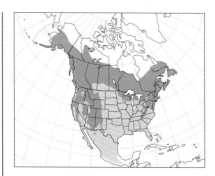

all juvenile *Catharus* have spotted plumage

thin eye ring

eastern juvenile

rufous tail

eastern

brownish buff flanks

IDENTIFICATION Common. Medium-size thrush—smaller than a robin—that has two habitual tics: it quickly raises its tail, then slowly lowers it, and it rapidly flicks its wings. Often seen hopping on the forest floor, keeping to the shadows, or visiting fruiting vines in migration or winter.
Plumage: Upperparts vary from rich brown to gray brown (in some western birds), but reddish tail is always the brightest part. Eastern birds have brownish flanks; western birds have grayish flanks. White eye ring; buff breast with dark spots. **Juvenile** has spotted upperparts.
Similar species: The face and eye ring of Swainson's Thrush (next page) are more buff, and the color of its tail matches its back. In the East, the Wood Thrush (page 167) is larger, bright rufous above, with bold black spots underneath. See also the Fox Sparrow (page 199).
Voice: Song is a serene series of clear, flutelike notes, with successive songs on different pitches. **Calls** include *chup* or *chup-chup* and a wheezy, rising *zhweee*.

RANGE Widespread species. Breeds widely in northern and mountain hardwood and coniferous forests. Quite hardy and migrates relatively short distances. In winter, found in more open forest with brushy (berry-producing) tangles, including residential areas, towns, and parks. Spring **migration:** April–mid-May; fall migration: late September–early November.

FOOD Mostly insects and fruit. Searches for food on the forest floor and in low trees, sometimes hovering briefly to pick off an insect or berry. In winter, about half of its diet is small fruits.

NESTING *Location:* On the ground, hidden by overhanging vegetation, or sometimes in a low tree. *Nest:* Bulky cup of grass, other plant fibers, and a layer of mud. *Eggs:* Usually 4; incubated by female for 12–13 days. *Fledging:* Leaves nest at 12–13 days.

SIGHTINGS

JAN FEB MAR APR MAY JUN JUL AUG SEP OCT NOV DEC

Swainson's Thrush
Catharus ustulatus, L 7" (18 cm)

Swainson's Thrush is a bird that backyard birders will most likely see during spring and fall migration. Berry-producing vines and shrubs often entice these retiring birds out into the open; the rest of the time, they stick to shady woodlands.

upperparts with a russet cast

olive gray upperparts

Pacific coast

buffy flanks

Alaska

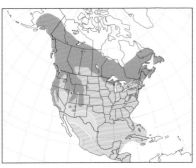

RANGE Widespread species; summer resident. Breeds in northern and mountain forests; Pacific coast birds also breed in streamside willows and shady canyons. Winters from Mexico to South America. Spring **migration:** mid-April–May; fall migration: September–mid-October.

FOOD Mostly insects and fruit. Searches for insects on the forest floor and in low trees. During fall migration, eats berries primarily.

NESTING *Location:* In a small tree, from 2 to 7 feet up. *Nest:* Compact cup of twigs, moss, and other plant material. *Eggs:* Usually 4; incubated by female for 10–14 days. *Fledging:* Leaves nest at about 14 days.

IDENTIFICATION Fairly common. Medium-size thrush. Unlike the Hermit Thrush, it does not flick its wings or cock its tail, but otherwise it has very similar behavior.
Plumage: Upperparts vary from russet brown (on the Pacific coast) to olive brown (in most other areas), with a similar-colored tail. The lighter parts of the face are buff, as are the eye ring and lores, giving it spectacled look.
Similar species: Hermit Thrush (previous page) has a white eye ring and a reddish tail that contrasts with its back. Other "spotted thrushes" seen in the East during migration include Veery and Gray-cheeked Thrushes (not illustrated).
Voice: Song is an ascending spiral of flute-like whistles. **Calls** include a sharp *quirk* and a liquid *whit* (Pacific coast).

buffy eye ring and supraloral line

olive brown upperparts

widespread subspecies

brownish flanks

Wood Thrush
Hylocichla mustelina, L 7¾" (20 cm)

Considered by many to rival the Hermit Thrush in vocal ability, the Wood Thrush moved Longfellow to write, "And where the shadows deepest fell / The wood thrush rang his silver bell."

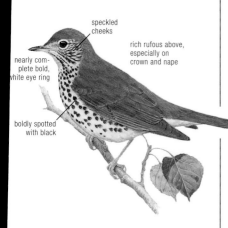

speckled cheeks

rich rufous above, especially on crown and nape

nearly complete bold, white eye ring

boldly spotted with black

Voice: Song is a dreamy, flutelike series of rising and falling notes—*eh-eh eee-o-lay*—followed by a complex trill. **Calls** include a staccato *pit pit pit pit.*

IDENTIFICATION Common. Medium-large thrush—larger and more robust than Hermit and Swainson's Thrushes, and much easier to identify. It sticks to the ground and understory of its eastern forest home and is particularly vocal in the early morning and at dusk. **Plumage:** Very bright cinnamon-rufous upperparts—brightest on the crown—but equally impressive below, with bold black spots on a pure white background. The large, dark eye and white eye ring are prominent. **Similar species:** Hermit and Swainson's Thrushes (page 165 and opposite) are smaller, less potbellied, less heavily spotted, and not as brightly colored, and they do not have a strong white eye ring. Larger Brown Thrasher (page 174) has a much longer tail and bill, and yellowish eyes.

RANGE Eastern species; summer resident. Breeds in moist hardwood and mixed forests with dense undergrowth. Backyards bordering good habitat and even large urban parks are sometimes suitable, but unfortunately, Wood Thrush numbers have declined since the 1970s. Forest fragmentation—both here and in its winter home in southern Mexico and Central America—and brood parasitism by Brown-headed Cowbirds are thought to be major causes. Spring **migration:** April–May; fall migration: October.

FOOD Mostly insects and fruit. Searches for insects on the forest floor (typically with several hops and a pause, like a robin) and in low trees. Small fruits and berries are consumed year-round.

NESTING *Location:* In a sapling or shrub, about 10 feet up. *Nest:* Open cup of leaves and grass, with a layer of mud. *Eggs:* Usually 3–4; incubated by female for 11–14 days. *Fledging:* Leaves nest at 12–15 days.

Varied Thrush
Ixoreus naevius, L 9½" (24 cm)

An extremely attractive thrush of the dark forests of the Pacific Northwest, the Varied Thrush is seen more often in winter, when some birds move south out of their forest havens into more open areas, such as backyards, gardens, parks, and shady oak canyons.

juvenile

orange wing bars and markings on wing

orange supercilium

♀

black breast band

♂

differently and followed by a pause. **Call** is a soft, low *tschook.*

IDENTIFICATION Common. Large thrush—almost robin size, and sometimes associates with robin flocks in winter. Hops on the ground, tossing debris aside to look for insects. Male often perches high up (out of sight) during long bouts of singing.
Plumage: Intricate orange wing pattern and prominent orange stripe above the eye. **Male** has orange underparts crossed by a black breast band and steely blue upperparts. **Female** is less intensely colored with a faint gray breast band and brownish-gray upperparts. **Juvenile** has scalier-looking breast and white belly.
Similar species: American Robin (pages 170–171) lacks the bold orange stripe over the eye and has brick red (not orange) underparts, with no dark breast band.
Voice: Song is a series of long, trilled whistles; each eerie whistle is pitched

RANGE Pacific coast and Alaska species. Breeds in moist coniferous and mixed forests with a closed canopy and also in alder and poplar groves farther north. In winter, many breeders move south and coastward (irregular to Southern California, in small numbers), but some stay put. Winter habitat is more diverse and includes urban parks and backyards (sometimes even open lawns). Typical time frame for winter visitors is October–April.

FOOD Insects, fruits, berries, and nuts. Searches for insects on the forest floor (typically taking several hops and a pause, like a robin). Small fruits and berries are consumed year-round, but are the primary food in winter.

NESTING *Location:* In a conifer, 4–20 feet up. *Nest:* Open cup of twigs, moss, and grass, with a layer of mud. *Eggs:* Usually 3–4; incubated by female for about 12 days. *Fledging:* Leaves nest at 13–15 days.

ROBIN EGG BLUE

Bird eggs come in all hues and patterns: brown, white, cream, red, green, speckled, and spattered. The eggs of ground-nesting birds are remarkably well camouflaged against their surroundings. But other colors are harder to explain. Why, for instance, does the American Robin lay bright blue eggs?

Across their range, robins build a cup-shaped nest of straw and mud. The female usually produces four unmarked eggs, in a beautiful shade very similar to Tiffany Blue—the cyan color trademarked by New York City's high-end jewelry company. Scientists have struggled to explain why a bird would lay such conspicuously colorful eggs.

A HEALTHY FAMILY

One interesting study showed that male robins take better care of chicks that hatch from brighter-colored eggs. In an egg-switching experiment, robins were given either dull blue or neon blue eggs to incubate. After hatching, the male parents with bright eggs fed their chicks twice as much as those with dull-colored ones.

Researchers theorized that egg color helps gauge the mother's fitness, and that males are more motivated to take care of chicks they believe are healthy.

NATURAL SUNSCREEN

Another possibility is that blue eggs are a trade-off for sun exposure. Light-colored eggs transmit more harmful ultraviolet rays to the embryo inside, while dark-colored eggs heat up faster in the sun (what researchers have called the "dark car effect"). For a bird that nests in dappled shade, like a robin, a medium color could balance the two extremes.

But that doesn't explain why some cavity-nesting birds, like Eastern Bluebirds, also lay blue eggs. You'd think sun protection would be unnecessary in a dark hole. This is a good question to ponder while gazing into the sky on a cloudless day: Why is a robin's egg blue?

Three blue robin's eggs sit in a nest.

Male and female American Robins look similar.

American Robin
Turdus migratorius, L 10" (25 cm)

This species' distinctive plumage and acceptance of human-dominated habitats make it one of our most familiar and beloved birds. In northern areas, the male's loud, caroling song is a welcome harbinger of spring. Exceptionally adaptable, robins nest from urban centers and backyards to remote wilderness areas above the Arctic Circle. State bird of Connecticut, Michigan, and Wisconsin.

IDENTIFICATION Identification is easy and usually obvious. The robin has a pot-bellied look and an upright stance as it searches for food with a distinctive run-stop-run rhythm. A stopped bird cocks its head to one side to look (not listen) for the presence of an earthworm or grub. Robins also poke into leaf litter, flipping leaves out of the way in their search for insects. In winter and migration, they often occur in large flocks.

Plumage: Brick red underparts are its most familiar attribute; also note its gray upperparts, yellow bill, white chin, and white eye arcs. Eastern birds have small white tail spots, visible in flight. **Male** has a darker head and deeper red underparts than **female**. **Juvenile** has a spotted breast.
Similar species: Compare to male Eastern Towhee (page 192). Juvenile might be confused with other spotted thrushes, such as the Hermit Thrush (page 165), but has gray upperparts and head.
Voice: Loud caroling **song** has a cheerful, bubbling quality. It is composed

juvenile

heavily spotted

♀

usually paler than male

white spot

bold white broken eye ring

yellow bill

♂

brick red underparts

Small berries are swallowed whole by American Robins, but larger fruits are pecked at.

of phrases broken with short pauses: *cheerily-cheer up-cheerio.* Its song can be confused with that of other birds that sing in phrases broken with pauses, such as tanagers and grosbeaks. **Calls** include a low mellow *pup* and a doubled or trebled *chok* or *tut.*

RANGE Widespread species. Robins are common and pervasive in North America, as both breeding and wintering birds. Most birds are migratory to some extent, but some southern breeders remain in the same area year-round. Spring **migration:** February–April; fall migration: October–November.

FOOD Insects, earthworms, and berries. From spring to fall, backyard robins forage conspicuously on lawns for earthworms. In many locations, winter flocks have no fixed address, but wander in search of fruit—after the trees or vines are stripped of food, the flock moves on. **Feeding:** Comes to a feeder that offers live mealworms. To promote earthworms (and robins) around your home, use organic fertilizers and avoid insecticides.

Fruiting trees, shrubs, and vines will encourage flocks to linger in winter—holly, sumac, crabapple, and pyracantha are good choices.

NESTING *Location:* Sheltered site in a tree, shrub, or man-made structure, from 5–15 feet up. *Nest:* Untidy, bulky, open cup of plant material, lined with mud and finished off with fine grass. *Eggs:* Usually 4; incubated by female for 12–14 days. *Fledging:* Leaves nest at 14–16 days. *Broods:* In most areas, 2 per season; sometimes 3.
Housing: Robins are not shy about nesting around homes, which may help to protect their nest from predators such as raccoons. If you have a porch with a suitable recess or even a protected windowsill, you might find robins nesting there. A nesting platform added to a sheltered location will attract them.

These hungry nestling American Robins will be ready to leave their crowded nest in about a week.

MOCKINGBIRDS & THRASHERS   Family Mimidae

Long-tailed songbirds noted for the rich variety and volume of their songs. Most species forage on or near the ground and have a solitary lifestyle.

Northern Mockingbird
Mimus polyglottos, L 10" (25 cm)

The male Northern Mockingbird is a masterful singer who weaves the songs of many other species into his own large repertoire. State bird of Arkansas, Florida, Mississippi, Tennessee, and Texas.

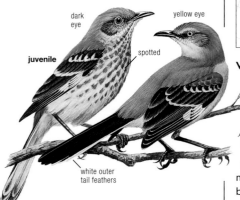

dark eye

yellow eye

juvenile

spotted

white outer tail feathers

Voice: Song is a mix of original and imitative phrases, each repeated several times. Unmated males often sing at night. Calls include a loud, sharp check.

RANGE Widespread species; year-round resident. Favors thickets and brushy areas with open ground nearby—a good description of many backyards.

IDENTIFICATION Common. Slender, long-tailed bird that is often conspicuous around backyards. Its habitual wing flashing exposes large white wing patches and may serve as a territorial defense, to startle predators, or to flush insects—no one is certain.
Plumage: Gray above, white below. Has dark wings with a large white patch, white outer tail feathers, and yellowish eyes.
Juvenile has faintly spotted breast and dark eyes.
Similar species: Loggerhead Shrike (not illustrated) is an uncommon predatory songbird with a similar overall pattern, but has a stubby, hooked bill, and a black face mask.

FOOD Eats a full menu of insects in spring and summer. Winter food is primarily berries—fruiting shrubs are vigorously defended from other birds.
Feeding: Will visit a suet feeder. Plant fruiting trees, shrubs, and vines for winter sustenance.

NESTING *Location:* In a dense shrub or tree, usually 3–10 feet up. *Nest:* Bulky open cup of twigs, grass, and other plant material. *Eggs:* Usually 3–4; incubated by female for 12–13 days. *Fledging:* Leaves nest at 12–16 days.

extensive white wing patch

SIGHTINGS | JAN | FEB | MAR | APR | MAY | JUN | JUL | AUG | SEP | OCT | NOV | DEC

Gray Catbird
Dumetella carolinensis, L 8½" (22 cm)

The thicket-loving Gray Catbird has a surprisingly wide distribution, reaching almost to the Pacific Ocean in the northern tier of states and southern Canada. The only mainland states that it avoids breeding in are Nevada and California.

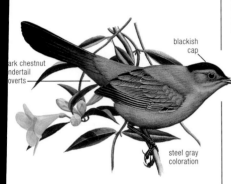

blackish cap

dark chestnut undertail coverts

steel gray coloration

RANGE Widespread species. Favors thickets, brushy forest undergrowth, tangled vines, and suburban backyards with dense shrub plantings. Winters along the East Coast, and south into the Caribbean and Central America. Spring **migration:** April–May; fall migration: September–early November.

FOOD Mainly insects in spring and summer; more small fruits and berries on migration and during the winter.

NESTING *Location:* In a dense shrub or tree, usually 3–10 feet up. *Nest:* Bulky open cup of twigs, weed stems, vines, and other plant material. *Eggs:* Usually 4; incubated by female for 12–14 days. *Fledging:* Leaves nest at 11–15 days.

IDENTIFICATION Common. Slender, long-tailed, dark gray bird, smaller than a mockingbird, that inhabits backyard shrubbery. Its behavior is somewhat furtive and skulking, with short, low flights that rarely take it far. However, around most backyards, a nesting pair of catbirds gets used to the hubbub, and you're almost as likely to see one perching openly on a lawn chair or visiting a birdbath.
Plumage: All gray except for a blackish skullcap, a long black tail, and inconspicuous chestnut undertail coverts. Juvenile has pale undertail coverts with a hint of rust color.
Similar species: None.
Voice: Song is a rapidly delivered mix of melodious, nasal, and squeaky notes, interspersed with catlike *mew* notes; also mimics other birds' **calls** and songs. Most frequent call is a nasal, down-slurred *mew*.

Even with a partial view, the gray plumage and blackish cap of the Gray Catbird are unmistakable.

Brown Thrasher
Toxostoma rufum, L 11½" (29 cm)

The only thrasher in the eastern half of North America (eight species of thrasher occur in the West). The East has more uniform habitat and climate than the West, and the Brown Thrasher is widespread throughout the region. State bird of Georgia.

 IDENTIFICATION Common to uncommon. Long-tailed, yellow-eyed, mostly rufous bird—larger than a mockingbird—that lurks in thickets and feeds mostly on the ground, sweeping aside leaf litter and soil in pursuit of hidden insects. In winter, when it eats mainly berries, it spends less time on the ground. Most flights are short, jerky affairs that hug the ground; however, a singing male usually selects a high perch to proclaim his breeding territory.
Plumage: Rich rufous upperparts and tail; two whitish wing bars. Underparts are extensively streaked.
Similar species: Wood Thrush (page 167) is short tailed with distinct spots (not streaks) on its underparts. In the South, a wintering Brown Thrasher often occupies the same habitat as the Hermit Thrush (page 165), which has less rufous upperparts, spotted underparts, and a shorter tail and bill. Long-billed Thrasher (not illustrated), a southern Texas specialty, is grayer above and has a longer bill.
Voice: Song is a series of varied melodious phrases, each phrase often repeated two or three times. **Calls** include a loud, smacking *spuck* and a low *churr*.

RANGE Eastern and midwestern species; scarce in the western part of its range. Favors thickets, brushy forest edges, briar tangles, shelterbelts, and suburban backyards with dense shrub plantings. Winters along the East Coast and throughout much of the South. Spring migration: late March–early May; fall migration: late August–early November.

FOOD Mainly insects in spring and summer; more small fruits and nuts (particularly acorns) on migration and during the winter.
Feeding: Comes to suet and seed feeders, particularly in winter.

NESTING *Location:* In a dense shrub or tree, usually 3–6 feet up; sometimes on the ground. *Nest:* Bulky open cup of twigs, weed stems, and other plant material. *Eggs:* Usually 4–5; incubated by both parents for 11–14 days. *Fledging:* Leaves nest at 9–12 days.

long rufous tail

rufous upperparts

streaked underparts

SIGHTINGS   JAN FEB MAR APR MAY JUN JUL AUG SEP OCT NOV DEC

Curve-billed Thrasher
Toxostoma curvirostre, L 11" (28 cm)

The Curve-billed Thrasher—the common thrasher from the Sonoran Desert of Arizona east to the brushlands of Texas—can be very conspicuous when calling loudly from atop a saguaro or prickly pear cactus (or street sign).

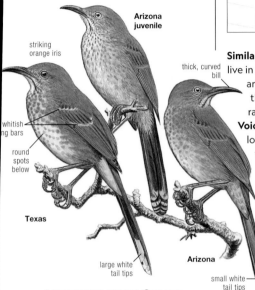

Arizona juvenile

striking orange iris

thick, curved bill

whitish ng bars

round spots below

Texas

Arizona

large white tail tips

small white tail tips

Similar species: Other similar thrashers live in the Southwest—Bendire's, Crissal, and Le Conte's (not illustrated)—but they are uncommon species, very rarely seen in backyards.
Voice: Long, melodic **song** consists of low trills and warbles. **Call** is a loud *whit-wheet* (in Arizona and New Mexico) or *whit-whit* (in Texas).

RANGE Southwestern species; year-round resident. Favors arid brush and cactus-rich desert. Often inhabits suburban desert communities, especially where cholla cactus grows or, in Texas, around prickly pear thickets.

IDENTIFICATION Common. A sturdy thrasher with strong legs and feet tough enough to perch on spiny cacti. Sometimes lurks in dense vegetation, but feeds on open ground, often walking or running from place to place. Most flights are short and jerky and keep near the ground. Has striking orange eyes and a heavy, downcurved bill.
Plumage: Overall dingy, brownish gray with spotted or mottled underparts and a white-tipped tail. **Juvenile** has a shorter bill and paler eyes. Southern Arizona subspecies has underparts with blurry mottling, less white in the tail, and no wing bars.

FOOD A wide variety of insect prey is uncovered or excavated from the ground. Diet is supplemented with seeds, wild berries, and cactus fruit.
Feeding: Comes to suet, mealworm, and seed feeders.

NESTING *Location*: In a dense shrub or tree, usually 3–6 feet up; sometimes on the ground. *Nest*: Bulky open cup of twigs, weed stems, and other plant material. *Eggs*: Usually 4–5; incubated by both parents for 11–14 days. *Fledging*: Leaves nest at 9–12 days.

SIGHTINGS

JAN   FEB   MAR   APR   MAY   JUN   JUL   AUG   SEP   OCT   NOV   DEC

STARLINGS   Family Sturnidae

Widespread Old World family of chunky, often glossy songbirds that also includes the mynas.

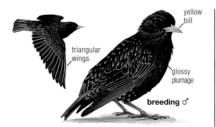

yellow bill
triangular wings
glossy plumage
breeding ♂

juven
overall grayish brown
dull, blurred streaks

European Starling
Sturnus vulgaris, L 8½" (22 cm)

First introduced in New York's Central Park in 1890—in a misguided plan to introduce all the birds mentioned in Shakespeare's works into the United States—it spread across the continent by the late 1940s.

IDENTIFICATION Abundant. Stocky and short-tailed songbird with a sharply pointed bill, often seen strutting about lawns and parking lots. Starlings form very large flocks in winter, often with blackbirds.
Plumage: Breeding bird is glossy black, with a yellow bill (blue-based in male; pink-based in female). **Fresh fall** bird is densely speckled with white and buff, with a black bill; by late winter, the speckles are worn off, revealing the glossy black feathering. **Juvenile** is uniformly grayish brown.
Similar species: Other blackish birds include the Brewer's Blackbird (page 219), Red-winged Blackbird (page 220), and Brown-headed (page 217) and Bronzed Cowbirds (page 216). Blackbirds have longer tails and

plumage heavily spotted with white

slender dark bill

short tail
fresh fall

shorter, never yellow bills.
Voice: Extremely varied. Elaborate, lengthy **song** with rattles, buzzes, clicks, and squealing notes. Often mimics other species. **Calls** include whistled *wheeeeoooo* and buzzy *dzeeer*, among others.

RANGE Widespread, non-native species. Very common around human structures but also occupies more natural settings. Avoids dense forest and unbroken desert.

FOOD Mixed, opportunistic diet of insects, berries, and seeds.

NESTING *Location:* In a tree cavity, sheltered building crevice, or nest box. Aggressively evicts many native species from scarce nest holes. *Nest:* Untidy cup of twigs, grasses, and other dried vegetation. *Eggs:* Usually 5–7; incubated by both parents for 12–15 days. *Fledging:* Leaves nest at 20–22 days.

JAN FEB MAR APR MAY JUN JUL AUG SEP OCT NOV DEC

MURMURATIONS

In fall and winter, European Starlings congregate in immense flocks—sometimes numbering into the millions—before settling into their evening roost.

This behavior can cause collateral damage, especially around airports and agricultural fields. In Rome, one particularly large starling party rained down so much poop that cars went skidding on roadways and pedestrians resorted to using umbrellas.

But viewed from a safe distance, a starling flock—poetically called a "murmuration"—can be an inspiring, otherworldly phenomenon. The birds fly so close to one another that they act as one organism, shape-shifting like a mythological animal. A murmuration is a three-dimensional ballet, stunningly choreographed, with a cast of thousands.

PARTICLE PHYSICS

It's appropriate that these flocks often occur in urban areas, as the birds act like busy traffic. They hardly slow down during their breathtaking aerial maneuvers, swooping and swerving together at full speed. How can they possibly avoid midair collisions?

The most interesting insights have come not from biologists, but from the world of physics. Computer models show that a starling flock has no leaders: Birds on the outside of a turn end up in the back of the group, while those in front end up on one side. This means that a starling flock behaves collectively, with the overall effect arising from many independent, individual decisions.

Those decisions are based on a few simple rules: Don't get too close to your neighbor (to avoid a mishap); don't stray too far from the group (to avoid sticking out); and align your direction with your seven closest neighbors (to keep the flock together). Each bird is like a particle, relying on those interactions to find safety—and beauty—in numbers.

A murmuration of European Starlings fills the evening sky like a shimmering cloud of smoke.

WAXWINGS   Family Bombycillidae

Waxwings have sleek crests, silky plumage, and yellow-tipped tails. Of three species in the world, two occur in North America.

Cedar Waxwing
Bombycilla cedrorum, L 7¼" (18 cm)

The curious name—waxwing—derives from the bright red, waxy secretions produced at the tips of the secondary wing feathers. Their function, if any, is unknown.

triangular wing shape

streaked underparts

juvenile

crest

yellowish belly

yellow tail tip

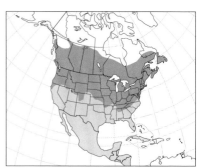

Similar species: Bohemian Waxwing (not illustrated) breeds in the far north, but occurs sporadically with Cedar Waxwings in the northern U.S. in fall and winter. Look for rufous (not white) undertail coverts and white wing markings.
Voice: No song (not territorial). **Call** is a soft, high-pitched, trilled whistle: *zeeee.*

IDENTIFICATION Common. A bluebird-size, extremely social bird with an arboreal lifestyle that revolves around fruiting trees. Amiable flocks feed high in fruiting trees and might go unnoticed but for their constant, high-pitched calling. When breeding, pairs may nest close together and do not defend a territory.
Plumage: Very sleek. Brown crest; black "bandit's mask"; toasty brown and yellow underparts; white undertail coverts; plain wings except for the red waxy tips. **Juvenile** is streaked below.

RANGE Widespread species. Breeds and winters in open forests, riparian corridors, orchards, and wooded (and berried) residential areas. **Migration** timing is difficult to assess; birds return to northernmost breeding areas in May–June and depart by late fall or early winter.

FOOD Searches for berry-producing trees and shrubs. Supplements its summer diet with insects.

NESTING Starts to breed as late as July–August in some areas. *Location:* In a tree, usually 6–20 feet up. *Nest:* Loose open cup of twigs, weed stems, and other plant material. *Eggs:* Usually 3–5; incubated probably by female for 12–14 days. *Fledging:* Leaves nest at 14–18 days.

FRUIT-EATERS

Even among fruit-eaters, the Cedar Waxwing is a connoisseur of sweet delights. Unlike many North American birds that grab an occasional berry for dessert, waxwings eat almost nothing but fruit. This diet affects every part of their lifestyle.

NESTING
When a male Cedar Waxwing wants to court a mate, he sidles next to her on a branch and presents a berry (or sometimes a flower petal). If she's keen, she accepts the gift and hops away, scoots back, and coyly returns it. They exchange the fruit several times, mimicking each other's movements, in an elegantly choreographed dance, sometimes touching bills.

To coincide with fruits' ripening in late summer, waxwings delay their nesting season somewhat. They lay eggs between June and August, when many songbirds have already hatched chicks.

If by chance a Brown-headed Cowbird sneaks its egg inside a Cedar Waxwing nest (as they are known to do), the cowbird's chick will often starve despite being fed by attentive waxwing parents. Cowbirds cannot handle the all-fruit diet.

DIGESTION
Waxwings digest very quickly: A cherry pit might be defecated within 10 minutes. Unlike most fruit-eating birds, which regurgitate or avoid seeds, waxwings pass them straight through. This helps spread their favorite plants around the forest.

Such efficient digestion also helps waxwings avoid absorbing alcohol if berries have fermented, but these birds do occasionally get tipsy. In extreme cases, they have been discovered lying under a berry bush, sleeping it off.

TAIL LIGHTS
Cedar Waxwings have yellow-tipped tails, but in the 1960s birders noticed individuals with orange-red tips. This color comes from a non-native honeysuckle berry laced with red carotenoid pigments; if eaten while the bird's tail feather is growing, it turns the tip orange.

The Cedar Waxwing has a taste for sweet fruits.

OLD WORLD SPARROWS   Family Passeridae

Two Old World sparrows were introduced to North America: the ubiquitous House Sparrow; and the Eurasian Tree Sparrow, found only in a small area of the Midwest around St. Louis.

House Sparrow
Passer domesticus, L 6¼" (16 cm)

House Sparrows (also called "English Sparrows") were introduced in New York City in 1851. By the early 1900s, the species had spread to California.

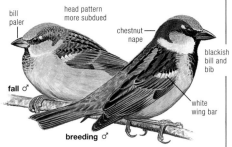

bill paler
head pattern more subdued
chestnut nape
blackish bill and bib
fall ♂
white wing bar
breeding ♂

IDENTIFICATION Abundant. Compared to our native sparrows, the House Sparrow looks big-headed with a heavy bill, stout build, and short tail. It hops on the ground, perches in bushes, and is usually found in flocks, except when breeding.
Plumage: Male: has a black bib, gray crown, and black bill. In fall, new plumage is edged with gray, and the bill is yellowish at its base. By spring, the gray edges wear away, revealing the black bib and chestnut colors. Nondescript **female** is best identified by the combination of buff eye stripe, streaked back, and dingy, unstreaked underparts.
Similar species: Compare to immature White-crowned Sparrow (page 205) and female House Finch (page 182).
Voice: Most common call is an honest-to-goodness *chirp*. Flocks chatter, sounding like a room full of talkative people.

RANGE Widespread non-native species; year-round resident. Abundant in human-altered habitats, especially urban parks, vacant lots, backyards, and farmyards.

FOOD Eats weed seeds and grain; also insects while breeding. **Feeding:** Visits feeders, often in unwanted numbers. Winter flocks "go to bed early" and are "late risers."

NESTING *Location:* In a cavity, building crevice, or nest box. *Nest:* Untidy construction of grasses, twigs, and bits of trash. *Eggs:* usually 4–6; incubated by both parents for 10–13 days. *Fledging:* Able to fly at about 14 days.

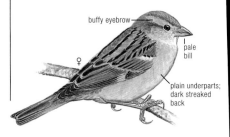

buffy eyebrow
♀
pale bill
plain underparts; dark streaked back

FINCHES   Family Fringillidae

Large, worldwide family of seed-eating birds. Many North American species nest in the North. In fall, flocks of "winter finches" may roam far to the south, but how far and how many birds vary from year to year.

Evening Grosbeak
Coccothraustes vespertinus, L 8" (20 cm)

During some winters in the East, flocks of these big noisy finches irrupt southward. Rarely, they'll travel as far as the Mid-Atlantic and Midwest. In recent decades, big irruptions have become rare.

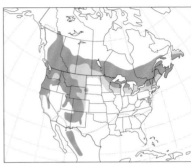

IDENTIFICATION Fairly common. A big, starling-size finch with a huge, pale bill, large head, barrel-chested body, and short tail. They frequent bird feeders, or forage in seed-bearing trees and on the ground below. **Plumage: Adult male** has a dark-brown-and-yellow body, yellow forehead and eyebrow, and single white wing patch. **Adult female** is grayish tan with a dark whisker below the bill, two white wing patches, and a white-tipped tail. **Juvenile male** resembles adult male, but is yellower.
Similar species: None.
Voice: Song is undeveloped, rarely heard. **Calls** include a loud, ringing *clee-ip* and shrill *peer.*

RANGE Breeds in coniferous and mixed forests. Winter irruptions vary from year to year and place to place; many birds spend the winter where they breed or move to lower elevations.

FOOD Seeds and insects (in summer), with some berries. Tree seeds, especially those of box elder, are a major component of its diet.

white primary patch

FEEDING Platform or hopper feeders are best. Prefers sunflower seeds.

NESTING *Location:* In a tree, often a conifer, usually 20–60 feet up. *Nest:* Loose cup of twigs, grass, and pine needles. *Eggs:* Usually 3–4; incubated by female for 12–14 days. *Fledging:* Leaves nest at about 14 days.

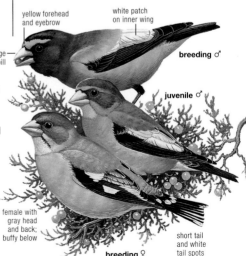

yellow forehead and eyebrow

white patch on inner wing

large bill

breeding ♂

juvenile ♂

female with gray head and back; buffy below

short tail and white tail spots

breeding ♀

House Finch
Haemorhous mexicanus, L 6" (15 cm)

Originally a bird of the semiarid West, House Finches spread throughout the East after caged birds were released on Long Island in 1940—about 50 years later, eastern birds met western birds on the Great Plains.

yellow to orange

variant ♂

broad reddish eyebrow

red throat and breast

typical ♂

brownish streaks on flanks

curved culmen

square-ended tail

muted brown back

very indistinct face pattern

♀

Similar species: Purple Finch (opposite) has a shorter, notched tail (not square tipped) and larger (not arched) bill; male Purple has less streaking below and a fully red cap; female Purple has a strongly patterned face, unlike the plain face of a female House Finch, and more distinct (not blurry) streaks below. Cassin's Finch (page 184), of the mountains of the West, has a longer, straighter bill; longer wings; and a forked tail tip.

Voice: Song is a lively warble of three-note phrases, usually ending in a nasal *wheer*. **Call** is a whistled *wheat*.

RANGE Widespread species; year-round resident. Mainly found around people and their dwellings, also in native habitats.

FOOD Seeds, buds, and fruit. Buds of trees are important in spring; fruits in fall and winter.
Feeding: Very common feeder visitor, often in large numbers.

NESTING *Location:* Often on a building, usually 5–7 feet up. *Nest:* Open cup of grass. *Eggs:* Usually 4–5; incubated by female for 13–14 days. *Fledging:* Leaves nest at 12–15 days.
Housing: Will use a nest box or nesting platform, or sometimes a hanging planter.

IDENTIFICATION Very common. A sparrow-size finch with a stubby bill, slightly curved on top. Some males are yellow or orange, a dietary deficiency.
Plumage: Male has red forehead, eyebrow, throat, breast, and rump, with long, brownish streaks on underparts. On a small percentage of males, the red plumage areas are yellow to orange. Female and juvenile are grayish brown, with a plain face and heavy streaking below.

Purple Finch

Haemorhous purpureus, L 6" (15 cm)

The male Purple Finch is raspberry red, not purple. In winter, it ranges irregularly south throughout much of the eastern United States and moves to lower elevations in the West. State bird of New Hampshire.

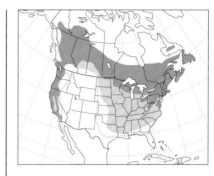

IDENTIFICATION Fairly common. About the size of a House Finch, but chunkier, with a larger head. Forages in trees and shrubs.
Plumage: Adult male is raspberry red on head, breast, and rump; its back and wings are tinged pinkish. **Female** and **juvenile** are brown and white, with a strongly patterned head and boldly streaked underparts. Western birds are buffier and diffusely streaked below.
Similar species: See House Finch (opposite) for differences. Cassin's Finch (next page), of the West, has a longer, straighter bill, longer wings, and streaked undertail coverts. Male Cassin's is brightest red on crown; female Cassin's has finer, sharper streaking below.
Voice: Song is a rich, continuous warble (shorter in the West). **Calls** include a musical *chur-lee* and a sharp *pit*.

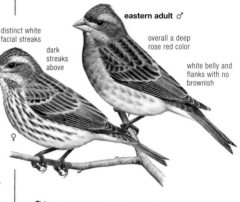

eastern adult ♂

distinct white facial streaks

dark streaks above

overall a deep rose red color

white belly and flanks with no brownish

♀

RANGE Widespread species. Favors moist coniferous forests (East) or oak-and-conifer woodlands and riparian areas (West). Spring migration: February–May; fall migration: September–December.

FOOD Seeds, buds, fruit; some insects.
Feeding: Feeder visitor, preferring black-oil sunflower seeds. Also feeds in berry-producing trees.

NESTING *Location:* In a tree, usually 15–20 feet up. *Nest:* Compact cup of twigs. *Eggs:* Usually 3–5; incubated mostly by female for 12–13 days. *Fledging:* Leaves nest at 13–16 days.

Pacific coast adult ♂

brownish tinge to back, flanks, and belly

pale facial stripes

Pacific coast ♀

browner, less contrasty streaking below against a buffier background color

SIGHTINGS

JAN FEB MAR APR MAY JUN JUL AUG SEP OCT NOV DEC

Cassin's Finch
Haemorhous cassinii, L 6¼" (16 cm)

If you live in the Rockies, Cascades, or Sierra Nevada and have yellow pines, firs, or quaking aspens as your backyard scenery, then Cassin's Finches are probably your avian neighbors.

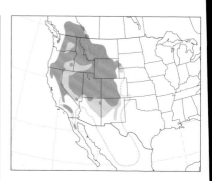

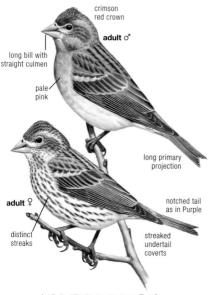

crimson red crown

adult ♂

long bill with straight culmen

pale pink

long primary projection

adult ♀

notched tail as in Purple

distinct streaks

streaked undertail coverts

IDENTIFICATION Fairly common. Slightly larger than either Purple or House Finch, with trimmer, more angular features, a longer and more sharply pointed bill, and longer wings. **Plumage:** Streaked undertail coverts, wings, and back with whitish edges and streaks ("frosty"). **Adult male** has a red cap, brown moustachial stripe, and pink wash on breast and rump. **Female** and **juvenile** are brown and white, with a lightly patterned head and underparts with fine, crisp streaking. **Similar species:** House Finch (page 182) has a shorter bill with a curved culmen and shorter wings. Male House Finch has a well-defined red bib and eyebrow; female House has heavily streaked underparts and is browner overall. Purple Finch (previous page) has a shorter, slightly more curved bill, shorter wings, and unstreaked undertail coverts. Male Purple Finch is more extensively washed with red (male Cassin's is brightest red on crown); female Purple has a more patterned face and coarser, blurry streaking below.
Voice: Song is a rich, continuous warble. **Calls** include a dry *kee-up* or *tee-dee-yip*.

RANGE Western species. Breeds in open coniferous forest in western mountain ranges. Movements are unpredictable, but in some years, birds are seen in nearby lowlands, especially in spring. Like other "winter finch" species, winter numbers vary from year to year.

FOOD Seeds, buds, and berries, plus some insects. Craves salt, and visits areas with mineral-rich soil.
Feeding: Feeder visitor, mostly in winter. Prefers black-oil sunflower seeds.

NESTING Semicolonial; defends only a 15- to 75-foot territory around its nest. *Location:* Often in a large conifer, usually 30–40 feet up. *Nest:* Loose cup of twigs, weeds, and other dried vegetation. *Eggs:* Usually 4–5; incubated by female for 12–14 days. *Fledging:* Leaves nest at about 14 days.

Common Redpoll
Acanthis flammea, L 5¼" (13 cm)

These attractive finches breed in the far North. They move south in fall, but some years they irrupt farther south. Birds west of the Rockies irrupt less frequently.

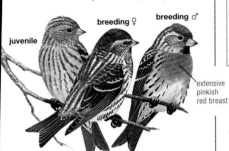

juvenile

breeding ♀

breeding ♂

extensive pinkish red breast

IDENTIFICATION Fairly common. A small "winter finch" with a blocky head, compact body, and deeply notched tail. The short bill is triangular shaped and mostly yellow. In irruption years, flocks frequent trees with winter seeds, such as birches and alders, or roam through weedy fields; some birds show up at feeders, where they are highly prized visitors.
Plumage: Both sexes have a red forehead ("poll") and black chin. **Winter male** has a rosy breast and sides (more intense in summer) and buff flanks with brown streaking. **Winter female** has whitish underparts with buff flanks and more streaking than male (darker in summer).
Similar species: Scarce Hoary Redpoll (not illustrated) breeds and winters even farther north. When seen, it is almost always with Common Redpolls. Differences from Common include: pale rump, unstreaked undertail coverts, smaller bill, faint flank streaks, and paler ("hoary") overall appearance.
Voice: Song combines trills and twittering. **Calls** include a rising *swee-ee-eet* when perched; flight call is a dry, scratchy *chit* or series of *chit* notes.

RANGE Northern species. Breeds in the boreal forest and Arctic tundra scrub. A winter visitor across northern North America (late October–April); unpredictable farther south.

FOOD Winter flocks feed on the ground or in seed-bearing trees. **Feeding:** Feeder visitor. Prefers nyjer and hulled sunflower seeds.

NESTING *Location:* In a low shrub. *Nest:* Untidy cup of fine twigs, grass, and moss. *Eggs:* Usually 4–6; incubated by female for 10–11 days. *Fledging:* Leaves nest at 11–14 days.

winter ♀

buffy flanks with streaks

streaked undertail coverts

winter ♂

pink

Pine Siskin
Spinus pinus, L 5" (13 cm)

The most common of the irruptive "winter finches," at first glance the Pine Siskin looks more like a small, streaky sparrow. Some winters, large numbers of this sociable bird move far to the south and are common at backyard nyjer feeders, where they join the ranks of American Goldfinches.

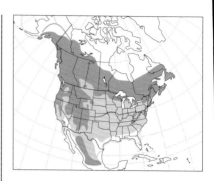

pale wing bars

thin, sharply pointed bill

juvenile

streaked underparts

 IDENTIFICATION Common. A small, goldfinch-size finch with a thin, sharply pointed bill and short, notched tail. In addition to frequenting feeders, winter flocks forage in seed-bearing trees and weedy patches, easily hanging upside down to extract seeds. **Plumage:** Sexes are similar, but female has less yellow on wings and tail. **Adult** is darker above, whitish below, and prominently streaked everywhere, with two whitish wing bars. A yellow wing stripe and the base of the tail are mostly hidden on perched bird, but conspicuous in flight. Rare **"green morph,"** probably male, is extensively yellow on wings, face, and underparts and greenish on back. **Juvenile** has an overall yellow tint, lost by late summer.
Similar species: Streaky female House Finch (page 182) is larger, has a thicker bill and longer tail, and lacks yellow in the wings and tail.

Voice: Song is lengthy jumble of sweet and buzzy notes; similar to that of American Goldfinch, but huskier. Most common **call** is a very buzzy, rising *zreeeeee*; also gives a harsh, descending *chee* in flight.

RANGE Widespread species. Breeds in coniferous and mixed forests of the North and mountainous West. An unpredictable migrant: winter irruptions vary from year to year and place to place, likely due to fluctuating food supply; in nonirruptive years, birds spend the winter mainly within their breeding range.

FOOD Seeds and tree buds; some insects.
Feeding: Common feeder visitor, preferring nyjer and hulled sunflower seeds. Although smaller, it is usually dominant over Purple Finches and American Goldfinches.

prominent yellow wing stripe and yellow patches at base of tail

NESTING Often in loose colonies. *Location:* In a tree, usually 10–40 feet up. *Nest:* Shallow cup of twigs, grass, and bark strips. *Eggs:* Usually 3–4; incubated by female for about 13 days. *Fledging:* Leaves nest at 14–15 days.

NORTHERN FINCHES

Once every few years, seed-bearing trees in northern forests—especially spruce, birch, and hemlock—have a poor seed crop. This can happen for any number of reasons, but one consequence is obvious for birders: seed-eating birds that depend on those cones have no food, and they fly south in search of better conditions.

Such events are called "irruptions," and they can be exciting some years. Suddenly, southern bird feeders may be flooded with northern finches like Pine Siskins, Purple Finches, Evening Grosbeaks, or Common Redpolls, which don't usually occur in your area. A few other seed- and fruit-eating birds may venture south as well, including Red-breasted Nuthatches, Mountain Chickadees, and Bohemian Waxwings.

NOMADS

These birds are nomadic, so they don't necessarily starve in an irruption year. Seed crops always vary, so northern seed-eating birds must follow their food supply. They typically move south in late fall and winter, and return to northern forests in spring. How far they go depends on food availability.

An irruption might happen every two to ten years, but bird ranges also shift. Evening Grosbeaks, common in the Northwest, haven't irrupted in the East in many years.

Winter finch irruptions are not to be confused with raptor irruptions, which are driven by prey availability. Snowy Owls famously push south in some winters, and these owl flights have been linked to productive summers—when more prey is available, owl parents have more chicks per nest, and young owls fly south in search of uncrowded territory. Like the finches, they generally return north in spring.

Common Redpolls and a Pine Siskin face off at a bird feeder.

American Goldfinch
Carduelis tristis, L 5" (13 cm)

Abundant, widespread, and beautiful, the American Goldfinch is a premier backyard bird. In early spring, you can easily observe the slow, patchy progression of feather replacement (molt) in the brownish winter male. It takes a period of weeks (late March–early April) until his transformation into a brilliant yellow-and-black bird is complete. State bird of Iowa, New Jersey, and Washington.

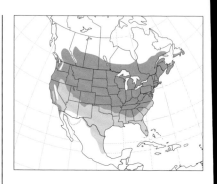

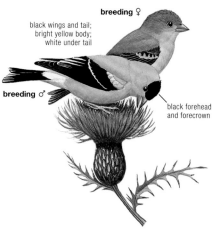

breeding ♀

black wings and tail; bright yellow body; white under tail

breeding ♂

black forehead and forecrown

IDENTIFICATION Common. Small, stocky finch with a short, notched tail. Most backyard birds congregate around feeders, but they are also very attracted to ornamental plantings of composite flowers, such as purple coneflower, black-eyed Susan, and sunflower. Bounds up and down in flight, often giving its distinctive "potato-chip" flight call (*per-chik-o-ree*) as it moves from place to place. Bill is pinkish in summer, dark in winter.
Plumage: All adult birds have white upper-tail and undertail coverts; white wing bars are thin (worn down) in summer, bold (fresh) in winter. **Breeding male** is bright

yellow with a black cap. **Winter adult male** is tan above, pale gray below, with a yellow face and throat. **Breeding female** is olive brown above, yellow below. **Winter female** is drab gray overall, with just a hint of yellow. **Juvenile** (until November) has buff wing markings and rump.
Similar species: Female Lesser Goldfinch (page 190) has yellow undertail coverts, which separates it in all plumages from American Goldfinch; it is also smaller and has a yellow belly, greenish upperparts, and a white patch at base of primaries.
Voice: Song is a lively series of trills, twitters, and *suwee* notes. **Call** is a rising *suwee*; its flight call, *per-chik-o-ree* (sounds like "po-ta-to chip").

The American Goldfinch molts its body feathers twice a year—the bright yellow male of summer molts into a coat of brown feathers in fall.

The American Goldfinch is mostly vegetarian, rarely consuming any insects. Its favorite foods are seeds, often pulled directly from a flower head.

RANGE Widespread species. Inhabits overgrown fields, pastures, and roadsides with shrubs and trees for nesting; often found near watercourses and in well-planted (or weedy) residential areas. Northern breeders migrate south in fall. Spring migration: April–May; fall migration: October–December.

FOOD Mostly seeds; very few insects. Favors seeds of thistles, wild sunflowers, other composite flowers, and many different weeds and grasses. Feeds nestlings a regurgitated mash of seeds with some insects.
Feeding: Very common feeder visitor. Prefers nyjer and hulled sunflower seeds.

NESTING Very late nester in the East (July–August), perhaps timed to coincide with peak of late-summer seed abundance. *Location:* In a vertical fork of a tree or shrub, usually 5–20 feet up. *Nest:* Compact cup of fine grass and plant fibers, often bound with spiderweb and lined with plant down. *Eggs:* Usually 4–6; incubated by female for 12–14 days. *Fledging:* Leaves nest at about 11–17 days.

yellow shoulder; brownish back

prominent wing bars

winter adult ♂

whitish undertail coverts

winter ♀

juvenile

notched tail

Lesser Goldfinch
Carduelis psaltria, L 4½" (11 cm)

This small, social finch is rarely found alone. Groups are often seen along brushy roadsides, particularly where thistles grow in abundance.

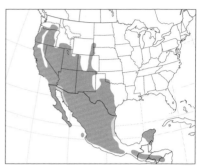

pale yellow underparts

♀

pale ♀

"black-backed" adult ♂

blackish cap contrasts with green back

"green-backed" adult ♂

white wing patch at base of primaries

immature ♂

IDENTIFICATION Common. Very small—smaller than an American Goldfinch—with a short, notched tail. Feeds quietly in weedy fields. Most easily detected when a flock takes flight and birds are calling. The male's white wing patch is prominent in flight.
Plumage: Two subspecies differ in adult male plumage: the **"black-backed"** (from Colorado to Texas) has solidly black upperparts; the **"green-backed"** (Southwest and West Coast) has a black cap but an olive back. **Adult female** is dull olive above and pale yellow below; dullest females are grayer above, paler below. **Immature male** has a blackish forehead.
Similar species: Female American Goldfinch (pages 188–189) is larger, has white undertail coverts, and lacks green tones to upperparts; it has a broad wing bar.

Voice: Song is a rambling, complex jumble of musical phrases and call notes, often including imitations of other species' calls. **Calls** include high, slurred whistles of *tee-yee?* or *tee-yur*.

RANGE Western species; primarily year-round resident. Most common in California and central Texas. Lives in a variety of habitats at different elevations, often in well-planted (or weedy) residential areas. In northern breeding areas, it arrives in April–May and departs in September–October.

FOOD Mostly seeds, tree buds, berries, and some insects. Favors seeds of thistle, purple coneflower, and other composite plants.
Feeding: Feeder visitor. Prefers black "thistle" (nyjer) and sunflower hearts.

NESTING Loosely colonial. *Location:* In a tree or shrub, usually 5–30 feet up. *Nest:* Compact cup of fine grass. *Eggs:* Usually 4–5; incubated by female for about 12 days. *Fledging:* Leaves nest at about 11 days.

SIGHTINGS

	JAN	FEB	MAR	APR	MAY	JUN	JUL	AUG	SEP	OCT	NOV	DEC

TOWHEES & SPARROWS   **Family Passerellidae**

Large family of seed-eating birds that contains many species that frequent backyard feeders. They all have conical bills for cracking open seeds, and most are seen on or near the ground.

Spotted Towhee
Pipilo maculatus, L 7½" (19 cm)

The Spotted and Eastern Towhees were once considered a single species, the "Rufous-sided Towhee."

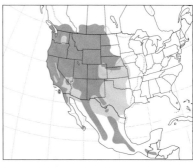

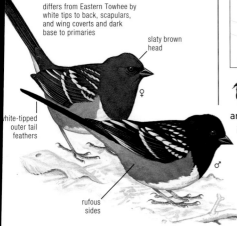

differs from Eastern Towhee by white tips to back, scapulars, and wing coverts and dark base to primaries

slaty brown head

♀

white-tipped outer tail feathers

rufous sides

♂

RANGE Widespread species; casual in the East. Breeds in chaparral, brushy mountain slopes, and riparian thickets. Resident in many locations. Spring **migration:** March–early May; fall migration: mid-September–October.

FOOD Eats insects all year, if available; winter diet includes berries, nuts, and seeds.
Feeding: Visits a platform feeder or takes seeds on the ground.

IDENTIFICATION Common. A large, chesty sparrow with a long tail that recalls a thrasher. Often stays out of sight in thickets or under shrubbery.
Plumage: The long tail has white-tipped outer tail feathers. **Male** has a black hood, ruby red eyes, and black upperparts neatly spotted with white. **Female** is slate brown where the male is black.
Similar species: Eastern Towhee (page 192) lacks the white spots on upperparts.
Voice: Song starts with short whistled notes and ends with a simple, loud, buzzy trill (coastal birds give just the trill).
Call is a scratchy, up-slurred *reee-eh?* or a descending, raspy mewing in the Rockies.

NESTING *Location:* Usually on the ground. *Nest:* Cup of dried leaves and grasses. *Eggs:* Usually 3–4; incubated by female for 12–13 days. *Fledging:* Leaves nest at 8–10 days.

juvenile

streaked

Eastern Towhee
Pipilo erythrophthalmus, L 7½" (19 cm)

Both the Eastern Towhee's song (*drink-your-tea*) and call (*chewink* or *towhee*) are easy to remember. That's very helpful, because this attractive sparrow has a talent for hiding in the underbrush.

milk chocolate upperparts and head

♀

white base to primaries in all plumages

black head and back

white-tipped outer tail feathers

♂

rufous sides

RANGE Widespread species. Is partial to forest edges with dense tangles, overgrown fields, and thickets. Year-round resident in some southern areas. Spring **migration:** March–early May; fall migration: late September–October.

FOOD Eats insects all year, if available; winter diet includes berries, nuts, and seeds.
Feeding: Common at platform feeders or takes seeds scattered on the ground.

NESTING *Location:* Usually on ground. *Nest:* Cup of dried leaves and grasses. *Eggs:* Usually 3–4; incubated by female for 12–13 days. *Fledging:* Leaves nest at 8–10 days.

IDENTIFICATION Common to uncommon. Like the related Spotted Towhee, a large and chesty bird with a long tail that recalls a thrasher. Its noisy foraging under the shrubbery will often alert you to its presence.
Plumage: Very dapper and neatly patterned. A white mark on the wings and white-tipped outer tail feathers are easy to see when a bird flushes. **Male** has a black hood, ruby red eyes, black upperparts, and rufous sides. **Female** is chocolate brown where the male is black. In Florida, adults have pale yellowish eyes.
Similar species: Spotted Towhee (page 191) has white spots on the upperparts. The two species overlap along rivers in the Great Plains and interbreed.
Voice: Full **song** is a loud, ringing *drink-your-tea!* or shortened *drink-tea*.
Calls include an up-slurred *chewink* or *towhee* and, in Florida, a clearer, even-pitched *swee*.

Florida ♂

yellowish white iris

juvenile

streaked

Canyon Towhee
Melozone fusca, L 8" (20 cm)

The Canyon Towhee and its Pacific coast relative the California Towhee (next page) were considered the same species, the "Brown Towhee," until 1989. Both are sedentary birds, and their ranges don't overlap.

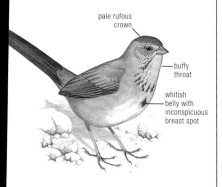

pale rufous crown

buffy throat

whitish belly with inconspicuous breast spot

 RANGE Southwest species; year-round resident. Lives in a variety of arid habitats: desert scrub, dry foothills, canyon slopes, arroyos, and desert-community backyards.

FOOD Mostly seeds. Supplements diet with insects. **Feeding:** Eats black-oil sunflower seeds, milo, or millet at a platform feeder or takes seeds scattered on the ground.

NESTING Nesting behavior not well known. *Location:* In a small tree or shrub, usually 3–12 feet up. *Nest:* Bulky cup of twigs and grasses. *Eggs:* Usually 3–4; incubated by female for 12–13 days. *Fledging:* Leaves nest at 8–10 days.

IDENTIFICATION Common. Large, long-tailed sparrow that sticks to the ground and low bushes. Fairly tame and approachable as it scratches and pecks for food, hopping from place to place. Sometimes becomes very tame around homes, even entering open doors. Usually seen alone or in a pair, occasionally with a small flock of other sparrows. **Plumage:** Plain brownish gray overall; rufous crown sometimes raised into a short crest; and a buff throat encircled by a "necklace" of dark streaks with a "stickpin" breast spot. **Juvenile** is faintly streaked below.
Similar species: Abert's Towhee (not illustrated) is a secretive, desert towhee with warm brown plumage, black face, and pale bill that is also seen in backyards.
Voice: Song opens with a call note, followed by sweet, slurred notes. **Call** is a shrill *chee-yep* or *chedep*.

This hopper feeder is large enough for a Canyon Towhee to perch on with ease.

California Towhee
Melozone crissalis, L 9" (23 cm)

From Southern California to southern Oregon, this simple brown bird enlivens many backyard feeders. A mated pair remains together throughout the year and is often seen foraging side by side or staying in touch by calling back and forth to each other.

IDENTIFICATION Common. Large, long-tailed sparrow that sticks to the ground and low bushes. Fairly tame and approachable as it scratches in the leaf litter or open ground looking for food. Hops from place to place or makes short, jerky flights on short, broad wings. **Plumage:** Very plain; medium-brown overall with a darker tail. Face and breast are suffused with orange-buff and bordered below by short, faint streaks; has a thin, orange-buff eye ring. **Juvenile** is faintly streaked below.
Similar species: Larger, darker brown California Thrasher (not illustrated) has a long downcurved bill and a very long tail, but occurs in similar habitat.
Voice: Song, heard mostly in late afternoon, is a series of *chink* notes strung into a loose accelerating series. **Call** is a sharp *chink,* like some Fox Sparrows.

RANGE West Coast species; year-round resident. Lives in a variety of brushy habitats from coastal lowlands up to about 4,000 feet in the mountains: chaparral, coastal sage, streamside thickets, open woodlands, and shrubby suburban and urban backyards. One of the most sedentary species, rarely moving far from where it nests.

FOOD Mostly seeds. Supplements diet with insects, especially when feeding young. Also feeds on small berries and green shoots.
Feeding: Very common feeder bird, where it is often seen in the company of White-crowned and Golden-crowned Sparrows. Prefers black-oil sunflower seeds, cracked corn, and millet at a platform feeder or seeds scattered on the ground. Vulnerable to free-roaming cats.

NESTING *Location:* In a small tree or shrub, sometimes on a sheltered building ledge, usually 4–12 feet up. *Nest:* Loosely constructed cup of twigs and grasses. *Eggs:* Usually 3–4; incubated by female for about 14 days. *Fledging:* Leaves nest at about 8 days, when still unable to fly well.

juvenile

crown fairly uniform with rest of head

no breast spot

blurry streaks

American Tree Sparrow
Spizella arborea, L 6¼" (16 cm)

Far to the north, in muskeg and brushy tundra, this hardy sparrow raises its family during the Arctic summer. In the fall, it migrates south to spend the winter months in weedy fields, at forest edges, and at backyard feeders, particularly after a heavy snow.

breeding

largest
Spizella

spot

 RANGE Widespread species. Breeds in Alaska and northern Canada. In winter, common in the northern tier of states, but scarce near the southern and western edge of its winter range. Spring **migration:** March–April; fall migration: mid-October–late November.

 FOOD Seeds in winter; mostly insects in summer.
Feeding: Common winter feeder bird in North (mostly in rural areas). Black-oil sunflower seeds and millet are preferred.

IDENTIFICATION Fairly common. Has a bicolored bill—dark above, bright yellow below. During winter, small flocks forage on the ground with juncos and other sparrows, or strip seeds from dried weed stalks. Despite its name, it is not particularly associated with trees, although flushed birds often alight there.
Plumage: Distinct rusty cap and eye line; rusty-striped back; two white wing bars. Underparts are mostly gray, with rufous sides of the breast and buff flanks. Note the central breast spot ("stickpin").
Similar species: Field Sparrow (page 198) is smaller, lacks the breast spot, and has a paler face and pink bill. Chipping Sparrow (next page) is also smaller, lacks the breast spot, and is duller below. Also, compare Song Sparrow (pages 200–201).
Voice: Song begins with several clear notes, followed by a variable, rapid warble; it is heard in late winter, before migration. **Call** is a cheerful, musical *teedle-eet*.

NESTING *Location:* On the ground or low in a dwarf willow. *Nest:* Cup of grasses and moss. *Eggs:* Usually 3–5; incubated by female for 12–13 days. *Fledging:* Leaves nest at about 9–10 days; able to fly 5–6 days later.

In winter, the American Tree Sparrow's central breast spot can be hard to see.

| JAN | FEB | MAR | APR | MAY | JUN | JUL | AUG | SEP | OCT | NOV | DEC |

Chipping Sparrow
Spizella passerina, L 5½" (14 cm)

The Chipping Sparrow ("Chippy") breeds in every mainland U.S. state and Canadian province or territory, except remote Nunavut. Its love of open areas with scattered trees—a good description of many backyards—has made it a well-known and popular bird. The male's loud trilling song is heard all day long in spring and early summer, although some people mistake it for an insect.

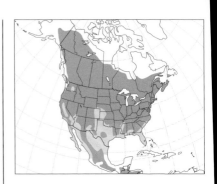

trace of rust on crown

grayish nape

winter adult

often buffy below

gray rump often hidden by wings

1st winter

IDENTIFICATION Common. Slender and well-proportioned sparrow, with a fairly long tail. In fall and winter, small flocks gather on lawns and at bird feeders, often loosely associated with other birds, such as bluebirds, wintering warblers, and other sparrows. If flushed, the whole group flies up to a nearby tree, but soon returns to the ground. The bill is black in summer, dull pinkish in winter.
Plumage: Dark eye line extends from the bill to behind the eye. **Breeding adult** has a chestnut cap, gray face, and white eyebrow; **winter adult** has streaked crown with some rufous, buff face and eyebrow. **First-winter** bird has little or no rufous in crown and a buff (not grayish) breast.

Juvenile (seen into October) has prominently streaked underparts.
Similar species: Field Sparrow (page 198) has a pale head and white eye ring, with no dark line through the eye. American Tree Sparrow (previous page) is larger and more richly colored below and has a breast spot and a sharply two-toned bill.
Voice: Song is a long, rapid trill of dry *chip* notes; all the notes are on one pitch, giving it a mechanical or insectlike quality. **Call** is a high, sharp *tsik* or *seep*.

RANGE Widespread species. Breeds across the continent in wooded suburbs and towns, city parks, golf courses, orchards, and farmland. Wilder breeding locations include open woodlands (especially pine woods), forest edges, and clearings—from lowlands to high in the mountains. Highly migratory, it winters in the southern tier of states and as far north as the Mid-Atlantic. Spring **migration:** mid-March–mid-May; fall migration: late August–early November.

FOOD Eats mostly insects in summer and feeds insects to nestlings. Insects are sometimes taken in midair after a short chase, but most are gleaned from the ground or vegetation. The rest of the

rufous crown and
white supercilium

dark eye line
in all plumages

breeding adult

juvenile

streaky plumage
held into Oct.

year, forages primarily on the ground for seeds of wild grasses and weeds.

Feeding: Common feeder bird, often seen in small flocks. It prefers to take seed scattered on the ground or on a platform feeder. Black-oil sunflower seeds, millet, and cracked corn are good choices.

NESTING *Location:* In a tree, often a conifer, shrub, or vine tangle, usually 3–20 feet up. *Nest:* Rather flimsy cup of grasses and rootlets. *Eggs:* Usually 4; incubated by female for 10–15 days. *Fledging:* Leaves nest at about 9–12 days. *Broods:* 2 per year.

In fall, Chipping Sparrows replace (molt) all their feathers.

In spring, Chipping Sparrows undergo a second molt that replaces only the head feathers.

Field Sparrow
Spizella pusilla, L 5¾" (15 cm)

This pale, wide-eyed sparrow breeds in brushy clearings and overgrown pastures. Its plaintive, whistled song is a delightful accompaniment to spring and summer days in many rural areas of the East.

IDENTIFICATION Common. Medium-size sparrow with a long tail. Easy to overlook in winter, when they are much quieter and infrequent at bird feeders. The stout bill is completely pink, as are the legs.
Plumage: Overall pale; gray and rufous tones combine for a "toasty" appearance (drabber in western part of range). Blank gray face with a bright white eye ring, a rusty patch behind the eye, and a rusty crown. Grayish underparts, suffused with tan on the breast and sides. **Juvenile** has a streaked breast.
Similar species: Chipping Sparrow (previous pages) has a dark eye line, no eye ring, and a darker bill. American Tree Sparrow (page 195) is larger and has a breast spot, and its bill is sharply two toned.
Voice: Song begins with several sweet whistles, then accelerates into a trill (tempo increasing "like a Ping-Pong ball dropped on a tabletop"). **Call** is a clear *chip.*

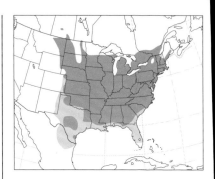

RANGE Widespread species, declining in many areas. Breeds in overgrown pastures, brushy woodlands with clearings, and power-line cuts. Winters in similar habitat and in large, less brushy fields of tall grasses. Some birds are resident; northern breeders move south. Spring **migration:** mid-March–early May; fall migration: mid-October–early November.

FOOD In summer, insects and small seeds. Primarily seeds in winter.
Feeding: Not particularly attracted to feeders. Visitors prefer millet and cracked corn scattered on the ground.

NESTING *Location:* On the ground or low in a small shrub or sapling. *Nest:* Cup woven of grass. *Eggs:* Usually 3–5; incubated by female for 10–12 days. *Fledging:* Leaves nest at about 7–8 days; able to fly 5–6 days later.

grayish median crown stripe

pink bill

buffy streaked breast

juvenile

some rufous color around edge of auricular

winter

breeding

Fox Sparrow
Passerella iliaca, L 7" (18 cm)

Fox Sparrows have plumage that varies from region to region, and the different groups may someday be split into different species.

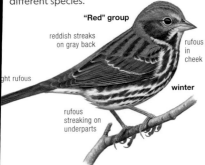

"Red" group
reddish streaks on gray back
rufous in cheek
bright rufous
winter
rufous streaking on underparts

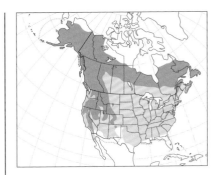

FOOD In summer, mostly insects; otherwise, primarily seeds.
Feeding: Seeds on the ground.

NESTING *Location:* On the ground. *Nest:* Open cup of grass. *Eggs:* Usually 2–4; incubated by female for 12–14 days. *Fledging:* Leaves nest at about 9–11 days.

IDENTIFICATION Common but shy. In the East, only the **"Red Fox Sparrow"** occurs. In the Rockies and Great Basin, only the **"Slate-colored"** occurs, and only in summer when it breeds there. **"Sooty"** breeds in the Pacific Northwest; **"Thick-billed"** (not illustrated) breeds in the mountains of California and Oregon. In winter, all three western types can occur together in the Pacific region.
Plumage: All are large and have underparts heavily marked with triangular spots that merge into a larger spot on the breast.
Similar species: Song Sparrow (pages 200–201) is much smaller and has a bold face pattern and streaked back.
Voice: Song combines sweetly slurred whistles and short trills; trills are harsher in western birds. **Call** of most birds is a smacking *tschup*, like a Brown Thrasher.

RANGE Widespread species. Different types breed in different habitats. In winter, found in undergrowth, also in suburban yards. Spring **migration:** early March–late April; fall migration: late September–late November.

on all "Sooty" subspecies, tail contrasts much less with back than other groups

"Sooty" group

"Slate-colored" group

small bill

all groups have yellow bills for nonbreeding, blue-gray during breeding season

broad dark, slightly blurry, streaking below

Song Sparrow
Melospiza melodia, L 6¼" (16 cm)

If you see a brown, streaky sparrow in your backyard, consider the Song Sparrow first—it's the most widespread and abundant American sparrow. In spring and summer, the male selects an exposed, eye-level perch and proclaims his territory with a loud and musical song.

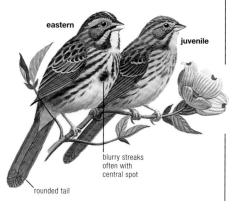

eastern

juvenile

blurry streaks often with central spot

rounded tail

IDENTIFICATION Very common. Medium-size sparrow with a fairly long, rounded tail. Backyard pairs are often quite tame and conspicuous as they move around the shrubby borders and undergrowth. Undulating flight has a jerky quality and the tail is constantly pumped up and down. In areas where they are resident, the male defends his territory year-round. Individual territories are often small, and it is not uncommon for multiple pairs to be present in large backyards with good habitat. In winter, migrant Song Sparrows from farther north may join the resident birds that come to your feeder, but never occur in big flocks. Song Sparrows vary regionally in color and size—more than 30 subspecies occur in the U.S. and Canada, from blackish streaked in coastal California; paler and smaller in the desert Southwest; darker and redder in the Pacific Northwest; and larger and grayer in Alaska—but they still look and sound undeniably like Song Sparrows.

Plumage: Striped face exhibits a dark crown, pale eyebrow, dark line through the eye, and two dark streaks ("whiskers," or more precisely, moustachial and malar stripes) below the eye. The underparts

Each male Song Sparrow has a repertoire of 8 to 10 songs; he usually repeats the same song 5 to 15 times before switching to a new one.

The short, rounded wings of the Song Sparrow make flying through brushy thickets easier.

FOOD Eats mostly insects in spring and summer; feeds insects to nestlings. The rest of the year, forages for seeds and birdseed at feeders and sometimes eats small berries. Often forages by scratching into leaf litter in dense cover; also picks insects from foliage.

Feeding: Common feeder bird, but comes most readily to a feeder placed close to good cover. It prefers seeds scattered on the ground or on a platform feeder. Black-oil sunflower seeds, millet, and cracked corn are good choices.

NESTING *Location:* On the ground or low in a shrub or vine tangle. *Nest:* Open cup of grasses, leaves, and rootlets. *Eggs:* Usually 3–5; incubated by female for 12–14 days. *Fledging:* Leaves nest at about 10–12 days; able to fly 5–6 days later.

are variably streaked on the sides and breast, and the streaking often converges into a central breast spot.

Similar species: Fox Sparrow (page 199) is larger and lacks a boldly striped face. Other common backyard sparrows lack heavily streaked underparts. Lincoln's Sparrow (not illustrated) is smaller and has a buff breast with fine streaking.

Voice: Song is a series of notes with a noticeable trill in the middle or as a final flourish. **Call** is a distinctive *chemp*.

RANGE Widespread species. Breeds across the continent in brushy areas, often near fresh or salt water. Also common around suburban homes, parks, rural hedgerows, farmland, and other altered habitats if there is sufficient shrubbery or brush for nesting and foraging. Northern breeders migrate south, where they winter in similar habitat. Spring **migration:** March–April; fall migration: October–November.

California races are very dark

northwestern races are dark and ruddy

dark malar stripe

southwestern desert races are small and pale

WATCHING SPARROWS

Many bird-watchers pass off sparrows as LBJs—"little brown jobs"—but don't discount this fascinating group of birds. Like an Italian sports car, sparrows reward a lingering, subtle sense of appreciation.

Can anything, after all, be as crisp as the profile of a White-throated Sparrow? Take a good look at those lines, like racing stripes, accented by the little yellow flame in front of each eye. There's a paint job straight from Formula One.

Or consider the Song Sparrow, with its brushed underparts, reminiscent of Monet's field of haystacks. The bird is canvas in motion, each feather its own work of art.

Identifying sparrows is not for dilettantes; the only difference between an expert bird-watcher and a novice is that an expert has misidentified more of these birds.

Anyone—expert or novice—can appreciate the aesthetics of a bird as intricately patterned as a Fabergé egg. The closer you look, the more you see.

MUSIC TO YOUR EARS

Don't forget to listen. In winter, each sparrow has a distinctive call note, packing its whole identity into a single syllable. The best sparrow listeners can separate species by tone, as if picking out a Stradivarius. Then, in spring, these diminutive birds suddenly tilt their heads back and sing, filling field and forest with cascading melodies. Is it language or music? Yes, it is both.

With a sweet, whistled song, the Fox Sparrow makes up for its somewhat drab appearance.

THE FALL OF A SPARROW

Even Shakespeare couldn't resist a bit of sparrowy nuance. "There is a special providence in the fall of a sparrow," quips Hamlet before a duel, musing on his own impending fate. The Prince of Denmark was probably referring to a House Sparrow—but, lacking details, we'll just never know.

The crisp profile of a White-throated Sparrow shows off its racing stripes.

Lark Sparrow
Calamospiza melanocorys, L 7" (18 cm)

The Lark Sparrow is a bird of open spaces. In the mid-1800s, when there was more cleared land in the East, Lark Sparrows colonized the new habitat. Today, most of those open fields are gone, reverted to forest or gobbled up by urban and suburban sprawl, and the Lark Sparrow is retreating to its core range in the Great Plains and the West.

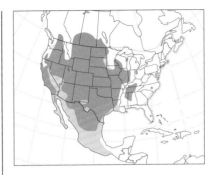

IDENTIFICATION Fairly common. This medium large sparrow has such a distinctive head pattern that, unlike many sparrows, its identification is easy. Lark Sparrows are often seen conspicuously perched along roadsides, on fences, utility lines, and shrubs, or feeding on open ground. In winter and migration, gathers in large flocks.

Similar species: None.

Voice: Song begins with two loud, clear notes, followed by a long jumble of clear notes, trills, and buzzes. **Call** is a soft, sharp *tsip*, often given in a rapid series and frequently delivered in flight.

RANGE Central and western species. Breeds and winters in open areas where grassy areas intermix with trees and shrubs, such as pastures, prairies, hedgerows, roadsides, sagebrush, and desert scrub. Year-round resident in some areas, but the majority vacate their breeding range, moving south into Mexico. Spring **migration:** March–May; fall migration: August–mid-October.

FOOD Weed and grass seeds are the primary food; insects make up about 25 percent of the diet. **Feeding:** Occasional feeder visitor; prefers millet and cracked corn scattered on the ground.

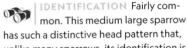

distinctive head pattern; dark breast spot

whitish at base of primaries

juvenile

extensive white in tail

subdued head pattern; streaked below

Plumage: Harlequin face pattern is unique; also note the dark central breast spot. In flight, the long black tail shows bold white corners (similar to an Eastern or Spotted Towhee). **Juvenile** has a subdued face pattern and light streaking on the breast.

NESTING *Location:* Usually on the ground. *Nest:* Cup woven of grass. *Eggs:* Usually 4–5; incubated by female for 11–12 days. *Fledging:* Leaves nest at about 9–12 days.

Harris's Sparrow

Zonotrichia querula, L 7½" (19 cm)

The heartland of North America is where you'll find the Harris's Sparrow—wintering on the Great Plains and breeding in northern Canada.

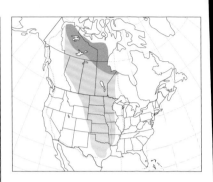

black crown and bib

large pink bill

breeding

Spring **migration:** late March–late May; fall migration: October–early November.

FOOD Insects, seeds, and berries. Winter diet primarily seeds and some berries.
Feeding: Visits feeders in winter.

NESTING *Location:* Breeds at the northern edge of the boreal forest in northern Canada—where there are no conventional backyards. Its nest went undiscovered until 1931!

IDENTIFICATION Fairly common. Large, bigger than a White-crowned Sparrow. Small winter flocks feed on the ground and often mix with more numerous smaller sparrows. Has pink bill and legs.
Plumage: Breeding adult has a mostly black head and gray cheeks. **Winter adult** has an all-black or partially black throat. **Immature** bird has less black on the head and a black whisker mark.
Similar species: Adult male House Sparrow (page 180) has a black bib, but is smaller and lacks the pink bill.
Voice: Song comprises two or three long, pure-toned whistles on the same pitch; rarely heard away from breeding grounds. **Call** is a loud *wink*.

RANGE Great Plains and northern Canada species. Winters in brushy areas on the southern Great Plains.

winter adults

dark postocular spot in all plumages

immature

dark chest patch

brownish flank streaking

White-crowned Sparrow
Zonotrichia leucophrys, L 7" (18 cm)

In many areas this attractive "crowned" sparrow is best known as a winter visitor to backyards—especially along the West Coast, where it is abundant.

brown and light tan head stripes

lower white stripe normally cut off just in front of eye

immature

pinkish bill

adult

Eastern subspecies with dark in front of eye; a similar subspecies breeds in the Rockies and other western mountains

IDENTIFICATION Common. Medium large, flocking sparrow. There are five subspecies with subtle geographic variation. Bill color varies from pinkish to orange to yellow.
Plumage: Adult has bold black and white crown stripes. **Immature** bird has brown and light tan crown stripes. **Juvenile** (seen only in nesting areas) has streaked underparts.
Similar species: White-throated Sparrow (next page) has a contrasting white throat and a yellow spot in front of the eye. Immature Golden-crowned Sparrow (page 207) on the West Coast has grayish bill and an indistinct crown pattern.
Voice: Song—heard all winter—is made up of mournful whistles, followed by jumbled notes and ending in a buzz or trill. **Calls** include a loud *pink* and a sharp *tseep*.

RANGE Widespread species. Breeds in Canadian tundra, in the western mountains, and along the West Coast north of Santa Barbara. Most birds are highly migratory, but some along the West Coast are resident. Spring **migration:** mid-March–mid-May; fall migration: September–mid-November.

FOOD In summer, eats mostly insects; primarily seeds the rest of the year; sometimes berries or buds. **Feeding:** Scattered seed on the ground.

NESTING *Location:* Usually on the ground or low in a bush. *Nest:* Open cup of grass and weed stems. *Eggs:* Usually 4–5; incubated by female for about 12 days. *Fledging:* Leaves nest at about 8–10 days.

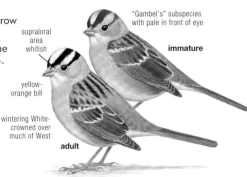

"Gambel's" subspecies with pale in front of eye

immature

supraloral area whitish

yellow-orange bill

wintering White-crowned over much of West

adult

White-throated Sparrow
Zonotrichia albicollis, L 6¾" (17 cm)

The two color morphs of this species behave differently—which is almost unheard of in the bird world. Tan-striped birds are nonaggressive and attentive parents; white-striped birds are socially dominant and poor parents. Mixed-morph pairs that strike the right balance of aggression and nurturing are most successful.

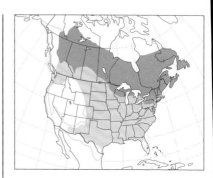

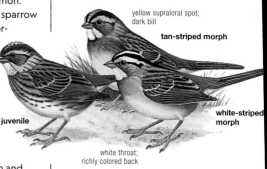

yellow supraloral spot; dark bill

tan-striped morph

white-striped morph

juvenile

white throat; richly colored back

IDENTIFICATION Common. Medium-large woodland sparrow that feeds on the ground along forested edges, darting for cover if disturbed. It may reemerge in response to pishing and can occur in large flocks in winter. **Plumage:** Conspicuous and strongly outlined white throat; also, a yellow spot in front of the eye. **White-striped morph** has clean black and white head stripes. **Tan-striped morph** has tan and dark brown head stripes, with duller, dingy-looking plumage on the face, throat, and underparts. **Juvenile** birds have heads like the tan-striped morph and a streaked breast.
Similar species: White-crowned Sparrow (previous page) lacks the contrasting white throat and the yellow spot in front of the eye.
Voice: Song—heard all winter—is a thin, mournful whistle, generally two single notes followed by three triple notes (*pure sweet Canada Canada Canada*). **Calls** include a sharp *pink* and a drawn-out, lisping *tseep.*

RANGE Widespread species. Very common to abundant in the East in winter; uncommon to rare along the West Coast. Winters in brushy woodland thickets, forest edges, wooded suburban neighborhoods, and urban parks. Breeds in coniferous and mixed forests, often in dense brush near water. Spring **migration:** late March–mid-May; fall migration: mid-September–early November.

FOOD In summer, eats mostly insects; primarily seeds the rest of the year, or sometimes berries or tree buds. **Feeding:** Scattered seeds on the ground or at a platform feeder. White-striped adults are dominant.

NESTING *Location:* Usually on the ground, concealed by shrubbery. *Nest:* Open cup of grass and weed stems. *Eggs:* Usually 4–5; incubated by female for 11–14 days. *Fledging:* Leaves nest at about 8–9 days; able to fly well about a week later.

Golden-crowned Sparrow
Zonotrichia atricapilla, L 7" (18 cm)

A West Coast specialty that breeds in western Canada and Alaska but winters from Vancouver to San Diego in brushy thickets and in shrubby backyards.

IDENTIFICATION Fairly common. Medium-large woodland sparrow. In winter, it is often found with flocks of White-crowned Sparrows, though it favors denser cover. Although close in size, the Golden-crowned is obviously larger and heavier set than the White-crowned.
Plumage: Breeding adult has an extensive black cap with a bright yellow forecrown and gray face. **Winter adult** has dusky brown cap with dingy yellow forecrown and browner face. **Immature's** face is very plain brown, with just a tinge of dull yellow on the forecrown (can be hard to see).
Similar species: Immature White-crowned Sparrow (page 205) is similar, but paler overall, with a light tan eyebrow, central crown stripe, and paler bill.
Voice: Song—a series of three or more plaintive, whistled notes *(oh dear me)* —is heard year-round. **Calls** include a soft *tseep* and a flat *tsick*.

RANGE West Coast species. Winters in dense brush, forest thickets, chaparral, backyard gardens, and urban parks. Breeds in mountain thickets at the tree line and also in alder and willow patches in coastal Alaska. Entire population is migratory. Spring **migration:** late March–mid-May; fall migration: late September–early November.

FOOD Not a seed specialist; eats a varied diet of seeds, buds, berries, and insects throughout the year.
Feeding: Scattered seeds on the ground or at a platform feeder.

NESTING *Location:* Usually on the ground, concealed by shrubbery. *Nest:* Bulky cup of grass and weed stems. *Eggs:* Usually 3–5; incubated by female for 11–12 days. *Fledging:* Leaves nest at 9–11 days; probably able to fly well about a week later.

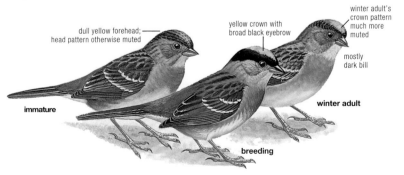

dull yellow forehead; head pattern otherwise muted

yellow crown with broad black eyebrow

winter adult's crown pattern much more muted

mostly dark bill

immature

winter adult

breeding

Dark-eyed Junco
Junco hyemalis, L 6¼" (16 cm)

Little flocks of these dapper sparrows—known to many as "snowbirds"—show up at backyard feeders across the continent as winter weather is about to set in. Juncos can also be summer breeding birds, for instance, throughout New England, across the mountainous West, and along much of the Pacific coast. Their plumage varies geographically more than any other American sparrow—the juncos in the East look quite different from those out West.

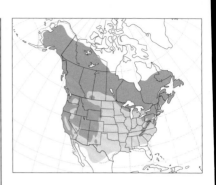

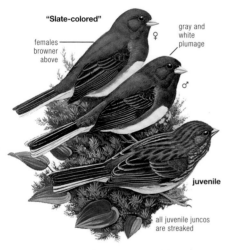

"Slate-colored"

females browner above

gray and white plumage

♀

♂

juvenile

all juvenile juncos are streaked

IDENTIFICATION Very common. There are two useful field marks that almost all juncos share: a pale pink bill, and flashing white outer tail feathers. The three most common subtypes are the "Slate-colored Junco" in Alaska and east of the Rockies; "Oregon Junco" in the northern Rockies and farther west; and "Gray-headed Junco" in the southern Rockies. Two other types with small western ranges are illustrated but not described: the "White-winged" (breeds in mountains of Wyoming, South Dakota, and Montana) and

"Pink-sided" (breeds mainly in central Montana and northern Wyoming). The "Red-backed" (not illustrated) breeds from mountains of central Arizona to western Texas.

Plumage: "Slate-colored" male is uniformly dark gray above and on breast, and white below; female is paler and brownish gray above. **"Oregon"** male has a slate black hood and rufous-brown back and sides; female has a gray hood. **"Gray-headed"** has a gray hood, gray underparts, and a neat rufous back. All **juveniles** are brown and streaky, but have white outer tail feathers.

Similar species: Distinctive, but complicated by regional varieties—in the Rocky Mountain states, different varieties mix together in winter. "Slate-colored" is uncommon to rare in the West.

Voice: Song is most often a simple trill, on

dark lores

pale gray head and underparts

pale bill

rufous back

"Gray-headed"

Although rare, birds with aberrant plumages, like this mostly white junco, are occasionally seen.

"Slate-colored" ♂

all subspecies have
white outer tail feathers

migration: March–April; fall migration: October–November.

FOOD Eats mostly insects in spring and summer, and feeds insects to nestlings. The rest of the year, forages for seeds and eats small berries. **Feeding:** One of the most common species at winter bird feeders. It prefers seeds scattered on the ground or on a platform feeder. Hulled sunflower seeds, millet, and cracked corn are good bets.

NESTING *Location:* Usually on the ground, sheltered by rocks or vegetation. *Nest:* Open cup of fine twigs, leaves, and rootlets. *Eggs:* Usually 3–5; incubated by female for 12–13 days. *Fledging:* Leaves nest at 9–13 days.

one pitch; it is also heard in winter. **Calls** include a sharp *dit* and rapid twittering, often heard in flight.

RANGE Widespread species. Breeds across the continent in a wide variety of forested habitats with open areas for foraging. Most populations are migratory, particularly the "Slate-colored." Small flocks of 10–30 birds stay together through the winter, concentrated around open areas with nearby trees, where they often mix with other sparrows and finches. Spring

grayish hood ♀

"Oregon"

blackish hood

buffy rufous sides

♂

faint white tips to coverts   "White-winged"

♂

bluish gray hood and dark lores

♂

broad pinkish buff sides and flanks

"Pink-sided"

BLACKBIRDS, GRACKLES, & ORIOLES   Family Icteridae

Large New World family of medium to large songbirds with sharply pointed bills. Plumage varies from all black to brilliant yellows and oranges.

Eastern Meadowlark
Sturnella magna, L 9½" (24 cm)

In spring, the male Eastern Meadowlark defends his few acres of meadow by singing from a conspicuous fence post or roadside bush.

 IDENTIFICATION Common, but decreasing due to habitat loss. A robin-size, chunky songbird with a short tail and long, pointed bill. White tail feathers are seen when a bird takes flight. Foraging is done on the ground. **Plumage:** Black V-shaped breast band on bright yellow underparts; upperparts are cryptically patterned. Head has bold stripes. **"Lilian's Meadowlark,"** a southwestern desert-grasslands subspecies, is much paler above and has more white in the tail. **Juvenile** has streaks on the breast. **Similar species:** Yellow of throat on Eastern does not extend up onto the face as in Western Meadowlark (opposite). **Voice: Song** is a clear, whistled *see-you see-yeereoo;* sings in winter. Distinctive **call** is a high, buzzy *drzzt,* given as a rapid chatter in flight.

spring

V-shaped breast band

extensive white

 RANGE Eastern and southwestern species. Inhabits native grasslands, old pastures, roadsides, and other open areas. Northern breeders move south for winter. Spring **migration:** March–April; fall migration: mostly in October.

more richly colored above than Western with stronger head pattern

fall

juvenile

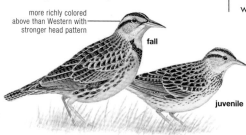

 FOOD Insects, especially grasshoppers and crickets, in summer; mostly weed seeds and grain in fall and winter.

NESTING *Location:* On the ground, in dense grass. *Nest:* Cup of grass with a domed roof woven into surrounding grass and a large side entrance. *Eggs:* Usually 3–5; incubated by female for 13–15 days. *Fledging:* Leaves nest at 11–12 days, when able to run but not fly.

Western Meadowlark
Sturnella neglecta, L 9½" (24 cm)

An emblematic bird of the wide-open western landscape. In the Great Plains and upper Midwest, its range overlaps that of the Eastern Meadowlark. Even though the two species look very similar, they sing different songs and rarely interbreed. State bird of Kansas, Montana, Nebraska, North Dakota, Oregon, and Wyoming.

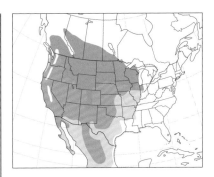

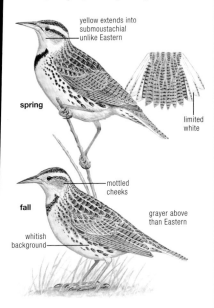

yellow extends into submoustachial —unlike Eastern

spring

limited white

—mottled cheeks

fall

grayer above than Eastern

whitish background—

song and call. Eastern (except "Lilian's") also has darker upperparts, less yellow in the face, paler cheeks, and more white in the tail (especially "Lilian's Meadowlark"); Western looks shorter legged, favors more sparsely vegetated fields, and flies with less rapid wing beats.
Voice: Long, melodious **song** starts off with several clear whistles and ends with complex gurgling and bubbling notes. **Call** is a blackbird-like *chuck*.

IDENTIFICATION Common. A robin-size, chunky songbird with a short tail and long, pointed bill. Behavior and structure very similar to Eastern Meadowlark.
Plumage: Black V-shaped breast band on bright yellow underparts; upperparts are cryptically patterned. Head with bold stripes; yellow of throat extends higher up onto the face than in Eastern Meadowlark. **Juvenile** has streaks on the breast.
Similar species: Eastern Meadowlark (opposite) has a diagnostically different

RANGE Western and midwestern species. Inhabits dry rangelands, native grasslands, roadsides, large pastures, desert grasslands, and, in winter, other open areas such as croplands, feedlots, large lawns, and golf courses. Northern breeders move south for winter. Spring **migration:** March–April; fall migration: September–October.

FOOD Insects, especially grasshoppers and crickets, in summer; mostly weed seeds and grain in fall and winter.

NESTING *Location:* On the ground, in tall grass. *Nest:* Cup of grass with a domed roof woven into surrounding grass and a tunnel side entrance. *Eggs:* Usually 3–5; incubated by female for 13–15 days. *Fledging:* Leaves nest at 10–12 days, when able to run but not fly.

Orchard Oriole
Icterus spurius, L 7¼" (18 cm)

The Orchard Oriole is North America's smallest oriole. Seen flitting through the shrubbery or gleaning insects in the treetops, an olive-and-yellow female can be reminiscent of a warbler.

IDENTIFICATION Fairly common. A small oriole—much smaller than a Baltimore Oriole—with a relatively short tail and a thin, picklike, downcurved bill with a bluish base. Actively forages in shrubs and deciduous trees, gleaning insects and sometimes probing flowers for nectar; often flicks its tail sideways. Is loosely territorial; in ideal habitat, several pairs may nest in the same tree.
Plumage: Adult male has a black hood and upperparts, with rich chestnut underparts (can look all dark in poor light). **Female** is olive green above, yellow below with two crisp white wing bars. **First-spring male** has a neat black bib and lores, but otherwise resembles female; sings like an adult male.
Similar species: Larger, stockier female Baltimore Oriole (page 215) has orangish underparts and a longer, heavier bill. All vireos and warblers are smaller and have shorter tails. Hooded Oriole (opposite) is larger with a longer bill.
Voice: Song is a short series of musical whistles with raspy notes, down-slurred at the end. **Calls** include a blackbird-like *chuck* and rapid chattering.

RANGE Eastern and midwestern species; summer resident. Favors forest edges and shade trees in suburbs, farms, and shelterbelts. Winters from Mexico to northern South America. Spring **migration:** late March–mid-May;

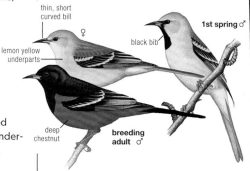

thin, short curved bill

♀

lemon yellow underparts

black bib

1st spring ♂

deep chestnut

breeding adult ♂

fall migration: mid-July–early September. Adult males are gone by early August.

FOOD Insects, spiders, fruits, and nectar. All ages shift to a fruit-based diet by the end of July, prior to migration. Usually forages lower than Baltimore Orioles and Bullock's Orioles.
Feeding: Occasionally visits hummingbird feeders and takes offerings of cut fruit.

NESTING *Location:* On the outer branches of a tree, 10–50 feet up; sometimes in loose colonies. *Nest:* Hanging cup about 4 inches long, attached to a forked branch and woven of grasses and long plant fibers; entered from the top. *Eggs:* Usually 4–6; incubated by female for 12–14 days. *Fledging:* Leaves nest at 11–14 days.

Hooded Oriole
Icterus cucullatus, L 8" (20 cm)

This striking oriole has benefited from the extensive planting of fan palms—a favorite nest location—in residential and urban areas of California and the Southwest.

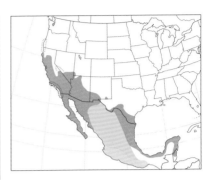

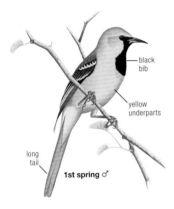

black bib

yellow underparts

long tail

1st spring ♂

 IDENTIFICATION Common. A slender, long-tailed oriole with a relatively thin, noticeably downcurved bill with a bluish base.
Plumage: Adult male is deep yellow (orange in Texas) with a black face and throat. **Female** is olive above, yellowish below (orange tinted in Texas). **First-spring male** has a black face and throat. **Similar species:** Stockier female Bullock's Oriole (next page) has a grayish-white belly and straighter bill. Orchard Oriole (opposite) is smaller with a shorter bill.
Voice: Song is a rapid series of jumbled whistles and short chatters. **Calls** include a rising, whistled *wheet* (loud and strident in males) and rapid chattering.

RANGE Primarily western species; summer resident. Commonly nests in ornamental fan palms and shade trees around suburban yards. Winters in Mexico and Belize. Spring **migration:** mid-March–April; fall migration: early August–mid-September.

 FOOD Insects, spiders, fruits, and nectar from flowering trees.
Feeding: Often visits hummingbird feeders and takes offerings of cut fruit.

NESTING *Location:* In a shade tree, palm, or shrub, 10–45 feet up. *Nest:* Suspended cup deftly woven of grasses and plant fibers, entered from the top. *Eggs:* Usually 4; incubated by female for about 13 days. *Fledging:* Leaves nest at about 14 days.

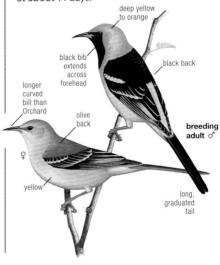

deep yellow to orange

black bib extends across forehead

black back

longer curved bill than Orchard

olive back

breeding adult ♂

♀

yellow

long, graduated tail

Bullock's Oriole
Icterus bullockii, L 8¼" (21 cm)

The striking adult male Bullock's Oriole looks obviously different from its eastern counterpart, the Baltimore Oriole, but from 1973 to 1995, the two species were considered the same species, called the "Northern Oriole." Their ranges overlap in a narrow corridor on the Great Plains, where they interbreed.

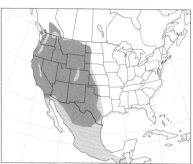

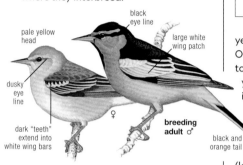

pale yellow head

black eye line

large white wing patch

dusky eye line

dark "teeth" extend into white wing bars

♀

breeding adult ♂

black and orange tail

yellowish below. Fall immature Baltimore Oriole (opposite) can look very similar to Bullock's, but is orangish (never lemon yellow) and lacks the dusky eye line, and its white upper wing bar is smooth and broad (not serrated).

Voice: Song is a mix of whistles and harsher notes. **Calls** include a harsh *cheh* and dry chattering (lower and slower than Hooded's).

IDENTIFICATION Common. The widespread "orange oriole" of the West. Stocky, with a relatively short tail and straight, pointed bill. Actively forages from low in shrubs to high in leafy treetops.

Plumage: Adult male is orange with a black eye line, crown, and chin stripe; black wings with a large white patch. **Female** and **immature** birds have a gray back, grayish white belly, and dull lemon yellow head, breast, and tail. Both show some trace of a dark eye line; upper wing bar has serrated ("toothed") pattern. **First-spring male** has a black chin and eye line; more orange than female.

Similar species: Female Hooded Oriole (page 213) is more slender, has a thinner, downcurved bill and longer tail, and is olive above and completely

black lores and chin

1st ♂ spring

RANGE Western species; mostly summer resident. Breeds in open woodland and where shade trees grow. Winters primarily in Mexico, with a few in coastal Southern California. Spring **migration:** mid-March–early May; fall migration: mid-July–mid-September.

FOOD Insects, spiders, fruits, and nectar.
Feeding: Visits hummingbird feeders and takes offerings of cut fruit or jelly.

NESTING *Location:* In a tree or shrub, usually 10–20 feet up. *Nest:* Hanging pouch about 4–5 inches long, suspended from a forked branch and woven of long plant fibers; entered from the top. *Eggs:* Usually 4–5; incubated by female for 11–14 days. *Fledging:* Leaves nest at about 14 days.

SIGHTINGS

JAN   FEB   MAR   APR   MAY   JUN   JUL   AUG   SEP   OCT   NOV   DEC

Baltimore Oriole
Icterus galbula, L 8¼" (21 cm)

This "meteor of birds," as Emily Dickinson described the stunning male Baltimore Oriole, breeds throughout much of the East. State bird of Maryland.

no eye line

fall immature

smooth wing bar

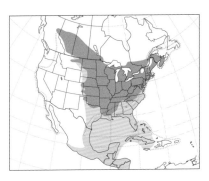

 IDENTIFICATION Common. The "orange oriole" of the East. Stocky, with a relatively short tail and straight, pointed bill. Actively forages high in the canopy.
Plumage: Adult male is bright orange with a black hood and back; orange shoulder bar. **Adult female** is pale orange below and has two white wing bars and a dull orange tail; some have an almost solidly dark hood and back (like male), but most have dusky orange to olive faces and backs. Most **immature females** are dull and have gray on their belly.
Similar species: Female Orchard Oriole (page 212) is much smaller and more slender, greenish above and completely yellow below. See Bullock's Oriole (opposite) for differences between fall immature birds.
Voice: Song is a sweet, flutelike series of notes. **Calls** include a rich *hew-li* and a series of rattles.

RANGE Eastern species; mostly summer resident. Breeds in deciduous woodlands and where shade trees grow, including residential areas. Winters primarily in Central

and South America, with small numbers in the Southeast. Spring **migration:** early April–late May; fall migration: late August–early October.

FOOD Insects, berries, and nectar.
Feeding: Visits hummingbird feeders and takes offerings of cut fruit and jelly.

NESTING *Location:* In a tall tree, near the end of a drooping branch, usually 20–30 feet up. *Nest:* Hanging pouch about 4–6 inches long, suspended from a forked branch and woven of long plant fibers; entered from the top. *Eggs:* Usually 4–5; incubated by female for 12–14 days. *Fledging:* Leaves nest at 12–14 days.

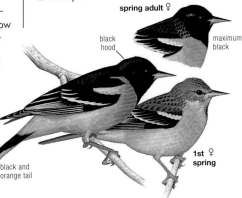

spring adult ♀

black hood

maximum black

black and orange tail

1st ♀ spring

Bronzed Cowbird
Molothrus aeneus, L 8¾" (22 cm)

Like its close relative, the better known Brown-headed Cowbird, the Bronzed Cowbird is a brood parasite, laying its eggs in other birds' nests.

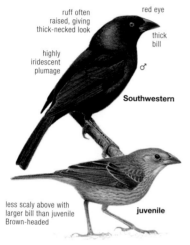

ruff often raised, giving thick-necked look
red eye
thick bill
highly iridescent plumage
Southwestern
♂

less scaly above with larger bill than juvenile Brown-headed
juvenile

Voice: Male's **song** is a series of odd, squeaky gurgles. **Call** is a rasping *chuck*.

RANGE South Texas and southwestern species. Inhabits open woodlands and suburban lawns. In winter, joins large flocks of other blackbirds around feedlots. **Migration** is not well known: there are spring movements in Texas in March, with southbound movements in September. Some winter in southern Louisiana and, increasingly, in Florida.

FOOD Seeds, grain, and some insects.
Feeding: Will visit feeders.

NESTING No nest and no parental care. Brood parasite of many different species—including jays, cardinals, sparrows, and orioles—which raise the cowbird's young. Usually 1 egg is laid in a nest and incubation takes 10–13 days.

IDENTIFICATION Common. Medium-size but heavyset blackbird, about the size of a Red-winged Blackbird. Has a thick-based bill, a thick neck ruff (male only), and red eyes. In spring, the male's bizarre courtship display includes strutting and bowing with his neck ruff expanded, interspersed with hovering flights above the female's head.
Plumage: Male is black with a bronzy gloss, becoming strongly blue-glossed on wings and tail. **Female** is brownish black (in Texas) or grayish (farther west); plumage is not glossy. **Juvenile** is dark brown (in Texas) to grayish and lightly streaked (farther west) and has dark eyes.
Similar species: Smaller Brown-headed Cowbird (opposite) has dark eyes and a shorter, smaller bill. Female Brewer's Blackbird (page 219) is darker brown and has dark eyes and a thinner, more pointed bill.

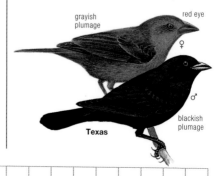

grayish plumage
red eye
♀

blackish plumage
♂
Texas

Brown-headed Cowbird
Molothrus ater, L 7½" (19 cm)

This pariah of the bird world is a brood parasite—it lays its eggs in other birds' nests to be raised by the hosts (see next page). Once a more restricted species, our fragmented agricultural and suburban landscapes have allowed it to spread across the continent. Its impact on many nesting songbirds can be substantial—a single female may lay 40 eggs per season.

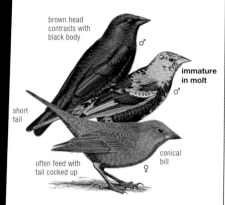

brown head contrasts with black body ♂

immature in molt ♂

short tail

often feed with tail cocked up

conical bill ♀

 IDENTIFICATION Common to abundant. This small, compact blackbird—about the size of a large sparrow—has a stout, sharp-tipped bill and a short tail. It usually feeds on the ground, typically walking around with its tail cocked up. In spring, the male conspicuously displays to and chases females; after mating, the female lurks at the forest's edge looking for nests to host her eggs. **Plumage: Male** is black with a greenish gloss and dark brown hood. **Female** is grayish brown above, paler below. **Juvenile** is paler than female, with pale scalloping on upperparts and lightly streaked below; molting males have patches of black plumage. **Similar species:** Larger Bronzed Cowbird (opposite) has red eyes (adults) and a much heavier bill. Female House Finch

(page 182) and female Red-winged Blackbird (page 220) are similar to juvenile. **Voice:** Male's **song** is a squeaky gurgling. **Calls** include a harsh rattle and squeaky whistles.

RANGE Widespread species. Inhabits open grassland with scattered trees, including woodland edges, fields, pastures, and residential areas; avoids unbroken forest. In winter, joins large flocks of starlings and other blackbirds. Northern breeders move south for winter. Spring **migration:** mid-March–mid-April; fall migration: August–October.

FOOD Seeds, grain, and some insects. **Feeding:** Will visit feeders. If cowbirds visit your feeders in spring and summer, consider taking them down rather than aiding this species.

NESTING No nest and no parental care. Brood parasite of many different species—including warblers, vireos, flycatchers, and sparrows—which raise the cowbird's young. Usually 1 egg is laid in a nest and incubation takes 11–12 days. The young cowbird develops very rapidly, leaving the nest at about 10 days and fed by the host parent for an additional 2 weeks.

UNDERSTANDING COWBIRDS

Few birds are so universally scorned as the Brown-headed Cowbird, simply because it lays eggs in other birds' nests and expects them to bring up the babies. By human standards, this is totally not OK—imagine secretly dumping your infant at a complete stranger's house. Cowbirds, accordingly, are considered lazy, unfair, trashy, ugly, offensive, indecorous interlopers.

But this reputation does a disservice to cowbirds, who are actually quite clever. Maybe we should not judge them by our morals, and instead value these birds on their own terms.

FOSTER PARENTS

Leaving your egg to be raised by another bird might seem easy, but this strategy requires work. Over the course of a season, a female cowbird might lay several dozen eggs. For each one, she must locate another bird's nest at the proper stage of incubation, then slip in unnoticed to deposit her egg. She can lay that egg in less than a minute, while it takes most birds 20 minutes to an hour to lay one.

Even so, only about 3 percent of cowbird eggs survive past the nestling stage. Some birds, like Yellow Warblers, construct a new nest over the top of the old one when they spot a foreign egg in their clutch. Others will abandon their nest and start over somewhere else. And some species, like thrashers and catbirds, toss the cowbird egg out on sight.

Cowbirds lay their eggs in other birds' nests, leaving them for other parents—like this Yellow Warbler—to rear.

YOUNG COWBIRDS

How does a cowbird chick know it's a cowbird, if it is raised by another species? Within a critical time period after it leaves the nest, the young cowbird must seek out other cowbirds to flock with, apparently by using some kind of innate directions. If the youngster doesn't interact with other cowbirds within a few months, it risks imprinting on whatever bird raised it—which means it will never find a mate, and won't pass on its genes to the next generation.

So even parasites like cowbirds have to work hard to survive and reproduce—and young cowbirds must make an effort to learn how to sing, eat, and act like cowbirds.

Brewer's Blackbird
Euphagus cyanocephalus, L 9" (23 cm)

Historically, Brewer's Blackbird was more of a western species, but over the past hundred years, it has pioneered new breeding territory to the northeast. From an ecological standpoint, this species replaces the Common Grackle, which is so common in the East.

males have yellow eyes

dark eye

♂

glossy

♀

grayish brown

wings uniformly dark

immature ♂

glossy, and in fall and winter it has a bold face pattern and feathers tipped broadly with rust.
Voice: Song is a wheezy, unmusical *que-ee* or *k-seee.* Typical call is a harsh *check.*

IDENTIFICATION Very common in many western locations. A slim blackbird that forages on the ground, walking with an alert, upright stance or probing the soil with its tail elevated. Occurs in a large winter flock with other species, such as cowbirds and Red-winged Blackbirds. Eyes are bright yellow in male, dark in female.
Plumage: Male is black, with strong purple iridescence on the head and greenish iridescence on the body. **Female** is a dull brownish gray. **Immature male** is grayish brown, like female, but usually has buff feather edges on the back and breast.
Similar species: Common Grackle (page 222) is larger and has a much longer tail; smaller Brown-headed Cowbird (page 217) has smaller, thicker bill and shorter tail; and female Red-winged Blackbird (next page) is streaked. Similar Rusty Blackbird (not illustrated) is uncommon in the East in fall and winter; its dark plumage is not

RANGE Mostly western species. Inhabits a wide variety of open habitats, from city sidewalks and suburban lawns to open woodlands and mountain meadows. In winter, large flocks congregate around agricultural operations. **Migration** is poorly understood, and wintering movements are somewhat nomadic, perhaps related to snow cover.

FOOD Insects, seeds, and berries; more insects in summer, more seeds and grains in winter.
Feeding: Will visit feeders.

NESTING *Location:* Usually in a tree, from 20 to 40 feet up. *Nest:* Bulky cup of twigs, grasses, and other dried vegetation. *Eggs:* Usually 4–6; incubated by female for 12–14 days. *Fledging:* Leaves nest at 13–14 days.

Red-winged Blackbird
Agelaius phoeniceus, L 8¾" (22 cm)

In northern areas, the male Red-winged Blackbird's song—*konk-la-ree*—signals the end of winter, even if the marsh he's staking claim to is just starting to thaw.

IDENTIFICATION Common to abundant. A stocky, short-tailed blackbird that forages on the ground, sometimes in immense winter flocks. The male's red shoulders are striking when he's singing and displaying, but largely hidden otherwise.
Plumage: Male is glossy black, with red shoulder patches broadly tipped in golden yellow. **Female** is dark brown above, heavily streaked below, and often orangish on face and throat. **First-year male**'s body is heavily scalloped with warm brown.
Similar species: Male Tricolored Blackbird (not illustrated) of California has a white border to the red shoulder patch; female has a blackish belly. Juvenile Brown-headed Cowbird (page 217) is smaller, with a thicker bill.

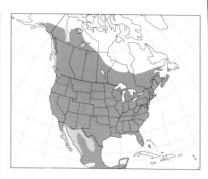

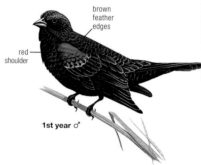

brown feather edges

red shoulder

1st year ♂

Voice: Song is a liquid, gurgling *konk-la-ree*, ending in a trill. **Call** is a flat *chack*.

RANGE Widespread species. In winter, large flocks (often including grackles, cowbirds, and starlings) sometimes roost in suburban neighborhoods. Spring **migration:** early February–early April; fall migration: September–November.

FOOD Insects, seeds, and berries, mostly grain in winter. **Feeding:** Will visit feeders.

NESTING Semicolonial. *Location:* Usually woven into marsh vegetation, from 3 to 15 feet up. *Nest:* Open cup of grass and reeds. *Eggs:* Usually 3–4; incubated by female for 11–13 days. *Fledging:* Leaves nest at 11–14 days.

distinct pale supercilium

back feathers edged buff

many with orangish throat

streaked belly against pale background color

adult ♀

red shoulders most visible when singing

adult ♂

| JAN | FEB | MAR | APR | MAY | JUN | JUL | AUG | SEP | OCT | NOV | DEC |

Great-tailed Grackle

Quiscalus mexicanus, L male 18" (46 cm);
female 15" (38 cm)

Twenty years ago, the Great-tailed Grackle was rare over most of California, but now it's common in the southern half of the state. The species continues to spread north and west, thanks to urbanization and irrigation.

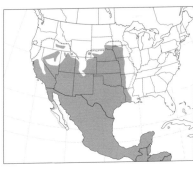

juvenile

long bill

shorter tail

very long, keel-shaped tail

flat crown and pale eye

♀

purple gloss

♂

Grackle (not illustrated) overlaps with Great-tailed on the Texas-Louisiana coast; Boat-taileds there have dark eyes.
Voice: Song is a loud series of whistles, trills, fast ratchet-like clacks, and other weird sounds. Most common **call** is a low-pitched *chuck.*

RANGE Widespread species. Inhabits farmlands, prairies, wetlands; also common in developed areas. **Migration** is not well understood; northern breeders usually move south for winter.

IDENTIFICATION Common to abundant. A large grackle with a very long, keel-shaped tail and piercing yellow eyes. Flocks often gather in town centers and city parks well after dark, proclaiming their presence with a cacophony of sound.

Plumage: Male is glossy black. **Female** is smaller and shorter tailed than male; dark brown above and cinnamon buff below. **Juvenile** has dark eyes and shows diffuse streaking below.

Similar species: Common Grackle (next page) is much smaller, with a shorter tail and shorter, thicker bill; gloss on head contrasts with body. Similar Boat-tailed

FOOD Omnivorous. Diet includes insects, small animals, bird eggs, plant matter, and human refuse.
Feeding: Will visit feeders, whether or not you want them. Considered a crop pest in some areas and a nuisance bird by many urbanites.

NESTING Colonial. *Location:* In dense shrubs, a low tree, or marsh vegetation (especially in West), usually 2–20 feet up. *Nest:* Bulky, woven cup of grass and reeds. *Eggs:* Usually 3–4; incubated by female for 13–14 days. *Fledging:* Leaves nest at 12–15 days.

Common Grackle
Quiscalus quiscula, L 12½" (32 cm)

Up close, the Common Grackle is a stunning species whose plumage shimmers with iridescent blue, purple, and bronze tones, set off by striking yellow eyes and a long, flared tail. However, it causes extensive crop damage, gathers in huge, noisome, winter flocks, and is therefore often officially "controlled" (killed) in large numbers.

IDENTIFICATION Abundant. A medium-size grackle with a long, graduated tail, yellow eyes, and a heavy bill. The male holds his tail in a deeply keeled shape—the central tail feathers lowered and the outer ones raised and flared—during the breeding season and engages in other ritualized display postures related to courtship (see photographs). This grackle is a familiar sight in many eastern backyards, striding across the lawn looking for an insect meal or singing its loud creaking song from the treetops, often in groups and sometimes

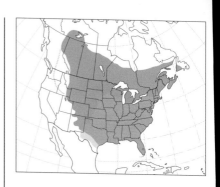

Common Grackles will visit all types of feeders and are not picky about what they eat.

The "bill-up" display is a threat given in response to the approach of another male.

well after dark. There are two basic plumage types with different glossy coloration in the male: the "Purple Grackle" is found in the Southeast and north along the coast to southern New England; the "Bronzed Grackle" occupies the rest of the range (mainly north and west of the Appalachians). From a distance, both types look plain black.

Plumage: Male "Bronzed Grackle" has a bronze-tinted body and wings that contrast with its blue head. **Male "Purple Grackle"** has a purplish body and head, with a green-glossed back (in Florida) or a more variegated, purple-green back (farther north). **Female** of both types is smaller, browner (less glossy), and shorter tailed than male. **Juvenile** is plain brown with dark eyes and faintly streaked breast.

Similar species: Brewer's Blackbird (page 219) has a shorter, unflared tail and smaller bill. Great-tailed Grackle (page 221) is much larger, with a longer bill, more striking tail, and uniform, purple gloss—not with different gloss colors on head and body as seen in "Bronzed Grackles." Boat-tailed Grackle (not illustrated), of the Atlantic coast and the Gulf Coast, is larger (almost Great-tailed size) and has a longer, more keel-shaped tail and longer bill. **Voice: Song** is a short, creaky *readle-eak*. **Call** is a loud, deep *chuck*.

RANGE Eastern and midwestern species. Inhabits fields with scattered trees, open woodlands, farmlands, and marshes; also common in developed areas, suburban yards, towns, and cities. Range is slowly expanding northward and westward. In the East, although still common, numbers have significantly decreased in the past 30 years. Northern "Bronzed Grackle" breeders move south for the winter. In winter, birds gather in large flocks that often seek out conifer stands for a night roost. Spring **migration:** mid-February–April; fall migration: late September–early November.

FOOD Omnivorous and opportunistic. Diet is mostly insects and some grain when breeding; otherwise, mainly grain (waste corn is a favorite),

The "song spread" display is a ritualized posture often seen early in the breeding season.

seeds (especially acorns), and some fruit and scavenged garbage. Usually forages in flocks when not breeding.
Feeding: Will visit feeders, whether or not you want them.

NESTING Semicolonial; typically nests in small colonies of 10–50 pairs, sometimes more. *Location:* Often in a conifer, usually 3–20 feet up. *Nest:* Bulky cup of twigs and grass. *Eggs:* Usually 3–4; incubated by female for 12–15 days. *Fledging:* Leaves nest at 12–15 days.

bluish head contrasts with bronze back

overall blackish; purplish gloss to head

keel-shaped tail

sooty brown

juvenile

bronze ♂

purple ♂

SIGHTINGS   JAN FEB MAR APR MAY JUN JUL AUG SEP OCT NOV DEC

GALLERY OF WARBLERS

Warblers steal bird-watchers' hearts, for they are the stars of spring and fall migration. More than 50 species nest in North America, and many of these colorful songbirds winter south of our borders. Here are some of the most gorgeous males in full breeding plumage.

WIDESPREAD WARBLERS

YELLOW WARBLER

WILSON'S WARBLER

COMMON YELLOWTHROAT

NASHVILLE WARBLER

WESTERN WARBLERS

BLACK-THROATED GRAY WARBLER

TOWNSEND'S WARBLER

HERMIT WARBLER

RED-FACED WARBLER

EASTERN WARBLERS

GOLDEN-WINGED WARBLER

NORTHERN PARULA

BLACK-THROATED GREEN WARBLER

BLACKBURNIAN WARBLER

CERULEAN WARBLER

MAGNOLIA WARBLER

PROTHONOTARY WARBLER

BLACK-AND-WHITE WARBLER

KENTUCKY WARBLER

AMERICAN REDSTART

RARE WARBLERS

KIRTLAND'S WARBLER

RUFOUS-CAPPED WARBLER

WOOD-WARBLERS Family Parulidae

More than 50 species of wood-warblers breed in North America. These colorful sprites are beloved by birders. Many backyards host migrating warblers in spring and fall.

Orange-crowned Warbler
Oreothlypis celata, L 5" (13 cm)

This widespread warbler is much more common in the West than in the East. The Orange-crowned is a hardy bird that winters farther north than most warblers.

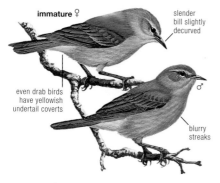

immature ♀
slender bill slightly decurved
even drab birds have yellowish undertail coverts
blurry streaks
♂

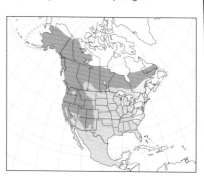

northern edge of the boreal forest. In the South or along the Pacific coast, look for this species in winter in backyard gardens. Spring **migration:** March–April in the West, mid-April–May in the East; fall migration: mid-August–October in the West, late September–October in the East.

IDENTIFICATION Common to uncommon. Plain warbler that often probes into dead leaf clusters.
Plumage: Very plain; olive green and yellowish overall; orange crown rarely visible. Note dark line through the eye, blurry streaks on the chest, and yellow undertail coverts. Western birds are more yellow; northern breeders (which winter in the Southeast) are duller.
Similar species: Pine Warbler (opposite) has wing bars and white undertail coverts. Very similar to Tennessee Warbler (not illustrated).
Voice: Song is a high-pitched staccato trill. **Call** is a sharp, metallic *chip*.

RANGE Widespread species. Breeds in brushy coastal canyons and mountain thickets and across the

FOOD Insects in summer; also small berries and nectar.
Feeding: Comes to suet and peanut butter feeders in winter and also to hummingbird feeders.

NESTING *Location:* On or near the ground. *Nest:* Open cup of twigs and other plant material. *Eggs:* Usually 4–5; incubated by female for 11–13 days. *Fledging:* Leaves nest at 10–13 days.

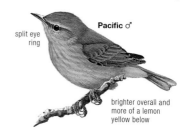

Pacific ♂
split eye ring
brighter overall and more of a lemon yellow below

Pine Warbler
Dendroica pinus, L 5½" (14 cm)

Unlike many bird names, this one rings true: Pine Warblers do indeed have a close connection to pine forests—they breed almost nowhere else. These hardy warblers winter almost entirely in the United States, in the Southeast and eastern Texas.

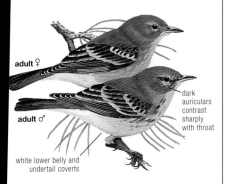

adult ♀

adult ♂

dark auriculars contrast sharply with throat

white lower belly and undertail coverts

 IDENTIFICATION Common. The Pine Warbler is long tailed and somewhat heavy billed for a warbler, and its feeding actions are slower and more deliberate than most warblers. Quite gregarious in winter, they often mix in with small flocks of Eastern Bluebirds, Yellow-rumped Warblers, and Chipping Sparrows.
Plumage: Unstreaked, olive upperparts; two wing bars; white undertail coverts. There is a sharp contrast between the dark ear coverts and throat. **Male** is yellow below with streaks on the sides and a white belly. **Female** is duller. **Immature female** is exceptionally drab.
Similar species: Orange-crowned Warbler (opposite) lacks wing bars and has yellow undertail coverts. Pine Warblers are very similar to fall Bay-breasted and Blackpoll Warblers (not illustrated).
Voice: Song is a twittering, musical trill that varies in speed. **Call** is a flat, sweet *chip*.

RANGE Eastern species. Breeds in southern pine forests and denser mature pine or mixed forests in the north. Spring **migration:** April; fall migration: late September–mid-October.

 FOOD Eats insects all year; winter diet is supplemented with small berries and seeds.
Feeding: Comes to suet feeders in winter and even takes sunflower seeds.

NESTING *Location:* Concealed in a pine, usually 30–50 feet up. *Nest:* Deep, open cup of twigs, pine needles, and other plant material. *Eggs:* Usually 4; incubated by both parents for about 10 days. *Fledging:* Leaves nest at about 10 days.

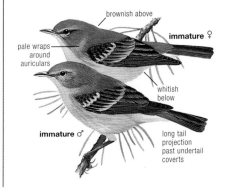

brownish above

immature ♀

pale wraps around auriculars

whitish below

immature ♂

long tail projection past undertail coverts

Yellow-rumped Warbler

Dendroica coronata, L 5½" (14 cm)

There are two regional groups with distinctly different head patterns that were once considered to be separate species— "Audubon's Warbler" in the West and the widespread "Myrtle Warbler."

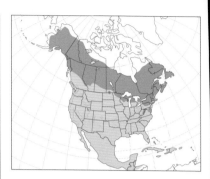

"Myrtle Warbler"

yellow crown patch

white throat

yellow patch

whitish supercilium

breeding ♀

breeding ♂

overall browner above than "Audubon's"

yellow rump

angled whitish throat

fall ♀

Voice: Song is a soft warble, trailing off at the end. **Call** of "Myrtle" is a flat *check,* a sharper *chip* is given by "Audubon's."

 RANGE Widespread species. Breeds in coniferous and mixed woodlands. Winters farther north than any other warbler. **Spring migration:** March–early May; fall migration: late September–October.

FOOD Eats insects all year; winter diet is often berries.

NESTING *Location:* Most often in a conifer, usually 4–50 feet up. *Nest:* Open cup of twigs, pine needles, and other plant material. *Eggs:* Usually 4–5; incubated by female for 12–13 days. *Fledging:* Leaves nest at 10–12 days.

IDENTIFICATION Common to abundant; often in winter flocks. It is often the first and last warbler you'll see during the year.
Plumage: A yellow rump patch and a patch of yellow on the sides are features of all ages, sexes, and regional groups. Northern and eastern birds **("Myrtle")** have a thin whitish eyebrow and a white throat that extends to a point behind the ear region; **breeding male** has a mottled black chest and bold white wing bars. Western birds **("Audubon's")** have a more rounded, yellow throat (sometimes whitish in immature females); **breeding male** has a black chest and large white wing patch.
Similar species: Magnolia and Cape May Warblers (not illustrated) are smaller "eastern warblers" with yellowish rumps.

most have pale yellow in rounded throat patch

"Audubon's Warbler"

fall ♀

yellow rump

yellow throat

extensive white

breeding ♂

The Northern Cardinal's red plumage and loud, clear song are admired by bird-watchers.

CARDINAL SONGS

A piercing *Birdie! Birdie! Birdie!* heralds the presence of a favorite feathered friend, the Northern Cardinal. This bird is the classic triple threat: Adding to its good looks and charm, the cardinal sings its heart out.

Within their range east and south of the Great Plains, cardinals are among the loudest and most familiar of songsters, belting out their whistles virtually anytime, anywhere. Unlike many songbirds, they commonly sing year-round, and are regularly reported singing in the middle of the night. Females sing as well as males, often while sitting on the nest. Youngsters learn their songs from adults and begin warbling (though not very well, at first) just days after fledging.

SHORT AND SWEET

Phrases are usually short, with repeating syllables in predictable sequences. The cardinal may not possess the vocal ingenuity of, say, a mockingbird (which incorporates all kinds of sounds into bewildering assortments), but it more than compensates for any creative shortcomings with an abundance of cheery enthusiasm.

Like an alarm clock, a cardinal on territory pipes up just before sunrise, and sings a hearty dawn chorus. Then, for the rest of the day, it bursts into song whenever it feels the urge.

SPECIAL VOCAL EQUIPMENT

It's hard for people to imitate their sounds because cardinals, like all birds, lack mammalian vocal cords. Instead they use an organ called a syrinx, which is located where the trachea splits—allowing birds to sing two notes at once, from deep inside the chest.

Cardinals excel at sweeping through pitches, combining low notes from the left lung and high notes from the right into one seamless whistle.

CARDINALS, TANAGERS, & ALLIES   Family Cardinalidae

This family of medium-size songbirds now includes all of the "tanagers" that breed in North America. Bright colors—reds, yellows, and blues—and bold patterns enliven the male plumage of many species, and most have heavy bills to deal with a diet of insects, seeds, and fruit.

Northern Cardinal
Cardinalis cardinalis, L 8¾" (22 cm)

The bright red male Northern Cardinal ("redbird"), with its conspicuous crest, is one of the most recognizable and popular birds in North America. Its stylish plumage has gotten it "elected" to state bird by seven states (more than any other) and enshrined as the name of numerous athletic teams. State bird of Illinois, Indiana, Kentucky, North Carolina, Ohio, Virginia, and West Virginia.

IDENTIFICATION Very common. Fairly large songbird with a pointed crest, triangular red bill, and long tail. Although sometimes secretive, the male cardinal sings from an exposed perch. The general public often mistakenly identifies any bright red bird as a cardinal, especially Westerners who grew up in the East. But with the exception of desert-dwelling cardinals in southern Arizona and New Mexico, there are no cardinals west of the Great Plains.
Plumage: Male is completely red, except for a small black mask and black chin. **Female** is tawny brown, tinged with red on the crest, wings, and tail. **Juvenile** resembles female, but has a blackish bill.
Similar species: Other prominently red birds include male Scarlet Tanager (page 232), Summer Tanager (page 233), male House Finch (page 182), and male Purple Finch (page 183), none of which has a crest. In the Southwest, Pyrrhuloxia (not illustrated) has a crest and some red plumage, but is grayer and has a rounded, yellow bill.
Voice: Loud, liquid whistling **song** with many variations, including *cheer cheer cheer* and *purty purty purty*; both sexes sing almost year-round. Common **call** is a sharp *chip*.

long crest

black surrounds red bill

♂

dark bill

♀

overall buffy brown and dull red

juvenile ♂

In spring the male Northern Cardinal is fiercely territorial. His own reflection in a window or car mirror may cause him to spend hours trying to repel the imaginary intruder.

RANGE Eastern and midwestern species; year-round resident. Found in a variety of habitats, including woodland edges, thickets, vine tangles, backyard gardens, towns, and urban parks. Abundant in the Southeast. Locally common around desert washes, mesquite groves, and riparian woodlands in the Southwest. Cardinals generally expanded their range to the north in the 20th century.

A baby Northern Cardinal may leave its nest before being able to fly adequately.

FOOD Varied diet consists mostly of insects in spring and summer, but also includes fruit, berries, leaf buds, flowers, and the seeds of weeds and grasses; feeds insects to nestlings. In winter, forages mainly for seeds and small berries.
Feeding: Very common at all types of feeders, but prefers seeds scattered on the ground, especially sunflower seeds, safflower seeds, and cracked corn. Fruiting trees and shrubs offer both food and nesting locations. A frequent victim of free-roaming cats.

NESTING *Location:* Hidden in a dense shrub or low tree, usually 3–10 feet up. *Nest:* Open cup of twigs, grasses, and bark strips. *Eggs:* Usually 3–4; incubated by female for 12–13 days. *Fledging:* Leaves nest at 9–11 days; male may care for the recently fledged young while female begins the next nesting attempt. *Broods:* 2–3 per year.

Scarlet Tanager
Piranga olivacea, L 7" (18 cm)

The luminous red plumage of the male Scarlet Tanager seems better suited to a tropical jungle than the eastern hardwood forests where it breeds. It does winter in the tropics, but by that time of year, the male has molted into a somber greenish plumage.

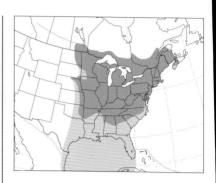

wings contrast darker to olive green back

small bill

1st spring ♂

♀

brownish

1st fall ♂

black shoulder contrasts with greenish wings

with loud, burry phrases. **Call** is a hoarse *chip-burr*.

RANGE Eastern species; summer resident. Breeds in mature deciduous forest with a high leafy canopy, often in oaks. Winters in South America. Spring **migration:** mid-April–late May; fall migration: September–mid-October.

FOOD Mostly insects, gleaned from leaves; sometimes hovers while gleaning. Small fruits and berries are important in late summer and during fall migration.

NESTING *Location:* In a tree, usually 20–50 feet up. *Nest:* Loosely woven cup of twigs, weed stems, and other plant material. *Eggs:* Usually 4; incubated by female for 13–14 days. *Fledging:* Leaves nest at 9–15 days.

IDENTIFICATION Common. Medium-size, compact songbird with a short tail and fairly heavy, pale bill. Forages slowly in the leafy treetops where, despite the male's brilliance, it can be hard to see. Your best looks will often be in spring before the leaves have fully emerged.
Plumage: Breeding male is vivid red and black, becoming a splotchy red and green in late summer when in molt. **Fall adult male** is bright olive green above and greenish yellow below with black wings. **Female** is like the fall male, but has greenish brown wings. **Immature male** is like female, but has partially black wings.
Similar species: Female Summer Tanager (next page) is larger and has mustard to orangish yellow (not greenish) plumage, a larger bill, and paler wings and tail.
Voice: Robin-like **song**, but much harsher,

breeding adult ♂

solid black wings and tail on adult males

fall adult ♂

Summer Tanager
Piranga rubra, L 7¾" (20 cm)

Bees and wasps may seem a hazardous food source, but the Summer Tanager specializes in them. The wasp or bee is usually caught in midair.

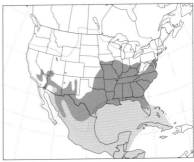

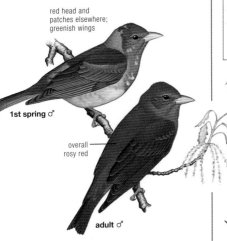

red head and patches elsewhere; greenish wings

1st spring ♂

overall rosy red

adult ♂

RANGE Widespread species; summer resident. Breeds in open deciduous woods, pine-and-oak woodlands, bottomland forests, and in the Southwest, riparian forests. Winters from central Mexico to South America. Spring **migration:** early April–early May; fall migration: late August–October.

FOOD Mostly insects in spring and summer. Small fruits and berries are part of its diet in late summer and during fall migration.

NESTING *Location:* In a tree, usually 10–35 feet up. *Nest:* Loosely woven cup. *Eggs:* Usually 4; incubated by female for 11–12 days. *Fledging:* Leaves nest at about 10 days.

IDENTIFICATION Common to uncommon. Medium-size songbird—bigger than Scarlet Tanager—with a large, pale bill. Forages sluggishly in the leafy treetops and often sits motionless, when only its loud call reveals its presence. **Plumage: Adult male** entirely rosy red. **Female** mustard yellow below, darker above; some females have blurry patches of red. **First-spring male** usually has red head and scattered patches of red plumage.
Similar species: Female Scarlet Tanager (opposite) is smaller and has greenish plumage, a smaller bill, and wings darker than upperparts. Also compare Northern Cardinal (pages 230–231).
Voice: Robin-like *song* of slurred, whistled notes with short pauses. **Call** is a staccato *ki-ti-tuck*.

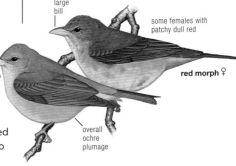

large bill

some females with patchy dull red

red morph ♀

♀

overall ochre plumage

Western Tanager
Piranga ludoviciana, L 7¼" (18 cm)

The striking black-and-yellow male Western Tanager, with its bright red head, is one of the most colorful summer species of western pine forests. Normally a treetop species, migrating birds are often seen foraging lower down in suburban gardens and urban parks.

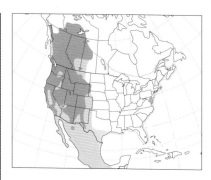

winter adult ♂
dusky
reddish head
breeding adult ♂
black back and yellow rump

IDENTIFICATION Common. Medium-size, compact songbird with a short tail and fairly heavy, pale bill. Although brightly plumaged, it can be quite inconspicuous when foraging high in the canopy.

gray back and white wing bars

Plumage: Breeding male has a red or orangish red head, but is otherwise bright yellow with black back, wings, and tail and two wing bars (front yellow, rear white).

larger bill ♀ than Scarlet

Fall adult male loses red on head (some are red-tinged on forehead and chin); back plumage has pale edges.
Female is olive green to olive gray above and dull yellow below, with two whitish wing bars.

Some females look quite gray and drab, with limited yellow below.
Similar species: Female Bullock's (page 214) and Hooded Orioles (page 213) have longer, pointy bills and much longer tails.
Voice: Robin-like **song**, but much harsher, with loud, burry phrases. **Calls** include a rising *pit-er-ick*.

RANGE Western species; summer resident. Breeds in open conifer and pine-and-oak woodlands, often at high elevations. Winters sparingly in coastal Southern California—mostly in residential gardens and around flowering eucalyptus—but primarily in Mexico and Central America. Spring **migration:** mid-April–early June; fall migration: mid-July–early October.

FOOD Mostly insects. Small fruits and berries are important in late summer and during fall migration.
Feeding: Will occasionally visit feeders for fruit.

NESTING *Location:* In a conifer, 8–60 feet up. *Nest:* Flimsy cup of twigs and weed stems. *Eggs:* Usually 4; incubated by female for 13–14 days. *Fledging:* Leaves nest at 10–11 days.

| JAN | FEB | MAR | APR | MAY | JUN | JUL | AUG | SEP | OCT | NOV | DEC |

Indigo Bunting
Passerina cyanea, L 5½" (14 cm)

Seen singing from an overhead wire against a bright sky, the male Indigo Bunting looks black—only when he is lower down can his electric blue coloration be appreciated.

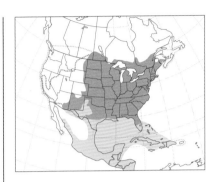

variable patchy blue and brown plumage

1st spring ♂

mostly brown but with some veiled dark blue showing

winter adult ♂

sweet-sweet. **Call** is a sharp *spit;* flight call is a husky *bzzzt.*

 RANGE Eastern and midwestern species; summer resident. Breeds in brushy thickets, overgrown fields, roadsides, and shelterbelts. Spring **migration:** mid-April–early June; fall migration: mid-September–mid-October. A rare but regular visitor throughout the West.

 FOOD Mixed diet of insects, seeds, buds, and berries. **Feeding:** Will occasionally visit feeders.

 NESTING *Location:* In a dense shrub or sapling, 1–3 feet up. *Nest:* Neat woven cup of dried vegetation. *Eggs:* Usually 3–4; incubated by female for 12–13 days. *Fledging:* Leaves nest at 9–12 days.

IDENTIFICATION Common. Small, compact songbird with a short, triangular, pale bill. Most foraging takes place in high weeds and brushy thickets. When flushed, swishes tail from side to side.
Plumage: Breeding male is entirely blue. **Winter adult male** and **first-spring male** are patchy brown and blue. **Female** and **immature** are all brown with two faint wing bars and diffuse streaking on the underparts.
Similar species: Blue Grosbeak (not illustrated) is larger and has a heavier bill and broad cinnamon wing bars. Also see Eastern Bluebird (page 162).
Voice: Cheerful **song** is a series of sweet, variously pitched phrases, usually paired: *sweet-sweet chew-chew*

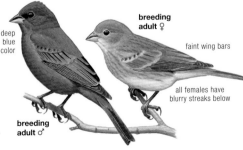

deep blue color

breeding adult ♀

faint wing bars

all females have blurry streaks below

breeding adult ♂

Rose-breasted Grosbeak
Pheucticus ludovicianus, L 8″ (20 cm)

The flashy male Rose-breasted Grosbeak sings his slow warbling song hidden in the treetops. His song is sweetly melodic, but the call note given by both sexes—*eek!* like the sound of a sneaker on a gym floor—is unique and easier to learn.

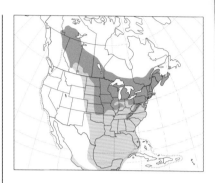

IDENTIFICATION Fairly common. Medium-large, robust songbird with a huge, pale, triangular bill. Usually forages in leafy treetops, but sometimes visits bird feeders.

Plumage: Breeding male is black and white, except for a rosy pink bib and underwings. **Winter adult male** (seen during fall migration) has brown-edged feathering on head and back. **Female** is brown above, with streaked underparts, a strong white eyebrow, and two wing bars. **First-fall male** resembles the female but is more buff, often with a few red feathers on the breast.

breeding adult ♂

rose red

Similar species: Female Purple Finch (page 183) is much smaller and has a smaller, darker bill and no white in the wings. Compare to female and immature Black-headed Grosbeak (opposite); their ranges have some overlap.
Voice: Warbling **song** is a series of singsong, robin-like phrases. **Call** is a sharp squeak *eek!*

RANGE Eastern and midwestern species; summer resident. Breeds in deciduous and mixed woodlands and woodland edges, pastures, orchards, and suburban and rural backyards. Winters in Central and South America. Spring **migration:** mid-April–early June; fall migration: late August–mid-October.

FOOD Mixed diet of insects, seeds, buds, and fruit. Feeds nestlings mostly insects. During fall migration, feeds almost entirely on fruit.
Feeding: Visits feeders, especially in spring. Prefers sunflower seeds.

NESTING *Location:* In a shrub or small tree, 4–20 feet up. *Nest:* Loose cup of twigs and dried vegetation. *Eggs:* Usually 4; incubated by both parents for 11–14 days *Fledging:* Leaves nest at 9–12 days.

winter adult ♂

breeding adult ♂

♀

streaked below

Black-headed Grosbeak

Pheucticus melanocephalus, L 8¼" (21 cm)

Even though male Rose-breasted and Black-headed Grosbeaks look completely different, the two species are closely related. They have almost identical songs and occasionally interbreed on the Great Plains. The females of the two species are very similar.

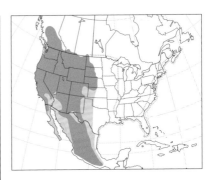

darker upper mandible than Rose-breasted

buffy breast; streaking largely limited to sides and flanks ♀

burnt orange

breeding adult ♂

Grosbeaks (previous page) tend to have heavier streaking on whiter underparts and a paler (not two-toned) bill; first-fall male usually has some pink feathers on the breast.

Voice: Warbling **song** is a series of sing-song, robin-like phrases. **Call** is a sharp *pik!* (not as squeaky as Rose-breasted's).

RANGE Western and Great Plains species; summer resident. Breeds in a variety of open woodlands (oak, conifer, piñon-juniper, riparian) from lowlands to mountains, as well as in woodsy suburban and rural backyards. Winters mainly in Mexico. Spring **migration:** early April–mid-May; fall migration: mid-July–September.

FOOD Mixed diet of insects, seeds, buds, and fruit. Feeds nestlings mostly insects. During fall migration, feeds almost entirely on fruit.

Feeding: Visits feeders; prefers sunflower seeds.

NESTING *Location:* In a thicket or tree 6–12 feet up, often near a stream. *Nest:* Loose cup of twigs, grasses, and other dried vegetation. *Eggs:* Usually 3–4; incubated by both parents for 12–14 days. *Fledging:* Leaves nest at about 12 days.

IDENTIFICATION Common. Medium-large, robust songbird with a huge triangular bill that is dark above and pale below. In late summer and fall, forages in fruiting bushes and trees.

Plumage: Breeding male has a black head, black-and-white wings, and cinnamon orange underparts. **Female** is brown above, with light streaking on tawny underparts, and has a strong white eyebrow and two wing bars. **First-fall male** is rich buff below, with little or no streaking.

Similar species: Female Purple Finch (page 183) is smaller overall and has a smaller, darker bill and no white in the wings. Female and immature Rose-breasted

JAN FEB MAR APR MAY JUN JUL AUG SEP OCT NOV DEC